Timea Havar-Simonovich,
Daniel Simonovich
(eds.)

Contemporary Theory and Practice of Organizations

Part I: Understanding the Organization

Timea Havar-Simonovich,
Daniel Simonovich
(eds.)

CONTEMPORARY THEORY AND PRACTICE OF ORGANIZATIONS

Part I: Understanding the Organization

ibidem-Verlag
Stuttgart

Bibliografische Information der Deutschen Nationalbibliothek
Die Deutsche Nationalbibliothek verzeichnet diese Publikation in der Deutschen Nationalbibliografie; detaillierte bibliografische Daten sind im Internet über http://dnb.d-nb.de abrufbar.

Bibliographic information published by the Deutsche Nationalbibliothek
Die Deutsche Nationalbibliothek lists this publication in the Deutsche Nationalbibliografie; detailed bibliographic data are available in the Internet at http://dnb.d-nb.de.

∞
Gedruckt auf alterungsbeständigem, säurefreien Papier
Printed on acid-free paper

ISBN: 978-3-8382-0747-6

© *ibidem*-Verlag
Stuttgart 2016

Alle Rechte vorbehalten

Das Werk einschließlich aller seiner Teile ist urheberrechtlich geschützt. Jede Verwertung außerhalb der engen Grenzen des Urheberrechtsgesetzes ist ohne Zustimmung des Verlages unzulässig und strafbar. Dies gilt insbesondere für Vervielfältigungen, Übersetzungen, Mikroverfilmungen und elektronische Speicherformen sowie die Einspeicherung und Verarbeitung in elektronischen Systemen.

All rights reserved. No part of this publication may be reproduced, stored in or introduced into a retrieval system, or transmitted, in any form, or by any means (electronical, mechanical, photocopying, recording or otherwise) without the prior written permission of the publisher. Any person who does any unauthorized act in relation to this publication may be liable to criminal prosecution and civil claims for damages.

Printed in the EU

Contents

Introduction 7

Section I: Modern Forms of Organization 9

Networked Organizations 11
    Sarah Breucker, Timea Havar-Simonovich

Project Organization 29
    Jonas Haake, Cristina Meinshausen

Virtual Organization 43
    Lea Gerharz, Philipp Marquardt

Team-based Organization 67
    Maximilian Geißinger, Jana Krennmayer

Section II: Organizational Properties 81

Organizational Identity 83
    Philipp Aich, Alexander Antusch

Organizational Complexity 95
    Fabio Kledt, Philippe Evers, Debora Benson

Organizational Agility 117
    Patrick Fuchs, Timea Havar-Simonovich

Organizational Alignment 131
    Timo Kallenbach, Hanna Epple

Organizational Resilience 147
    Gabriel Martin Böhm, Alexandre Dietz, Debora Benson

Section III: Group and Team Aspects 165

Team Dynamics 167
    Annika Franziska in der Beek, Florian Pahl

Virtual Teams 193
    Stefan Wieland, Jens Wolf

Leading International Teams 209
    Christina Ungerer, Jan Plachta

Introduction

This is the first of two volumes dedicated to the state of research and practice in organizations. It is a joint effort of graduates of the Master's in International Management at ESB Business School at Reutlingen University in Germany. Although organizations have been studied and researched for decades, their state of practice and theory is still evolving. This first volume is dedicated to three broad themes: non-traditional forms of organization, organizational characteristics and team level aspects.

The non-traditional organizations treated in the first section of this volume include project-based, team-based, virtual and network ways of organizing. To be distinguished from traditional structuring philosophies, such as functional, divisional, geographic or matrix structures, these modern elements, often combined with their traditional counterparts, have been practiced with varying degrees of success and understanding over the last few decades. The first four articles in this volume present and synthesize the current knowledge available in this domain. In particular, they discuss different interpretations of the networked organization, the right choice of project organization, disparate phenomena considered in the context of virtual organizations, and ongoing research gaps about ways of organizing.

The second section of this book contains a handful of papers highlighting different properties studied in organisations, all of which have created excitement among researchers and practitioners alike: identity, complexity, agility, alignment and resilience. Some properties, such as identity and complexity provide a deeper understanding of organizations and their interactions with their environment. Other organizational characteristics, such as agility, alignment or resilience have been proposed as sources of competitive advantage. What this second section highlights is the extent to which further research is necessary and what concrete research gaps need to be addressed in order to better inform business leaders and managerial practitioners about how to better understand and shape their organizations.

The final section of this volume turns the attention to virtual and international teams, as well as to the more foundational theme of team dynamics. While team dynamics is a well-published domain, recent research investigations undertaken in this decade suggest that this topic is far from being entirely understood in the corporate context. Virtual teams are a means of utilizing the most qualified employees for a specific project. Here, critical success factors are of great interest and therefore discussed in the dedicated article. As with virtual teams, international teams have become a form of work that has become a necessity nowadays. The effectiveness of global leaders is of particular concern in international team setups. All these team-related subjects are screened for their state of research and practice prior to suggesting further research.

Overall, this volume brings together twelve contemporary topics relevant for understanding today's organizations, while showing to what extent research efforts have achieved to supply substantiated knowledge and guidance.

Section I: Modern Forms of Organization

Networked Organizations

Sarah Breucker, Timea Havar-Simonovich

Abstract. This article discusses the topic "networked organization" with a focus on terminology, definitions and in recent literature. Authors agree on the rising importance of networked organizations, but introduce different, at times contradictory perspectives on the topic. The different research approaches and focuses, as well as remaining research gaps, are examined in this article. It is found that due to inconsistencies in terminology, definition and characterization of networked organizations, the current state of research neither provides a satisfactory foundation for the academic field, nor for management practice, as research, theories and solutions are either too holistic or too specific to be applicable.

Keywords: Networked organizations, networked enterprises, organizational networks, collaboration

1 Introduction

Undoubtedly, the importance of networked organizations (NOs) has increased during the last decades, driven by the need to "respond to the increasing need of strong adaptability to the constantly changing economic context" (Camarinha-Matos, Pereira-Klen, & Afsarmanesh 2011, p. V). Today, networked organizations can be found in various forms, acting in diverse industries, including manufacturing, knowledge based-industries (Goldman 2012), public services (Provan & Milward 2001), banking and insurance (Mukherjee 2009).

This article discusses the state of research on the topic "networked organizations". Many authors have contributed to it, introducing different, somewhat heterogeneous perspectives. To reduce complexity here, the focus has been set on terminology, definitions and characteristics given during the last 14 years. Additionally, findings of exemplary earlier contributions that were often cited in current literature have been included. In total, 49 articles from journals and three more recently edited books (Camarinha-Matos, Afsarmanesh, & Ollus 2008b; Camarinha-Matos et al. 2011; Putnik & Cruz-Cunha 2012) have been reviewed.

After a short introduction, similarities and contradictory opinions in the focus area are examined. Subsequently, a cluster of the differences in research focuses and approaches in the reviewed literature is provided and gaps in research are pointed out. The article closes with a conclusion on the state of research in relation to further academic studies and management praxis.

2 Literature contributions to the field of networked organizations

The following section discusses literature contributions to the topic with focus on terminology, definitions and characteristics, while pointing out similarities and disagreement among authors.

2.1 Terminology and definitions

In a literature review about network organizations from the year 1997, the author already mentioned the „remarkable diversity of ideas and nomenclature on networks" (Alstyne 1997, p. 1). A number of terms, such as agile enterprise, small firm network or modular corporation, are linked to the "concept of an association of distinct business units operating in tandem" (Alstyne 1997, p. 1). Further years of literature contributions did not lead to more consensus, but to even more diversity. Many authors are aware of this problem and seek to find a definition for their own studies (Baum & Schütze 2012, 2013; Camarinha-Matos, Afsarmanesh, Galeano, & Molina 2009).

The following paragraph gives an overview of the nomenclature and definitions after 1997. The term collaborative network (CN) is used as an overall term to describe multiple independent entities (companies, individuals, or machines), which collaborate towards a common goal, often supported by computer technology. The single entities have different, often complementary corporate cultures, operating environments, competences and skills (Camarinha-Matos et al. 2009; Camarinha-Matos et al. 2008b; Ferreira, Cunha, Carneiro, & Sá 2011; Shadi & Afsarmanesh 2011).

As soon as an organizational structure is involved that establishes governance rules, legal regulations and takes care of the overall management of the network, the terms collaborative networked organization (CNO) (Camarinha-Matos & Afsarmanesh 2008; Camarinha-Matos et al. 2009; Camarinha-Matos et al. 2008b; Chituc & Azevedo 2005; Chituc & Nof 2007; Dutton 2008; Lavrac et al. 2007; Yassa, Hassan, & Omara 2012) or collaborative enterprise network (CEN) (Alfaro-Saiz, Rodríguez-Rodríguez, & Verdecho 2011; Baum & Schütze 2012, 2013) are used. Other authors use the terms networked organizations (NO) (Dangelmaier & Dürksen 2012; Lavrac et al. 2007; Smirnov, Pashkin, Levashova, Chilov, & Krizhanovsky 2003; Smirnov, Shilov, Levashova, Sheremetov, & Contreras 2007) or networked enterprise (NE) (Mukherjee 2009; Noori & Lee 2004) as synonyms.

A different view is the concept of a virtual enterprise (VE), which is considered to be a collaboration, which is temporary or focused on a singular project (Camarinha-Matos, Afsarmanesh, & Ollus 2008a; Chesbrough & Teece 2002; Kumar & Harding 2011; Lavrac et al. 2007; Stefanovic et al. 2012). Arsovski et al. share this understanding, but use the term virtual organization (VO) (Arsovski, Arsovski, Aleksic, Stefanovic, & Tadic 2012). Thus, VEs and VOs can be seen as sub-categories of the concepts described above. Other authors do not limit the term virtual organization to temporary, but also to permanent collaborations of different enterprises (Jansson, Karvonen, Ollus, & Negretto 2008; Tamošiūnaitė 2011).

Various specific models of NOs for certain industries or purposes are found in the literature, such as a "collaborative virtual laboratory" (Camarinha-Matos et al. 2009, p. 47) in in the science and engineering context or the "Intelligent Learning Extended Organizations" (Kieslinger, Pata, & Fabian 2009, p. 1), which describe temporary networked organizations that include businesses and educational institutions.

Another term that needs clarification is the virtual organization breeding environment (VOBE), which can be seen as a CNO "on standby", without a current task, "prepared to collaborate and thus rapidly respond to a collaboration opportunity or necessity" (Vargas Vallejos, Macke, & Faccin 2011, p. 58). Authors referring to this are Camarinha-Matos and Afsarmanesh (2008), Camarinha-Matos et al. (2009), Camarinha-Matos et al. (2008a, 2008b), Chituc & Azevedo (2005), Chituc and Nof (2007). In the following, the terms networked organizations and collaborative networked organizations will be used as synonyms, and, given the definition mentioned above, further described. Figure 1 provides an overview of characteristics of the networked organization.

2.2 Characteristics of networked organizations

"Due to the absence of this generic description, a general characterization and differentiation of individual types of CEN becomes difficult." (Baum & Schütze 2012, p. 549) Figure 1 shows the seven characteristics concluded to be the features that most authors agree on in building a profile of a NO.

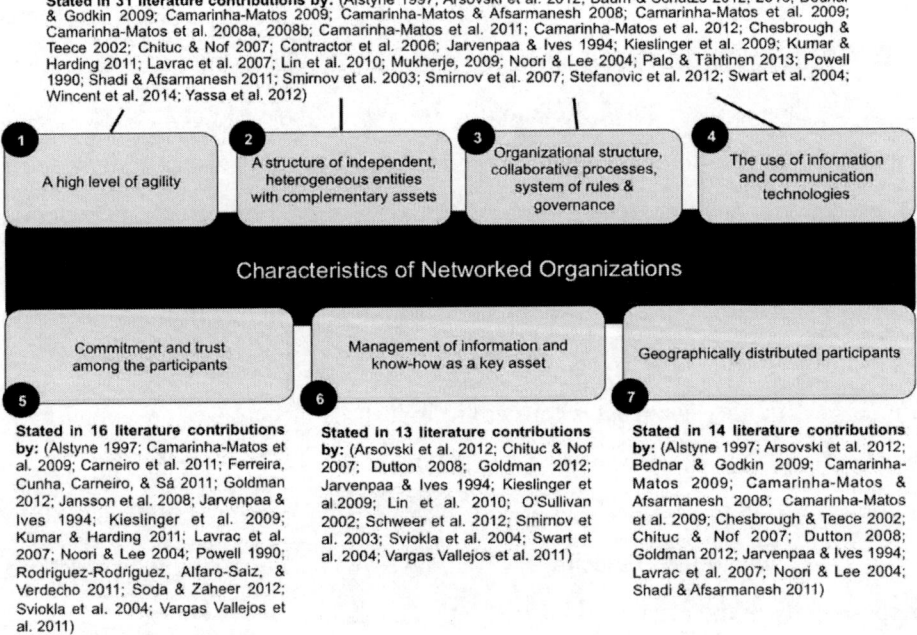

Figure 1: Characteristics of a networked organization

These characteristics distinguish the concept of networked organizations from other concepts, such as centralized, vertically integrated organizations or markets (Alstyne 1997; Camarinha-Matos et al. 2009; Contractor, Wasserman, & Faust 2006; Goldman 2012; Jarvenpaa & Ives 1994; Lin, Desouza, & Roy 2010; Lorenzoni, Shank, & Silvi 1999; Powell 1990).

The figure demonstrates that characteristics 1 – 4 are the most common and undisputed, as they were stated in 31 literature contributions. The fact that characteristics 5 – 7 are mentioned less frequent suggests that they might not be regarded as indispensable: they can be, but are not necessarily feature of a networked organization. E.g., Smirnov et al. state that NOs are independent companies, "often with different geographic locations" (Smirnov et al. 2003), but not always. The factor trust among the participants is mainly discussed by authors looking "one step ahead", e.g. towards the avoidance of conflicts in NOs (Carneiro, Novais, Lemos, Andrade, & Neves 2011; Grugulis, Vincent, & Hebson 2003).

2.3 Disagreements in literature on the definition and characteristics

Nevertheless, there are some characteristics that oppose contradictory views. As described in section 2.1, the time limitation is a factor that some authors apply to NOs in general (Chituc & Azevedo 2005; Chituc & Nof 2007 and Yassa et al. 2012), while others only apply it to the concept of a virtual enterprise (Camarinha-Matos et al. 2008a; Chesbrough & Teece 2002; Kumar & Harding 2011; Lavrac et al. 2007 and Stefanovic et al. 2012). Figure 2 summarizes four more fields of disagreement: while the left column shows the predominant opinion and lists exemplary authors, contradictory opinions are summarized on the right.

Predominant Opinion	Contradictory opinion
Participants of a NO are individuals, units, institutions and companies from more than one enterprise. (Baum & Schütze 2012, 2013; Camarinha-Matos et al. 2009; Yassa et al. 2012)	NO describe collaborating individuals or units of one single enterprise (Dutton 2008; O'Sullivan 2002; Schweer, Assimakopoulos, Cross, & Thomas 2012; Tamošiūnaitė 2011; Yuk-kwan Ng & Höpfl 2013)
The entities in a NO work towards a **common or compatible goal**. This can, but does not have to be, profit maximization, e.g. stated by (Baum & Schütze 2013; Goldman 2012).	In a NO, every participant follows its own goals which are unknown to the others (Vetschera 1999). This is particularly true in the non-profit or public sector, since profit maximization does not apply (Provan & Milward 2001).
To make a NO work, a **central responsible entity** is needed (Chesbrough & Teece 2002; Lavrac et al. 2007; Palo & Tähtinen 2013; Wincent, Thorgren, & Anokhin 2014).	A NO should be a system where all units have equal power, which is a challenging task to fulfill (Vetschera 1999).
A NO only exists with the presence of at least one **collaborative task**, e.g. stated by (Baum & Schütze 2012, 2013).	In the VOBE described above, the NO is in a "standby-mode" without a current task (Camarinha-Matos & Afsarmanesh 2008; Camarinha-Matos et al. 2009; Camarinha-Matos et al. 2008a, 2008b; Chituc & Azevedo 2005; Chituc & Nof 2007; Vargas Vallejos et al. 2011).

Figure 2: Contradictory opinions on characteristics of a NO

3 Clusters of reviewed literature

In this section, literature contributions will be clustered and contrasted according to their research focus and approach.

3.1 Research focuses

Evidently, authors look at networked organizations from different perspectives. Figure 3 provides an overview of the three main research foci and the corresponding authors identified in the reviewed literature: (1) information systems & technology, (2) theoretical framework development and (3) management of NOs. The numbers and sizes of the bubbles represent the number of authors that are grouped by focus themes.

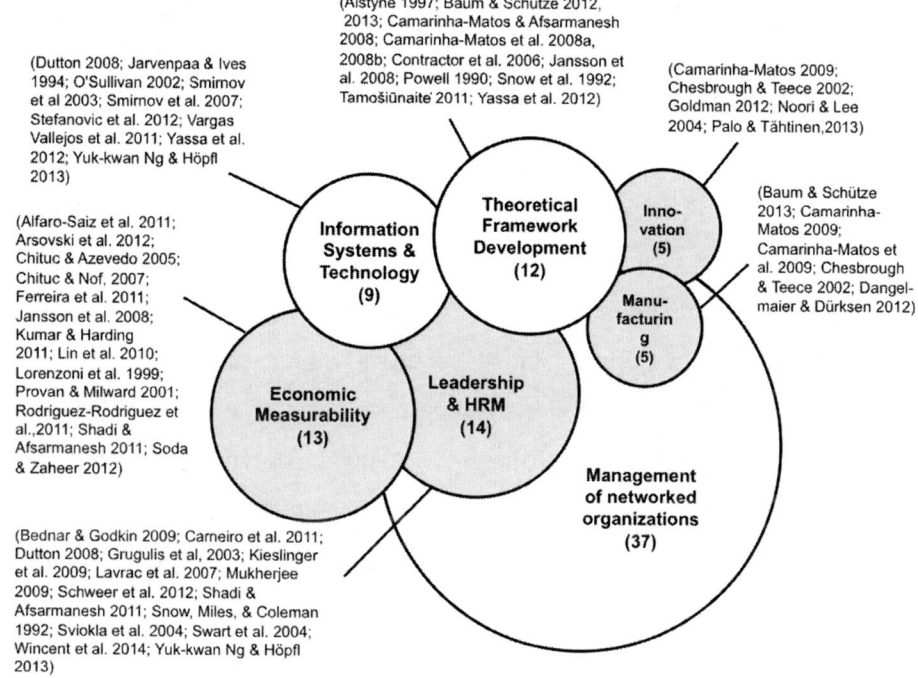

Figure 3: Research Focuses

It becomes obvious that the majority (37) contributed to advances in the understanding of managerial aspects. According to the specific focus, this field is divided into four sub-categories, shaded in grey. In the following, the research focuses and exemplary contributions will be further described, according to the references listed in figure 3.

The first research focus examines information systems and technology enabling networked organizations. It discusses the design and operation of information systems and knowledge logistic systems for communication, process integration or quality documentation purposes (Dutton 2008; Stefanovic et al. 2012).

The second research focus deals with theoretical framework development. Leading authors from the early stages of literature contributions are Powell, who already contributed to this topic in 1990 by differing networked organizations from hierarchies and the marketplace, Powell (1990) as well as Snow, Miles and Coleman, who suggested the typology of internal, stable and dynamic networked organizations two years later (Snow, Miles, & Coleman 1992). Many current authors have referred to these concepts in their work (Alstyne 1997; Baum & Schütze 2013; Noori & Lee 2004).

During the last 10 years, Camarinha-Matos, Afsarmanesh and Ollus can be seen as the leading contributors to the development of a theoretical framework. They were responsible for the ECOLEAD project (European Collaborative Networked Organizations Leadership Initiative), a four-year initiative (2004-2008), including 28 academic and industrial partners from 14 countries, which conducted research on CNOs from a holistic point of view (Camarinha-Matos et al. 2008a). One major goal of ECOLEAD was "the establishment of a sound theoretical foundation, and a reference model, as a pre-condition for the next generation of CNOs" (Camarinha-Matos et al. 2009, p. 58).Several authors either directly contributed or referred to the ECOLEAD project with their work (Baum & Schütze 2012, 2013; Chituc & Nof 2007; Ferreira et al. 2011; Jansson et al. 2008; Lavrac et al. 2007; Vargas Vallejos et al. 2011).

Most contributions focus on the management of networked organizations, including different issues of the formation and operation of networked organizations from a management perspective on macro- and micro-level (Vetschera 1999). Some authors focus on the manufacturing sector, where NOs have the advantages to be more responsive to changing market requirements (Baum & Schütze 2013; Camarinha-Matos 2009; Camarinha-Matos et al. 2009; Chesbrough & Teece 2002; Dangelmaier & Dürksen 2012). Another "hot topic" is innovation in networked organizations, e.g. discussing open innovation concepts within a NO to enhance product or technology development (Camarinha-Matos 2009; Chesbrough & Teece 2002; Goldman 2012; Noori & Lee 2004; Palo & Tähtinen 2013). Furthermore, there have been contributions on the challenge of economic measurability of certain factors in networked organizations, such as performance measurement (Alfaro-Saiz et al. 2011; Chituc & Nof 2007; Ferreira et al. 2011; Provan & Milward 2001; Soda & Zaheer 2012). It was also stated that qualitative and intangible features, such as motivation and collaboration spirit (Jansson et al. 2008) or intellectual capital (Rodriguez-Rodriguez, Alfaro-Saiz, & Verdecho 2011) have to be measured. Other contributions cope with risk assessment in the formation of NOs (Kumar & Harding 2011), the introduction of strategic cost analysis (Lorenzoni et al. 1999), or the measurement of the organization's agility (Lin et al. 2010). The last sub-category is leadership and human resource management (HRM). The leadership challenges in NOs that are most widely discussed include the need for an adaptation of strategy, e.g. (Sviokla, Schneider, Calkins, & Quirk 2004), and HR policies (Swart, Kinnie, & Purcell 2004), the increased requirements on talent-management, e.g. (Schweer et al. 2012), and the establishment of a trust-based culture (Lavrac et al. 2007). Others deal with the anticipation and resolution of conflicts that typically evolve in such an environment (Carneiro et al. 2011; Mukherjee 2009). An exemplary leadership approach to improve the success of NOs is to introduce incentives, which improve individual behavior, thereby lead to more effectiveness on collaborative levels and also provide a measurable system (Shadi & Afsarmanesh 2011). This example shows that the research focuses overlap to some extent (in this case leadership and measurability). Figure 3 illustrates this through the intersection of the bubbles. Another example is the discussing of an open innovation approach in the context of manufacturing (Camarinha-Matos 2009; Chesbrough & Teece 2002).

3.2 Research approaches

There have been diverse approaches by different authors in the revised literature towards the topic, which are summarized in Figure 4. While literature reviews (1) and the development of theoretical frameworks (2) are approaches under a holistic perspective, case studies (3) and analyses with statistical or mathematical models (4) conduct research with a specific approach that is focused on singular problems or industry cases. Some contributions are not listed, as they are a mixture of different approaches. In the following paragraph, some exemplary contributions will be pointed out.

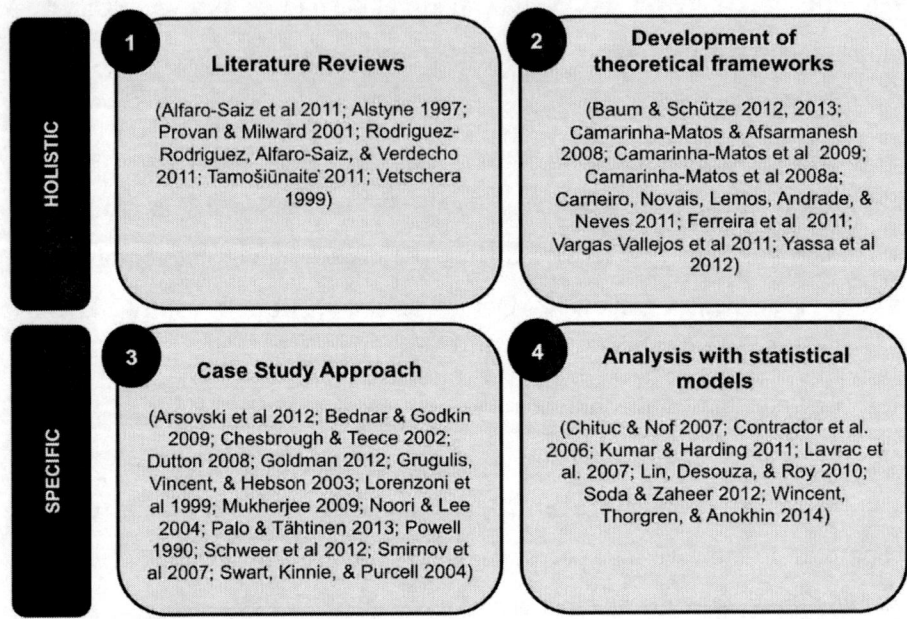

Figure 4: Research Approaches

In literature reviews, authors predominantly examine literature for similarities and differences regarding terminology, characteristics and concepts of networked organizations (Alstyne 1997; Tamošiūnaitė 2011).

A variety of authors, especially those engaged in the ECOLEAD project, use the state of research combined with theoretical approaches to set up theoretical frameworks for the concept of networked organizations (Camarinha-Matos et al. 2008a). Various theoretical concepts have been applied to describe the formation, operation and dissolution of NOs, including field theories, system theories and cognitive theories (Baum & Schütze 2012).

On the specific side, a common approach is to explore the topic with cross-sectional case studies. Some examples are Swart et al. (2004), who conducted a case study on software firms to discuss the application of HRMs in networks or Lorenzoni et al. (1999), who examined strategic cost management in the Italian motorbike industry. Authors following a more holistic approach have criticized the case study technique: "The definitions of CEN are usually subjective point of view considerations of the individual authors. Many times, various types of CEN are described case-driven and not reflected by a normative understanding." (Baum & Schütze 2012, p. 550).

More rarely, statistical models were applied in order to discuss a certain question concerning networked organizations, such as in the statistical analysis by Contractor et al. (2006), who analyzed social and organizational behavior in a NO composed of representatives of three U.S. Army agencies and four corporations, which collaborate for the commercial production of software.

4 Research gaps in the field of networked organizations

The previous sections have exposed the heterogeneity in the understanding of NOs and the diversity of research focuses and approaches. Under these conditions, a state of research has evolved that fails to balance the holistic, theoretic perspective against the preoccupation with short-term, singular issues. Nevertheless, three major research gaps have been identified among the presented research foci: (1) a standard definition and framework, (2) systems for economic measurement and (3) specific research gaps from the management literature.

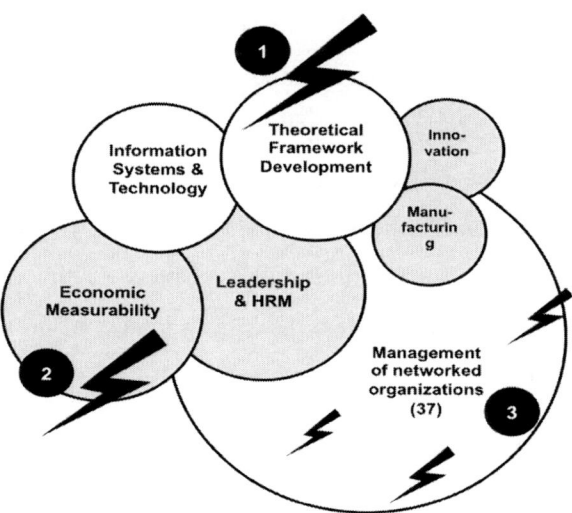

Figure 5: Research Gaps

Many authors seek clarification of nomenclature and concepts. They claim a unifying, holistic model, as a standard, instead of further theoretical "ad-hoc approaches" (Camarinha-Matos et al. 2009, p. 58). It is criticized that prior clarification attempts have not been holistic, but too focused on single disciplines (e.g. either business or technology) and thus biased (Camarinha-Matos & Afsarmanesh 2008; Yassa et al. 2012). „The lack of a reference model that could synthesize and formalize the base concepts, principles, and recommended practices, is an obstacle for an easier and more consistent development of the area" (Camarinha-Matos & Afsarmanesh 2008, p. 2453). Although there have been endeavors to close this research gap, e.g. through the ECOLEAD project, it is still not fully explored.

Another major research gap is the lack of research on (performance) measurement systems for networked organizations as stated by Lin et al. (2010, p. 2824): "Research is needed to examine how to measure the performance of networked organizational structures or organizational networks." Many other authors also mention (Alfaro-Saiz et al. 2011; Bednar & Godkin 2009; Chituc & Azevedo 2005; Chituc & Nof 2007; Ferreira et al. 2011; Rodriguez-Rodriguez et al. 2011).

Thirdly, research perspectives so far have been either too holistic or too specific to be applicable in management praxis. As stated by Yassa et al.: "Decision makers need more comprehensive information about CNO system to support their decision." (Yassa et al. 2012, p. 1). Consequently, various specific research gaps in management literature have been claimed. Examples include "the issues of appropriate collaboration forms for micro and small enterprises" (Baum & Schütze 2013, p. 55), research on business modeling in NOs (Palo & Tähtinen 2013) and "additional longitudinal case studies to test the lasting effects of networks" (Bednar & Godkin 2009, p. 341).

5 Conclusion

Authors agree on the rising importance of networked organizations, as these organizations "have the power to reshape not only organizations but also industry dynamics" (Mukherjee 2009, p. 24). Although the topic can be traced back in literature to the early 1960s (Snow et al. 1992), no mature state of research has developed until today. It is claimed that networked organizations are „common in practice, but are surprisingly under-researched" (Wincent et al. 2014, p. 329). The variety and inconsistencies in terminology, definition and characterization of a NO have been described in this article. Also, the varying research focuses and approaches were outlined. The analysis of the research gaps showed that the lack of consensus in these areas has led to a lack of comprehensive theoretical frameworks, (performance) measurement systems and investigations regarding specific management challenges. It can thus be concluded that the current state of research on networked organizations neither provides a satisfactory solution for the academic field, nor for the management praxis, as research, theories and solutions are either too often broad or too specific to be applicable.

References

Alfaro-Saiz, J.-J., Rodríguez-Rodríguez, R., & Verdecho, M. a.-J. (2011). Performance Management in Collaborative Networks: Difficulties and Barriers. In L. M. Camarinha-Matos, A. Pereira-Klen & H. Afsarmanesh (Eds.), *Adaptation and Value Creating Collaborative Networks. 12th IFIP WG 5.5 Working Conference on Virtual Enterprises, PRO-VE 2011 São Paulo, Brazil, October 17-19, 2011 Proceedings.* (Vol. 362, pp. 133-139). Heidelberg: Springer.

Alstyne, M. V. (1997). THE STATE OF NETWORK ORGANIZATION: A SURVEY IN THREE FRAMEWORKS. *Journal of Organizational Computing, 7(3)*.

Arsovski, Z., Arsovski, S., Aleksic, A., Stefanovic, M., & Tadic, D. (2012). Resilience of Virtual and Networked Organizations: An Assessment. In G. D. Putnik & M. M. Cruz-Cunha (Eds.), *Virtual and Networked Organizations, Emergent Technologies, and Tools. First International Conference, ViNOrg 2011 Ofir, Portugal, July 6-8, 2011. Revised Selected Papers* (pp. 155–164). Berlin Heidelberg: Springer Verlag.

Baum, H., & Schütze, J. (2012). A Model of Collaborative Enterprise Networks. *Procedia CIRP, 3*, 549-554. doi: 10.1016/j.procir.2012.07.094

Baum, H., & Schütze, J. (2013). An Organizational Concept for Collaborative Enterprise Networks. *Procedia CIRP, 7*, 55-60. doi: 10.1016/j.procir.2013.05.010

Bednar, D. H., & Godkin, L. (2009). Organizational Learning and the Development of a Networked Company. *Review of Policy Research, 26*(3), 329-343. doi: 10.1111/j.1541-1338.2009.00385.x

Camarinha-Matos, L. M. (2009). Collaborative networked organizations: Status and trends in manufacturing. *Annual Reviews in Control, 33*(2), 199-208. doi: 10.1016/j.arcontrol.2009.05.006

Camarinha-Matos, L. M., & Afsarmanesh, H. (2008). On reference models for collaborative networked organizations. *International Journal of Production Research, 46*(9), 2453-2469. doi: 10.1080/00207540701737666

Camarinha-Matos, L. M., Afsarmanesh, H., Galeano, N., & Molina, A. (2009). Collaborative networked organizations – Concepts and practice in manufacturing enterprises. *Computers & Industrial Engineering, 57*(1), 46-60. doi: 10.1016/j.cie.2008.11.024

Camarinha-Matos, L. M., Afsarmanesh, H., & Ollus, M. (2008a). ECOLEAD and CNO base concepts. In L. M. Camarinha-Matos, H. Afsarmanesh & M. Ollus (Eds.), *Methods and Tools for Collaborative Networked Organizations* (pp. 3-32). New York: Springer.

Camarinha-Matos, L. M., Afsarmanesh, H., & Ollus, M. (Eds.). (2008b). *Methods and Tools for Collaborative Networked Organizations*. New York: Springer.

Camarinha-Matos, L. M., Pereira-Klen, A., & Afsarmanesh, H. (Eds.). (2011). *Adaptation and Value Creating Collaborative Networks. 12th IFIP WG 5.5 Working Conference on Virtual Enterprises, PRO-VE 2011 São Paulo, Brazil, October 17-19, 2011 Proceedings.* (Vol. 362). Heidelberg: Springer.

Carneiro, D., Novais, P., Lemos, F. v., Andrade, F., & Neves, J. (2011). Issues on Conflict Resolution in Collaborative Networks. In L. M. Camarinha-Matos, A. Pereira-Klen & H. Afsarmanesh (Eds.), *Adaptation and Value Creating Collaborative Networks. 12th IFIP WG 5.5 Working Conference on Virtual Enterprises, PRO-VE 2011 São Paulo, Brazil, October 17-19, 2011 Proceedings.* (Vol. 362, pp. 271-278). Heildelberg: Springer.

Chesbrough, H. W., & Teece, D. J. (2002). When Is Virtual Virtuous? *Harvard Business Review, 80(8)*, 127-135.

Chituc, C.-M., & Azevedo, A. L. (2005). Multi-Perspective Challenges on Collaborative Networks Business EnvironmentsCollaborative Networks and Their Breeding Environments. IFIP TC5 WG 5.5 Sixth IFIP Working Conference on VIRTUAL ENTERPRISES, 26–28 September, 2005, Valencia, Spain (Vol. 186, pp. 25-32). doi: 10.1007/0-387-29360-4_3

Chituc, C.-M., & Nof, S. Y. (2007). The Join/Leave/Remain (JLR) decision in collaborative networked organizations. *Computers & Industrial Engineering, 53*(1), 173-195. doi: 10.1016/j.cie.2007.05.002

Contractor, N. S., Wasserman, S., & Faust, K. (2006). Testing Multitheoretical, Multilevel Hypotheses About Organizational Networks: An Analytic Framework and Empirical Example. *Academy of Management Review, 31*(3), 681-703. doi: 10.5465/amr.2006.21318925

Dangelmaier, W., & Dürksen, D. (2012). A Planning System Using a Four Level Approach for the Planning of Production in a Networked Organization. In G. D. Putnik & M. M. Cruz-Cunha (Eds.), *Virtual and Networked Organizations, Emergent Technologies, and Tools. First International Conference, ViNOrg 2011 Ofir, Portugal, July 6-8, 2011. Revised Selected Papers* (Vol. 248, pp. 145-154). Berlin Heidelberg: Springer.

Dutton, W. H. (2008). The Wisdom of Collaborative Network Organizations: Capturing the Value of Networked Individuals1. *Prometheus, 26*(3), 211-230. doi: 10.1080/08109020802270182

Ferreira, P. S., Cunha, P. F., Carneiro, L. s., & Sá, A. (2011). An Approach to Performance Management in Collaborative Networks Based on Stakeholders' Key Success Factors. In L. M. Camarinha-Matos, A. Pereira-Klen & H. Afsarmanesh (Eds.), *Adaptation and Value Creating Collaborative Networks. 12th IFIP WG 5.5 Working Conference on Virtual Enterprises, PRO-VE 2011 São Paulo, Brazil, October 17-19, 2011 Proceedings.* (Vol. 362, pp. 140-147). Heidelberg: Springer.

Goldman, S. L. (2012). Smart Communities and Networked Organizations. In G. D. Putnik & M. M. Cruz-Cunha (Eds.), *Virtual and Networked Organizations, Emergent Technologies, and Tools. First International Conference, ViNOrg 2011 Ofir, Portugal, July 6-8, 2011. Revised Selected Papers* (pp. 304–315). Berlin Heidelberg: Springer.

Grugulis, I., Vincent, S., & Hebson, G. (2003). The rise of the 'network organisation' and the decline of discretion. *Human Resource Management Journal, 13*(2), 45-59. doi: 10.1111/j.1748-8583.2003.tb00090.x

Jansson, K., Karvonen, I., Ollus, M., & Negretto, U. (2008). Governance and Management of Virtual Organizations. In L. M. Camarinha-Matos, H. Afsarmanesh & M. Ollus (Eds.), *Methods and Tools for Collaborative Networked Organizations* (pp. 221-238). New York: Springer.

Jarvenpaa, S. L., & Ives, B. (1994). The Global Network Organization of the Future: Information Management Opportunities and Challenges. *Journal of Management Information Systems, 10*(4), 25-57.

Kieslinger, B., Pata, K., & Fabian, C. M. (2009). A Participatory Design Approach for the Support of Collaborative Learning and Knowledge Building in Networked Organizations. *International Journal of Advanced Corporate Learning (iJAC), 2*(3). doi: 10.3991/ijac.v2i3.999

Kumar, S. K., & Harding, J. (2011). Risk Assessment in the Formation of Virtual Enterprises. In L. M. Camarinha-Matos, A. Pereira-Klen & H. Afsarmanesh (Eds.), *Adaptation and Value Creating Collaborative Networks. 12th IFIP WG 5.5 Working Conference on Virtual Enterprises, PRO-VE 2011 São Paulo, Brazil, October 17-19, 2011 Proceedings.* (Vol. 362, pp. 450-455). Heidelberg: Springer.

Lavrac, N., Ljubic, P., Urbancic, T., Papa, G., Jermol, M., & Bollhalter, S. (2007). Trust Modeling for Networked Organizations Using Reputation and Collaboration Estimates. *IEEE Transactions on Systems, Man and Cybernetics, Part C (Applications and Reviews), 37*(3), 429-439. doi: 10.1109/tsmcc.2006.889531

Lin, Y., Desouza, K. C., & Roy, S. (2010). Measuring agility of networked organizational structures via network entropy and mutual information. *Applied Mathematics and Computation, 216*(10), 2824-2836. doi: 10.1016/j.amc.2010.03.132

Lorenzoni, G., Shank, J. K., & Silvi, R. (1999). Networked Organizations: A Strategic Cost Management Perspective. http://papers.ssrn.com/sol3/papers.cfm?abstract_id=1012643

Mukherjee, A. S. (2009). Leading the networked organization. *Leader To Leader, 2009*(52), 23-29.

Noori, H., & Lee, W. B. (2004). Collaborative design in a networked enterprise: the case of the telecommunications industry. *International Journal of Production Research, 42*(15), 3041-3054. doi: 10.1080/00207544042000208385

O'Sullivan, D. (2002). Framework for managing business development in the networked organisation. *Computers in Industry, 2002*(47), 77-88.

Palo, T., & Tähtinen, J. (2013). Networked business model development for emerging technology-based services. *Industrial Marketing Management, 42*, 773–782.

Powell, W. W. (1990). Neither market nor hierarchy: Network forms of organization. *Research in Organizational Behavior, 12:*, 295–336.

Provan, K. G., & Milward, H. B. (2001). Do networks really work? A framework for evaluating public-sector organizational networks. *Public Administration Review, 61*(4), 414-423.

Putnik, G. D., & Cruz-Cunha, M. M. (Eds.). (2012). *Virtual and Networked Organizations, Emergent Technologies, and Tools. First International Conference, ViNOrg 2011 Ofir, Portugal, July 6-8, 2011. Revised Selected Papers* (Vol. 248). Berlin Heidelberg: Springer Verlag.

Rodriguez-Rodriguez, R., Alfaro-Saiz, J.-J., & Verdecho, M.-J. (2011). A Review on Intellectual Capital Concepts as a Base for Measuring Intangible Assets of Collaborative Networks. In L. M. Camarinha-Matos, A. Pereira-Klen & H. Afsarmanesh (Eds.), *Adaptation and Value Creating Collaborative Networks. 12th IFIP WG 5.5 Working Conference on Virtual Enterprises, PRO-VE 2011 São Paulo, Brazil, October 17-19, 2011 Proceedings.* (Vol. 362, pp. 41-47). Heidelberg: Springer.

Schweer, M., Assimakopoulos, D., Cross, R., & Thomas, R. J. (2012). Building a Well-Networked Organization. *MIT Sloan Management Review, 53*(2), 35-42.

Shadi, M., & Afsarmanesh, H. (2011). Addressing Behavior in Collaborative Networks. In L. M. Camarinha-Matos, A. Pereira-Klen & H. Afsarmanesh (Eds.), *Adaptation and Value Creating Collaborative Networks. 12th IFIP WG 5.5 Working Conference on Virtual Enterprises, PRO-VE 2011 São Paulo, Brazil, October 17-19, 2011 Proceedings.* (Vol. 362, pp. 263-270). Heidelberg: Springer.

Smirnov, A., Pashkin, M., Levashova, T., Chilov, N., & Krizhanovsky, A. (2003). High-level business intelligence service in networked organizations. *Frontiers of E-Business Research.* http://citeseerx.ist.psu.edu/viewdoc/download?doi=10.1.1.97.2438&rep= rep1&type=pdf

Smirnov, A., Shilov, N., Levashova, T., Sheremetov, L., & Contreras, M. (2007). Ontology-driven intelligent service for configuration support in networked organizations. *Knowledge and Information Systems, 12*(2), 229-253. doi: 10.1007/s10115-007-0067-5

Snow, C. C., Miles, R. E., & Coleman, H. J. (1992). Managing 21st Century Network Organizations. *Organizational Dynamics*(20(3)), 4-20.

Soda, G., & Zaheer, A. (2012). A network perspective on organizational architecture: performance effects of the interplay of formal and informal organization. *Strategic Management Journal, 33*(6), 751-771. doi: 10.1002/smj.1966

Stefanovic, M., Arsovski, S., Arsovski, Z., Aleksic, A., Nestic, S., Rajkovic, D., & Punosevac, Z. (2012). Integration of Virtual and Networked Organization Using Server Oriented Architecture. In G. D. Putnik & M. M. Cruz-Cunha (Eds.), *Virtual and Networked Organizations, Emergent Technologies, and Tools. First International Conference, ViNOrg 2011 Ofir, Portugal, July 6-8, 2011. Revised Selected Papers* (Vol. 248, pp. 165-175). Berlin Heidelberg: Springer.

Sviokla, J., Schneider, A., Calkins, C., & Quirk, C. (2004). The Rise of the Networked Organization. *DiamondCluster Whitepaper, Spring 2004.*

Swart, J., Kinnie, N., & Purcell, J. (2004). Human Resource Advantage in the Networked Organisation. *Management Revue, 15*(3), 288-304.

Tamošiūnaitė, R. t. (2011). Organization virtual or networked. *Social Technologies (Socialines Technologijos), 1*(1), 49-60.

Vargas Vallejos, R., Macke, J., & Faccin, K. g. (2011). Establishing Knowledge Management as an Important Factor to Develop Social Capital for Collaborative Networks. In L. M. Camarinha-Matos, A. Pereira-Klen & H. Afsarmanesh (Eds.), *Adaptation and Value Creating Collaborative Networks. 12th IFIP WG 5.5 Working Conference on Virtual Enterprises, PRO-VE 2011 São Paulo, Brazil, October 17-19, 2011 Proceedings.* (Vol. 362, pp. 58-65). Heidelberg: Springer.

Vetschera, R. (1999). Economic analysis of network organizations: Possibilities, limitations and open questions. *Central European Journal of Operations Research, 7*(4), 225-247.

Wincent, J., Thorgren, S., & Anokhin, S. (2014). Entrepreneurial orientation and network board diversity in network organizations. *Journal of Business Venturing, 29*, 327–344.

Yassa, M. M., Hassan, H. A., & Omara, F. A. (2012). New Federated Collaborative Networked Organization Model (FCNOM). *International Journal of Cloud Computing and Services Science (IJ-CLOSER), 1*(1), 1-10.

Yuk-kwan Ng, R., & Höpfl, H. (2013). *Beyond the image of Big Brother: Towards a Trustworthy, Autonomous and Collaborative Networked Organization.* Paper presented at the 3rd Annual International Conference on Business Strategy and Organizational Behaviour.

Project Organization

Jonas Haake, Cristina Meinshausen

Abstract. Project Management has evolved into a significant and indispensable discipline in a wide array of industries and businesses. Nonetheless a majority of projects fail and academics, as well as practitioners, consider the poor implementation of projects within existing organizational structures as major root cause. The purpose of this article is to shed light on this topic by systematically reviewing the existing literature on different organizational structures in project management. It further seeks to highlight specific factors for choosing a suitable organizational structure for certain types of project. The paper discusses particulalry three different wys to organize projects, namely the functional project organization, the project-based organization and the matrix organization. There is a consensus that the efficacy and practicality of functional organizational structures is relatively limited, especially for comprehensive projects. By contrast, matrix organizations appear to gain increasing importance in contemporary project management, although relevant empirical research on the effectiveness of matrix structures is limited.

Keywords: Functional project organization, project-based organization, matrix organization, organizational structures in project management, organization, corporation, enterprise

1 Introduction

Businesses across a variety of different industries as well as public and social institutions make use of project management to achieve satisfying results with limited resources under critical time constraints (Meredith & Mantel 2012). However, it must be noticed that too many projects are still subject to failure. For instance, in 2012 only 39 percent of software development and IT projects were successful. With regard to large and complex software projects the rate of success even diminishes to six percent (Standish Group 2014; Standish Group 2013). Academics and practitioners agree that one major cause for project failure is the poor implementation of projects within the existing organizational structure of a company (Standish Group 2013; Perkins 2006; Pinto & Mantel 1990; Pinto & Prescott 1988). Consequently, the question arises as to how to successfully integrate projects within the organization (Frese 2012; Sayles 1976). Furthermore, organizations need to decide whether a project should be granted full autonomy or whether it should be embedded in a functional department (Hill & White 1979).

Since the early 1960s, extensive academic research has been conducted to find an answer to the aforementioned question. Meanwhile reserachers and practitioners developed varied advice on project related organizational forms and frameworks to enhance the effectiveness of project management within an organization. The purpose of this article is to review the relevant literature on these alternative project organizations.

The research reviewed in this article is structured into three sections: the first section reviews the literature on the development of project organizational structures since the 1950s. The second section discusses the distinctive features of these structures. Hereafter, the third part reviews frameworks and criteria, which serve as a guidance for management to decide which project organization is applicable in certain project environments.

2 Evolution of alternative project organizational structures

According to the majority of academic researchers, the rapidly changing business environment has been the major influential factor for organizational change and the development of new organizational structures in the past thirty years (Kerzner 2009; Kolodny 1979; Gailbraith 1971).

Circumstances such as global market opportunities, increasing competitiveness, rapidly changing marketplaces and technology, unpredictable consumer demands and overall increased complexity forced management to change in order to guarantee the survival of the company (Meredith & Mandel 2012; Kerzner 2009; Bodera 2008). The U.S. American aerospace of the 1960s was one of the first industries which encountered many of the aforementioned challenges and the players in this sector realized that traditional vertical structures proved to be inadequate. Instead, the application of projects became significantly important and managers began implementing more innovative organizational structures such as matrix and pure-project organizations (Larson & Gobeli 1987; Knight 1976; Mee 1964).

With regard to this evolutionary process, Kolodny (1979) built his "evolutionary model" (p. 543), which illustrates the organizational development through four phases, namely function, project, product/ matrix and matrix. However, prior to Kolodny's concept, Davis and Lawrence (1977) already pointed out that organizations may not necessarily follow these particular stages of development as they may skip a phase or stop at a certain point in their evolutional process. In addition, in his empirical study, Burns (1989) could not find evidence for any such developmental trend.

Another model, which has been validated and used by the majority of writers on organizational development and project management, is Gailbraith's work (Ford & Randolph 1992). In his 1971 article entitled "Matrix Organization Designs" he proposed a continuum of alternative organizational structures, which is based upon the idea that the choice of a suitable organizational structure for projects depends on the level of authority, and responsibility senior management is ready to delegate to the project manager (Verma 1995). At one extreme of this continuum is the traditional functional line approach to organization with a vertical hierarchy and top-down management (Gray et al. 1990; Youker 1977). On the other end of the continuum is the project-based organization, in which the project is the primary unit of all organizational activities (Hobday 2000). At the center of this framework is the matrix organization which is characterized by "dual or multiple managerial accountability and responsibility" (Stuckenbruck 1981, p.69).

3 Project organizational structures

3.1 The functional project organizational structure

In the literature, the term functional organization (Figure 1), traditional management structure and vertical hierarchy are often used as synonyms. There is consensus among academics that all of these terms refer to a type of organization that is divided along functional lines such as research & development, procurement, production or marketing (Daft 2010; Jones & Bouncken 2008; Schreyögg 2005). Furthermore, its line of command can be compared to that of a pyramid with the senior management at the top and middle to lower management spreading down to the middle and lower levels (Youker 1977).

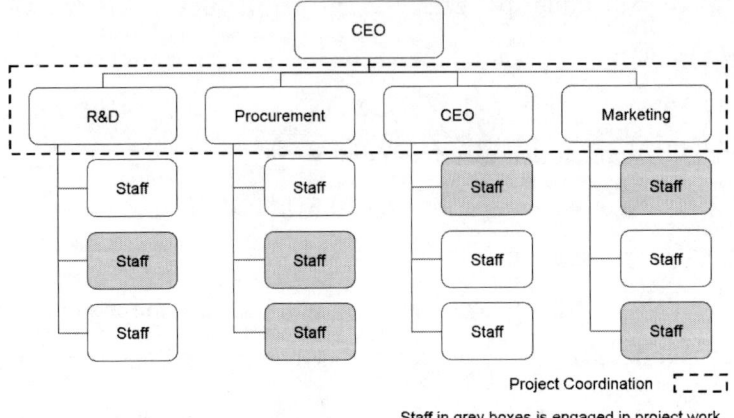

Figure 1: The functional project organization (adapted from PMBOK 2008)

In the early days of management, and in the absence of more project-oriented organizational forms, enterprises used their existing functional organization for the execution of projects without altering or adapting any aspects of the organizational structure (Frese 2012; Youker 1977). Thus, projects had been structured into different segments, which were allocated to the relevant functional departments and were placed under the supervision of the respective functional heads (PMBOK 2008; Gobeli & Larson 1987).

The literature provides a range of advantages for this particular project environment such as cost efficiencies, low complexity and flexibility (Meredith & Mantel 2012); effective allocation of expertise within the functional departments (Verma 1995); and simple post-project transition of project participants (Youker 1977). However, there is agreement among scholars and practicing project managers that functional project organizations can yield several drawbacks, which become particularly evident in complex and broad projects (Stuckenbruck 1981). First and foremost project commitment and project customer orientation are relatively low, since functional units are mainly concerned with their daily operations (Kerzner 2009). Furthermore, authority issues are likely to appear, because no individual within the organization has total responsibility for the project and its outcomes (Bodera 2008).

Finally, coordination of projects along functional departments and the transfer of information are rather complicated and requires additional lead time (Morris & Pinto 2007). Based upon these disadvantages Frese (2012) suggests that functional organizational structures are only applicable to small-sized projects and should be neglected if complexity is involved. This conclusion is underpinned by empirical evidence. Larson & Gobeli (1987) revealed that already in the late 1980s over 75 percent of enterprises were applying matrix organizational structures to effectively carry out projects. In another study Larson & Gobeli (1989) further detected that development projects carried out in functional organizations were significantly less successful than those processed in matrix or project-based organizations. More recently Hyväri (2006) underpinned these findings as he investigated that only less than ten percent of the questioned respondents were integrating projects within the existing functional organizations. Instead matrix organizations and pure-project structures were the organizational types most commonly used.

3.2 The project-based organizational structure

Since the 1950s, influential developments such as the race to space, rapid technological advancements and the explosive production of goods and services increased the importance of project management and induced the development of project oriented organizations (Turner & Keegan 1999). Here the most extreme organizational form is the pure project-based organization, which is also referred to as PBO. Contrary to the classic functional organization, in PBO's the project is at the center of all main business functions such as R&D, production or marketing (Hobday 2000).

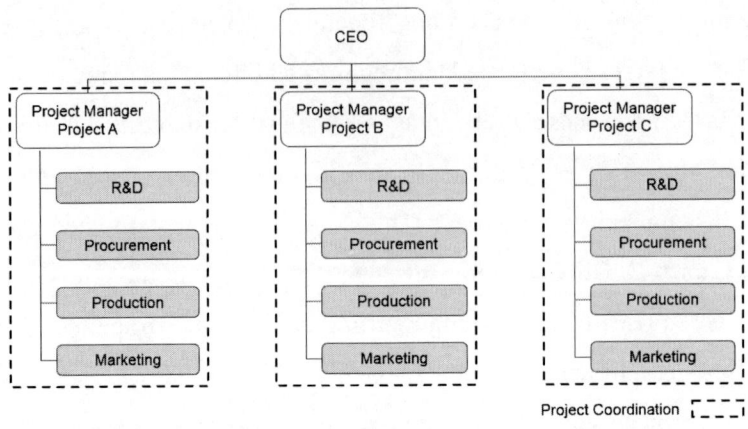

Figure 2: The project-based organization (adapted from PMBOK, 2008)

Larson & Gobeli (1987) define the PBO as duplicate of the functional organization, yet business functions and personnel are organized under the command of the project manager. According to Lindkvist (2004) a pure project-based organization is existent, when the majority of business processes is operated in a temporary project mode.

One major advantage of this organizational form is that project managers are provided with considerable authority and responsibility, making them capable of allocating the necessary resources from inside or outside the organization in order to achieve the desired project outcome (Youker 1977). Aside from this full line authority over the project, PBO's have a range of other benefits. For example, there is a consolidation of expertise from several functional areas within one project group, which in return positively influences the quality of the project activities, as well as the project outcome (Keller 1986). Furthermore, project commitment, motivation and group cohesiveness is likely to increase within project-based structures (Meredith & Mantel 2012). In this regard there is empirical evidence that group cohesiveness is positively correlated to project performance (Keller 1986). Finally, flexibility to project changes, elimination of coordination difficulties and strong project customer focus are other merits, which further justify the application of this particular organizational form in project management (Kerzner 2009).

Nonetheless, Youker (1977) suggests that regardless of all the associated merits, the PBO is not universally applicable to all project settings and further contains a variety of drawbacks. For instance, he pointed out that in multi-project enterprises the duplication of functional units, facilities and staff results in inefficient use of resources. In the same vein, complex products with high technology background may be better handled by the competent functional department than in heterogeneous project teams (Bodera 2008). Finally, job security for project participants upon project termination is rather uncertain and personnel are often put into overhead labor pools until they are assigned to new projects (Kerzner 2009; Youker 1977). Early empirical evidence suggests that employment uncertainties and career retardation are more of a problem among individuals of project-based organizations than in functional organizations (Reeser 1969).

3.3 The matrix organizational structure

As an attempt to leverage the advantages of functional and project-based organizations, matrix structures evolved and awakened interest among academics, particularly during the 1970s and 1980s, and hence, were subject to extensive research ever since that time (Sy & D'Annunzio 2005). Nevertheless, it appears neither academics nor practitioners cannot not agree on a precise and universal definition that comprises all of the distinctive features of a matrix (Frese 2012). This discord can be explained by the versatile application of matrix structures across a wide range of industries, such as the aerospace industry (Poirot 1991), the health care industry (Burns 1989) or marketing and financial organizations (Davis & Lawrence 1977). Nonetheless, most of the reviewed definitions have three aspects in common: A matrix organization is a cross-functional structure or "web of relations" (Mee 1964, p.72) in which functional lines are overlaid with lateral lines of authority and communication (Baber 1990; Larson & Gobeli 1987; Knight 1976), and in which people are placed in teams to work on tasks for a finite period of time (Ford & Randolph 1992). In a typical project matrix organization, the project represents the lateral lines of authority whereas the different business functions are structured along the vertical or functional lines (Turner et al. 1998; Youker 1977).Figure 3 illustrates such a typical project matrix organization in which a full-time project manager has considerable authority and responsibility over the project and the involved functional units (PMBOK 2008).

In the reviewed literature, three distinct types of matrix organizations are commonly mentioned, namely functional matrix, balanced matrix and strong matrix. In their 1987 article "Matrix Management: Contradictions and Insights", Larson & Gobeli introduced these terms for the first time. Based on the notion of Gailbraith's continuum of alternative organizational forms, the scholars suggest that matrix organizations can occur in several ways, depending on how much authority is granted to project management. Figure four depicts the key characteristics of the functional, balanced and strong matrix organizational structure.

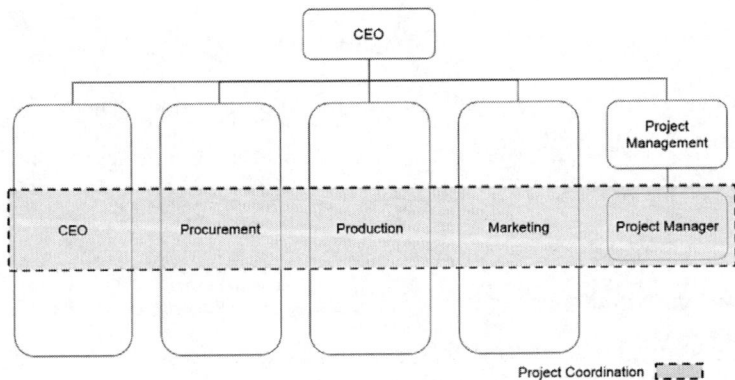

Figure 3: A strong project matrix organization (adapted from Youker 1977)

The reviewed literature on matrix organizations provides a range of advantages particularly in relation to project management. Proponents argue that the implementation of horizontal communication channels increases the frequency of communication and improves transfer of information, which in return enhances project coordination and the overall project quality (Larson & Gobeli 1987; Kolodny 1979). A further key merit of matrix structures is the efficient and flexible use of human and capital resources, since both can be shared across projects (Larson & Gobeli 1987; Stuckenbruck 1982). Based upon these merits and many other advantages mentioned in the literature (Meredith & Mantel 2012; Kerzner 2009; Ford & Randolph

1992; Gobeli & Larson 1987), many academics and practitioners believe that matrix organizations are the "epitome of modern, sophisticated management thinking" (Baber 1990, p.235). In fact, there have been some empirical findings, which stated that project performance is particularly high in matrix organizations (Kuprenas 2003; Hovmark & Nordqvist 1996).

Project characteristics	Matrix		
	Functional	Balanced	Strong
Project manager's authority	Limited	Low to moderate	Moderate to high
Resource availability	Limited	Low to moderate	Moderate to high
Control of project budget	Functional Manager	Mixed	Project Manager
Project manager's role	Part-time	Full-time	Full-time
Project management administrative staff	Part-time	Part-time	Full-time

Figure 4: Key Project Characteristics of matrix organizational structures (adapted from PMBOK 2008)

Nonetheless, matrix organizational structures have been subject to criticism for several reasons. Peters and Waterman (1982) argued that such structures are "hopelessly complicated and ultimately unworkable" (p.49). This statement was based upon earlier publications dealing with drawbacks of matrix organizations. For instance, in his research Argyris (1963) identified complexity, impracticability, mistrust among employees and the continued focus on functional units as major pathologies. Davis and Lawrence (1978) complemented the aforementioned issues with nine further problems of matrix management such as tendencies toward anarchy, power struggles, [...], and decision strangulation" (p.132). In a social experiment, Joyce (1986) revealed that matrix structures may have negative impacts on the employees' role perceptions and job satisfaction. More recently Arvidsson (2009) came to the same conclusion and followed that differences in organizing principles, identification issues among employees and complexity were the main sources for organizational tensions.

4 Effective choice of an organizational structure in project management

Due to the fact that the aforementioned project organizations have been subject to extensive research for the last forty to fifty years, one might suggest that the literature is full of concepts, frameworks and guidelines which aid in answering the question on how to choose the right structure to meet the requirements of a certain project. The contrary is the case and research into this area is rather limited. Most of the reviewed articles on that matter provide a range of key factors senior management and project managers should consider when designing a suitable organizational structure for the purposes of completing a project. For instance, uncertainty, level of technology, complexity or customer aspects are worth of consideration (Youker 1977; Gailbraith 1971). Youker (1977) in particular provided a comprehensive set of criteria illustrated in figure 5.

	Functional	Balanced	Strong
Uncertainty	Low	High	High
Technology	Standard	Complicated	New
Complexity	Low	Medium	High
Duration	Short	Medium	Long
Size	Small	Medium	Large
Importance	Low	Medium	High
Customer	Diverse	Medium	One
Interdependency (Within)	Low	Medium	High
Interdependency (Between)	High	Medium	Low
Time criticality	low	Medium	High
Resource criticality	Depends	Depends	Depends
Differentiation	Low	High	Medium

Figure 5: Guidelines for the decision on organizational design (Youker 1977)

Other authors focused on the design of matrix organizations and assert that this form is the optimal solution, when an enterprise is operating in rapidly changing marketplaces with changing consumer demands and where various competencies from different organizational units are needed to effectively complete the project (Grinnell & Apple 1977). However, all of the aforementioned suggestions are of conceptual nature only and empirical data on the effectiveness of certain structures on project management is relatively scarce (Kuprenas 2003).

5 Critical review and conclusion

This article illustrates the state of knowledge about the integration of project work within existing organization structures. An extensive body of knowledge has been created regarding alternative organizational structures and their respective impact on project management. There is an agreement among academics that functional organizational structures are only of minor importance for project management, due to its considerable disadvantages. By contrast, matrix organizations and their application in project management has been an area of controversy. Proponents of a matrix base their argumentation mainly on assumptions and conceptual considerations, whereas opponents partially ground their line of thoughts on empirical data. Nonetheless, the empirical foundation of both sides is rather thin and consists mostly of "a few well-done analytic case studies and numerous anecdotal reports" (Baber 1990, p.236). Hence, the impact on alternative organizational structures could be a field for further empirical research.

The same can be said for the choice of an effective organizational structure in project management. Most of the reviewed articles on this matter were published in the 1970s and it appears that since then no further breakthrough research has been undertaken. This can be partially explained by the fact that in the present time, organizations make use of all organizational structures depending on the specific requirements of a project (PMBOK 2008). Yet further empirical research should be undertaken regarding the relative effectiveness or influence of organizational structures on project success.

Finally, knowledge on the reciprocal influence of project management activities on the performance of the overall organization is relatively limited, and hence, provides another source for future research (Thiry & Deguire 2007).

References

Argyris, C. (1967). Today's Problems with Tomorrow's Organization, Journal of Management Studies, 4(1). 31-55.

Arvidsson, N. (2009). Exploring tensions in projectified matrix organisations, Scandinavian Journal of Management, 25(1), 97-107.

Baber, W., F.; Bartlett, R., V. & Dennis, C. (1990). Matrix Organization Theory and Environmental Impact Assessment, The Social Science Journal, 27(3), 235-252.

Bodera, D. (2008). Project Management Organization, Management Information Systems, 3(1), 3-9.

Burns, L., R. (1989). Matrix Management in Hospitals: Testing Theories of Matrix Structure and Development, Administrative Science Quarterly, 34(3), 349-368.

Daft, R., L. (1995). Organization Theory & Design (5th ed.). St. Paul: West Publishing Company

Davis, S., M. & Lawrence, P., R. (1977). Matrix. Reading: Addison-Wesley Publishing Company

Davis, S., M. & Lawrence, P., R. (1978). Problems of matrix organizations, Harvard Business Review, 56(3), 131-142.

Ford, R., C. & Randolph, W., A. (1992). Cross-Functional Structures: A Review and Integration of Matrix Organization and Project Management, Journal of Management, 18(2), 267-294.

Frese, E.; Graumann, M. & Theuvsen, L. (2012). Grundlagen der Organisation: Entscheidungsorientiertes Konzept der Organisationsgestaltung (10th ed.). Wiesbaden: Springer Fachmedien

Gailbraith, J., R. (1971). Matrix organization designs. Harvard Business Review, 37(3), 89-96.

Gray, C.; Dworatschek, S.; Gobeli, D.; Knoepfel, H. & Larson, E. (1990). International comparison of project organization structures: use and effectiveness, International Journal of Project Management, 8(1), 26-32.

Grinnell, S., K. & Apple, H., P. (1977). When Two Bosses Are Better than One, IEEE Engineering Management Review, 5(3), 72-75.

Hobday, M. (2000). The project-based organisation: an ideal form for managing complex products and systems?, Research Policy, 29(7-8), 871-893.

Hovmark, S. & Nordqvist, S. (1996). Project Organization: Change in the work atmosphere for engineers, International Journal of Industrial Ergonomics, 17(5), 389-398.

Hyväri, I. (2006). Project management effectiveness in project-oriented business organizations, International Journal of Project Management, 24(3), 216-225.

Jones, R., G.; Bouncken, R., B. (2008). Organisation: Theorie, Design und Wandel (5th ed.). München: Pearson Education Deutschland GmbH

Joyce, W., F. (1986). Matrix Organization: A Social Experiment, Academy of Management Journal, 29(3), 536-561.

Keller, R., T. (1986). Predictors of the performance of project groups in R&D Organizations, Academy of Management Journal, 29(4), 715-726.

Kerzner, H. (2009). Project management: a systems approach to planning, scheduling and controlling (10th ed.). New Jersey: John Wiley & Sons, Inc.

Kolodny, H., F. (1979). Evolution to a matrix organization, Academy of Management Review, 4(4), 543-553.

Knight, K. (1976). Matrix organization: A review, Journal of Management Studies, 17(2): 111-130.

Kuprenas, J., A. (2003). Implementation and performance of a matrix structure, International Journal of Project Management, 21(1), 51-62.

Larson, E., W.; Gobeli, D., H. (1987). Matrix Management: Contradictions and Insights, California Management Review 29(4), 126-138.

Larson, E., W.; Gobeli, D., H. (1989). Significance of Project Management Structure on Development Success, IEEE Transactions of Engineering Management, 36(2), 119-125.

Hill, R. & White, B., J. (ed.) (1979). Matrix Organization & Project Management. Michigan: Michigan Business Papers

Mee, J. (1964). Matrix organizations. Business Horizons, 7(2), 70-72.

Meredith, J. R.; Mantel, S. J. (2012). Project Management: A Managerial Approach (8th ed.). Singapore; John Wiley & Sons Pte. Ltd.

Morris, P., W. & Pinto, J.; K. (2007). Project Organization & Project Management Competencies. New Jersey: John Wiley & Sons, Inc.

Peters, T. & Waterman, R., H. (1982). In Search of Excellence. New York: Harper & Row, Publisher

Perkins, T., K. (2006). The Core Problem of Project Failure, Journal of Quality Assurance Institute, 20(4), 6-9.

Pinto, J., K. & Mantel, S., J. (1990). The Causes of Project Failure, IEEE Transactions of Engineering Management, 37(4), 269-276.

Pinto, J., K. & Prescott, J., E. (1988). Variations in critical success factors over the stages in the project life cycle, Journal of Management, 14(1), 5-18.

Poirot, J., W. (1991). Organizing for quality: Matrix organization, Journal of Management in Engineering, 7(2), 178-186.

Project Management Institute (PMBOK Guide. (2008). A Guide to the Project Management Body of Knowledge (4th ed.). Pennsylvania: PMI Publishing

Reeser, C. (1969). Some Potential Human Problems of the Project Form of Organization, Academy of Management Journal, 12(4), 459-467.

Schreyögg, G. (2008). Organisation: Grundlagen moderner Organisationsgestaltung (5th ed.). Wiesbaden: Gabler Fachverlage GmbH

Sayles, L., R. (1976). Matrix management: The structure with a future, Organizational Dynamics, 5(2), 2-17

Standish Group (2013), Chaos Manifesto 2013: Think Big, Act Small, Boston, MA: The Standish Group International, Inc.

Standish Group (2014), Big Bang Boom, Boston, MA: The Standish Group International, Inc.

Sy, T. & D'Annunzio, L., S. (2005). Challenges and Strategies of Matrix Organizations, Human Resources Planning, 28(1), 39-48.

Stuckenbruck, L., C. (1981). The implementation of project management: The professional's handbook. Reading: Addison-Wesley Publishing Company

Thiry, M. & Deguire, M. (2007). Recent developments in project-based organisations, International Journal of Project Management, 25(7), 649-658.

Turner, S., G.; Utley, D., R. & Westbrook, J., D. (1998). Project Managers and Functional Managers: A Case Study of Job Satisfaction in a Matrix Organization, Project Management Journal, 29(3), 11-19.

Turner, J., R. & Keegan, A. (1999). The Versatile Project-based Organization: Governance and Operational Control, European Management Journal, 17(3), 296-309.

Verma, V., K. (1995). The Human Aspects of Project Management: Organizing Projects for Success. Pennsylvania: Project Management Institute, Inc.

Youker, R. (1977). Organization alternatives for project managers, Management Review, 66(11), 46-53.

Virtual Organization

Lea Gerharz, Philipp Marquardt

Abstract. The term of virtual organization has been used for over more than 20 years and is linked to a range of disparate phenomena. Based on advanced networking and the technology used, the platform design changed and eased the implementation and design of new products. As a basis for virtual organizations, there can be seen the areas of software provisioning, value creation, legal frameworks, partition of profit, loss and trust. Using these three domains as a basis, a holistic understanding of an area, which is as complex as virtual organizations, is to be created. An overview of knowledge, ideas and definitions is given and the various aspects of virtual organizations are reflected and contrasted. Furthermore, the main drivers and contrasting viewpoints are shown and further research areas are listed.

Keywords: virtual organization, virtuality, virtual reality, network organization, virtual office, dimensions of virtual organization

1 Introduction

The notion of a virtual organization was mentioned already 20 years ago by Bleecker (1994) and was from there on analyzed in a wide contextual range. Initially, virtual organizations were still limited and used for instance to communicate with homeless people to inform them about their progress in finding a work placement (Bleecker 1994). Therefore the question that has to be asked is what is known about virtual organizations and which different viewpoints on this topic exist.

In regards to the structure, the theoretical framework for virtual organization is set by an overview of knowledge, ideas and definitions. Directly after the key terms, three different clusters following the structure of Riemer and Vehring (2012) are introduced and different point of views are related to one of the types, and furthermore contrasted. In addition to this structure, a further possible way of forming groups within virtual organizations is explained following Kürümlüoglu et al. (2005) and connection is drawn between the ways of structuring. Next the main drivers for virtual organization are shown and are followed by the dimensions in which this structure is present. Underlining possible causes for virtual organizations, the main advantages as well as disadvantages and limitations are contrasted. Finally possible areas for further research within the topic of virtual organizations are pointed out.

2 Definition and ideas

Several definitions and ideas can be found in literature regarding virtual teams. In the following part, the term of virtual organization will be reflected through the findings of different authors. Mowshowitz (1997) sees virtual organizations as a possibility to manage goal-oriented activities and giving them a structure, while Turoff (1985) is explaining the term *virtuality* in a broader frame as he is generalizing it to *virtual reality*. Therefore he is referring to real systems, which were transformed out of computer-based systems (Turoff 1985). The term of virtual organization was conceptualized in the early 1980's by Mowshowitz (1994), which created a sort of agreement in literature on what is meant by it. Mowshowitz (1997) himself however states in his articles the lack of a universally definition, as he considered it being a new idea. According to Linston et al. (2008) virtual organizations are entities within an organization, which are having a specific purpose and are existent only for a period of time. Other authors in contrast see virtual organization as long-term elements of structures (Camarinha-Matos & Afsarmanesh 2007; Larsen & McInerey 2002; Franke 1999). Such networks are having the aim to achieve a defined goal and reach it by using their core competencies and resources (Lin & Lu 2005). Consequently virtual organizations are seen as interdependent and geographical dispersed structures (Stoica & Ghillic-Micu 2009) and are connected to several different areas such as "[...] virtual memory, virtual reality, virtual classrooms, virtual teams and virtual offices" (Mowshowitz 1997, p. 30). Moreover virtual organization is used to discuss a broad variety of different organizational phenomena and the appropriate managerial challenges, which can cause problems and be seen as an unsatisfying explanation (Mowshowitz 1997).

3 Theoretical framework and different author's views

According to Riemer and Vehring (2012) virtual organizations were sorted and clustered through 67 instances and definitions. As a result the term was classified in three groups: *Internal, network and outsourcing virtual organization* (Riemer & Vehring 2012). In the following figure an overview is shown:

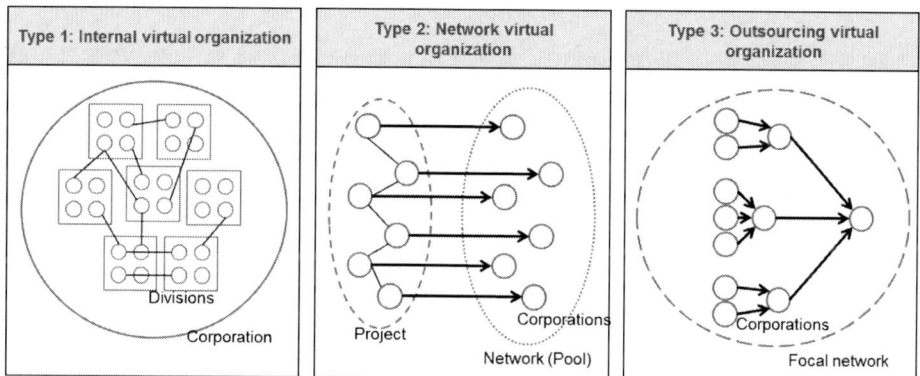

Figure 1: Main structural features of virtual organization types (Riemer & Vehring 2012)

These groups will be explained and contrasted in the following part. The first type of *internal virtual organization* sees the organization as one corporation. Blocks are set up and are focusing on virtual communities and teams (Breu & Hemingway 2004). Within this corporation, there are different divisions, where virtual teams are working together through ICT (information and communication technology). Through technologies such as remote and mobile work practices, the organization can efficiently handle geographic and distribution distances. Value is created geographically, shared through ICT information and communicated internally (Riemer & Vehring 2012). Multi-national corporations are making particularly use of ICT and are hence organizing their value creation (Kock 2000). Typically the organization is spread over the globe, so that the geographical distance between the locations is vast (Breu & Hemingway 2004; Davenport & Pearlson 1998; Berger 1996). Following Moller (1997) travelling to exchange information because of geographical distances is rare trough ICT. Tianfield and Unland (2003) argue that the need of having locations of organizations close to each is decreasing. Likewise this progress would not have been possible without networked ICTs (Breu & Hemingway

2004). Some authors use the term *virtual office* to show how work environments changed in virtual organizations (Scholz 1996; Davenport & Pearlson 1998). For instance, the variety increased trough mobile and high distance offices and employees can work from home, close to their home or wherever they can connect themselves (Davenport & Pearlson 1998; Kock 2000; Shao, Liao & Wang 1998; Bortolot 2014). Msanjila and Afsarmanesh (2008) see the main aim of virtual organization in breeding environments (VBE) to create effective virtual organization by measuring trust within an organization.

Usually virtual organizations are seen as *network organizations* (Bekkers 2003) according to type 2. Teams come together quickly with the aim of fast exploitation of upcoming market opportunities (Coyle & Schnarr 1995). Typically these teams consist of diverse entities concerning their functionality and culture (Lin & Lu 2005). Concerning the time horizon of network virtual organizations, the majority of authors see virtual organizations as rather short term oriented (Christie & Levary 1998) through project teams (Kasper-Fuehrer & Ashkansasy 2001). In most of the cases, these organizations are disassembling when the purpose for creating them is met (Christie & Levary 1998). Some authors see on the other hand a high need in a long term orientation of collaborative structures in order to enable them to emerge. Long-term oriented organizations can be seen as a pool (Larsen & McInerey 2002), web based platforms (Franke 1999) or breeding environments (Camarinha-Matos & Afsarmanesh 2007). One main goal is the selection of qualified partners to enhance a long term relationship (Camarinha-Matos & Afsarmanesh 2007).

The third type of *outsourcing virtual organization* is described as an organization, where value-creating activities are outsourced to a supplier network (Riemer & Vehring 2012; Liston et al. 2008), while the core player is specifying the strategy (Lawton & Michaels 2001). In the manufacturing area outsourcing is one of the major drivers for the increase of virtual organizations according to Liston et al. (2008), while in general the network is contract-based (Werther 1999). Separating the process of value creating geographically and temporary (Alt, Legner & Österle 2005), the supply chain can be used efficiently. The production process, transport and distribution can be improved through virtual logistics and therefore modern simulation techniques as a part of modern supply chain management (Firescu, Filip & Vlad 2013).

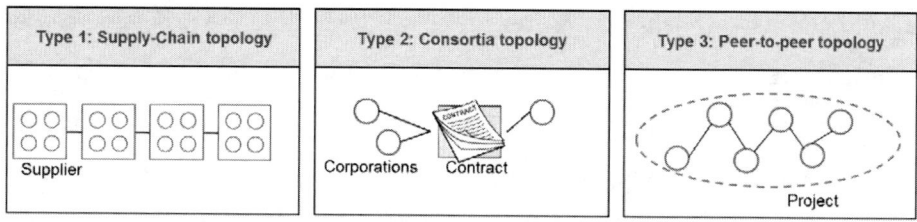

Figure 2: virtual organization Topology (Kürümlüoglu, Nostdal & Karvonen 2005)

According to figure 2, a further option of structuring virtual organizations can be through their organizational topology (Abuelmaatti & Rezgui 2008; Kürümlüoglu, Nostdal & Karvonen 2005). Therefore virtual organizations were divided up into *Supply-Chain, Consortia and Peer-to-Peer topologies*. The *Supply-Chain topology* includes supply chain networks and is connected to type 3 outsourcing *virtual organizations* (Riemer & Vehring 2012). It is following a hierarchical process and the principles of the SCOR (Supply Chain Operations Reference Model) model. The *Consortia topology* is usually driven by contractual based structures and is seen as a hub and spoke network. In regard to the contractual based structure, a connection to type 3 outsourced virtual organizations exists (Riemer & Vehring 2012). The *Peer-to-peer-Topology* is focusing on networks, which are based on projects. These organizations can be re-assembled quickly. Especially the long lasting character is supported by type 2 network virtual organization (Riemer & Vehring 2012; Camarinha-Matos & Afsarmanesh 2007).

In regards to the dimensions of virtual organization, there is set a framework for creating value within an alliance. Following Abuelmaatti and Rezgui (2008), virtual organizations can be narrowed trough *organizational, legal, economic* and *socio-cultural* dimensions. The *legal* dimension is referring to processes like the inclusion or removal of participants and two legal entities cooperating through virtual organizations (Plump & Ketchen 2013; Abuelmaatti & Rezgui 2008). The *economic dimension* is including the transformation of former economic systems to smart new economies, while they are pressured to behave adaptive, agile and focusing on innovative approaches (Lipnack & Stamps 2000). Trust, the structure of the team members, social cohesion and organizational culture is included in the *socio-cultural* dimension (Abuelmaatti & Rezgui 2008). Regarding the *technological* dimension of virtual organizations, central business processes need to be supported and systems need to be integrated and work together properly. Moreover the support of interaction between organization members and individuals needs to be provided by a technological solution (Rezgui & Wilson 2005; Shao, Liao & Wang 1998).

4 Main causes and relevance

In the following section the main causes are reflected, as they underline the importance of virtual organizations. One of the main drivers for virtual organizations are the environmental developments in markets and the raise of new technologies dealing with information and communication. Organizational structures were fundamentally impacted in the role of value creation (Bleecker 1994; Riemer & Vehring 2012). Making use of new technologies people, companies and networks can be easily linked together on a global level (Bleecker 1994). Cooperation between firms in order to get access and create resources, technological risk sharing and facilitated market entry are possible reasons for changed structures. Furthermore changing market requirements require a more flexible and responsive internal organization, according to Bekkers (2003) especially in the public sector (Riemer & Vehring 2012).

The following section will show why virtual organization is relevant and what main opinions exist. In business press and in academic reviews, virtual organizations received increased attention (Reinicke 2011). In nearly any place on the world internet is accessible, far distance communication is possible and therefore the basis for virtual organizations is set (Drucker 1998). Particularly Abuelmaatti and Rezgui (2008) highlight the fact of a grown demand for individual, high quality services and products through technological progress and a global and therefore complex economy. Creating a competitive advantage can according to Barrett and Sexton (2006) only be reached through innovation. Value is created by virtual organizations and is therefore an answer to complex business environments (Workman, Kahnweiler & Bommer 2003). Reacting accordingly to these developments, many firms remodeled their structure to virtual organizations (Reinicke 2011). According to Camarinha-Matos and Afsarmanesh (2007) virtual organizations are even seen as a survival mechanism being faced with market turbulence. They point out the extreme case of the necessity to coordinate activities and engage numerous units and the upcoming challenges for management within the disaster rescuing processes. virtual organizations can be set up rapidly and throughout their goal-oriented structure provide great agility (Camarinha-Matos & Afsarmanesh 2007).

5 Advantages and disadvantages

virtual organization can be a competitive advantage and a possible strength for companies dealing with current environmental challenges. Being a *flexible system* and *increasing responsiveness*, virtual organization can increase the quality level of services and products, reduce costs, optimize the use of resources and improve managerial control (Mowshowitz 1997; Gökmen 2012). Abuelmaatti and Rezgui (2008) are going further and see the advantage in a better market position, profitability and the ambition to create value. Especially in the area of b2b (business to business) and for small or medium sized companies (Franke 1999), the *low cost and rapid development* and manufacturing of products virtual organization is seen as an advantage for partner companies. Within the virtual organization, partners like suppliers, manufacturers and retailers can set up their resources and be therefore more competitive as a whole (Preece 2001; Drucker 1998). Mainly the ability of using a *home office* or working in an office which is located close to home, is increasing the comfort for the employee as well as reducing costs in general (Davenport & Pearlson 1998). Concerning the lifecycle of virtual organization, the characteristics of informal and managerial nature adhere to economic systems were measured by Stoica et al. (2009). Notably significance has the *ability to learn* of virtual organizations and therefore the behavioural accordance with changes within the environment (Stoica & Ghillic-Micu 2009).

Adapting the concept of virtual organization can be challenging (Abuelmaatti & Rezgui 2008) and create disadvantages. Especially if there is no information about matching partners accessible and the possible partners are internally not prepared for being part of a virtual organization (Camarinha-Matos & Afsarmanesh 2007). Camarinha-Matos and Afsarmanesh (2007) disagree partly in the point of virtual organizations being a low cost advantage for organization (Drucker 1998; Preece 2001). They argue that especially partner selection and the establishment to found virtual organizations can be *costly concerning* time and effort. Therefore virtual organizations can even hinder the goal of being agile (Camarinha-Matos & Afsarmanesh 2007). According to this point of view, the demand for new skills will challenge leaders especially in traditional organizations. Human spirit and capabilities can only be designed by an adequate *HR (Human Ressource) system* (Coyle & Schnarr 1995). Coming from the need of enterprises to cooperate with other enterprises, *trust* can be seen as a basis for interactions. Only with trust in virtual organizations, acting without uncertainty and the high risk of negative outcomes becomes possible (Mun, Shin & Jung 2011; Camarinha-Matos & Afsarmanesh 2007). Concerning the *legal* dimension of virtual organization (Riemer & Vehring 2012), there increases the difficulty to address claims within the entity, as it is seen as one enterprise and as there was not found a coherent framework yet (Shelbourn, Hassan, & Carter 2005). Plump et al. (Plump & Ketchen 2013) are pointing out the risk of harming the reputation of a company, financial risks and loosing key personnel due to legal issues like the violation of labor and personnel laws.

6   Questions concerning virtual organization that need further research

There are discussed several topics concerning virtual organization in literature and authors suggest further research in certain areas. Especially information about working procedures and managerial structures within virtual organizations was not provided yet by research. Moreover the *software provisions* within technological progress need further research (Abuelmaatti & Rezgui 2008). Particularly flexible crawlers and text analyzers is a challenge that needs further research (Camarinha-Matos & Afsarmanesh 2007). Especially the "combination of technology, organizational, and ultimately legal and ultimately legal and economic considerations" (Abuelmaatti & Rezgui 2008, p. 8) is *creating value* in an organization. Consequently these issues must be included in future research on the potential of virtual organizations. Additionally there is asked for a *roadmap* which will focus on social and organizational aspects and is applicable for all categories of staff within an organization (Abuelmaatti & Rezgui 2008). Shelbourn et al. (2005) point unanswered *legal questions*, as there was not found a consistent *legal framework*, while a rough overview of legal questions is provided by Plump et al. (2013). Especially confidential issues, IP (intellectual property) rights, issues concerning confidentiality, responsibility, distribute liability and defining a legal entity will be challenging (Abuelmaatti & Rezgui 2008; Plump & Ketchen 2013).

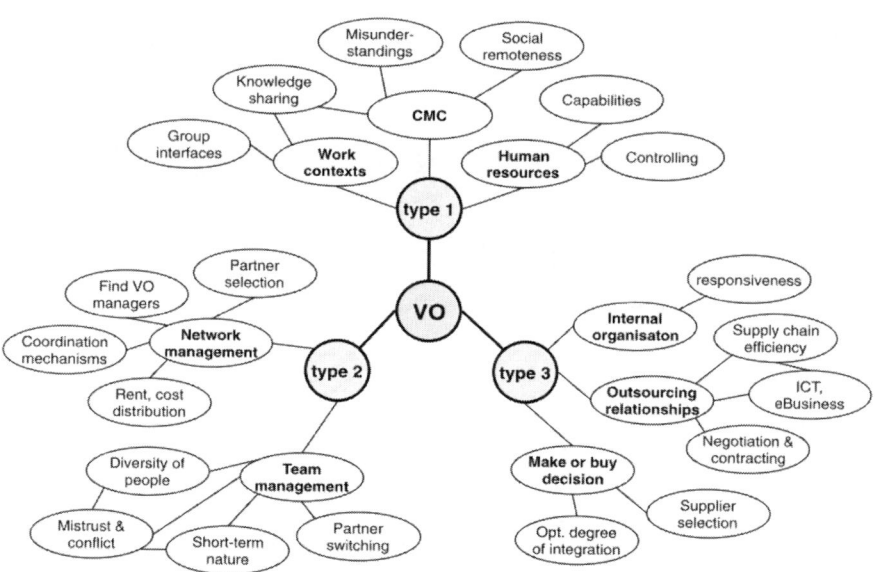

Figure 3: Network of management challenges to the three virtual organization types (Riemer & Vehring, 2012 p. 277)

From an economic perspective the *partition of profit and losses* within the virtual organization and the consistent evaluation and determination of costs across the network needs to be researched (Abuelmaatti & Rezgui 2008). Regarding the socio-cultural dimension of virtual organizations or network virtual organization (Riemer & Vehring 2012) further research is needed in terms of *trust* within the organization, which working infrastructures can support trust and how relationship management can foster teams in virtual organizations (Abuelmaatti & Rezgui 2008). Msanjila and Afsarmanesh (2008) already set a basis for these studies by an approach to the objective trust analysis within virtual organization breeding environments (VBE) as well as Pangil and Chan (2014) within the influence of limitation of communication in virtual teams. Mun et al. (2011) furthermore established a more practical and goal-oriented model to evaluate the values of trust within an enterprise and applied this model even in project based virtual organizations.

In addition to that, *the coefficients that influence trust* in virtual organizations need investigation, since the evaluation model has a fuzzy structure (Mun, Shin & Jung 2011). Hence the *identification and relation between organization members* and their manager can be as well a basis for further research (Msanjila & Afsarmanesh, 2008; Abuelmaatti & Rezgui, 2008). In addition the selection process of partner search and suggestions in regards of soft issues needs to be analyzed more detailed (Camarinha-Matos & Afsarmanesh 2007). A summary of the challenges that management can be confronted with according to the three types provided by Riemer and Vehring (2012) provides figure 3.

7 Conclusion

Being treated in literature since more than 20 years, virtual organization still has a broad spectrum of further research. The areas of software provisions, creating value, legal frameworks, partition of profit and loss and trust can be seen as a basis for virtual organizations. Regarding these areas, solutions for virtual organizations need to be blended towards them (Abuelmaatti & Rezgui 2008).

Riemer and Vehring (2012) point out the need for a *clear concept* and the definition of the *characters* of virtual business modes on which future research needs to be based on (Abuelmaatti & Rezgui 2008). A possible concept is the division of virtual organization into three types of virtual organizations: Internal, network and outsourcing virtual organization. They are especially useful as virtual organization has its roots in areas, which are linked closely together, but are still different areas (Riemer & Vehring 2012).

Using these categories as a basis, the area of virtual organization can gain credibility and make a value adding contribution to research in IS (Riemer & Vehring 2012). Hence a holistic understanding of an area, which is as complex as, virtual organizations can be created.

References

Abuelmaatti, A., & Rezgui, Y. (2008). virtual organizations in Practice: A European Perspective. *AMCIS 2008 Proceedings*, pp. 1-9.

Alt, R., Legner, C., & Österle, H. (2005). Virtuelle Organistaionen: Virtuelle Organisation: Konzept, Realität, Umsetzung, Herausforderungen. In H. Heilmann, *Virtuelle Organisationen* (pp. 7-20). Heidelberg: dpunkt-Verlag.

Barrett, P., & Sexton, M. (2006). Innovation in Small, Project-Based Construction Firms. *British Journal of Management, Vol. 17*, pp. 331-346.Abuelmaatti, A., & Rezgui, Y. (2008, January). Virtual Organizations in Practice: A European Perspective. *AMCIS 2008 Proceedings*, pp. 1-9.

Alfadly, A. A. (2011). Managing Complexity in Kuwaiti Organizations . *International Journal of Business and Management*, Vol. 6(3), pp. 142-145.

Alt, R., Legner, C., & Österle, H. (2005). Virtuelle Organistaionen: Virtuelle Organisation: Konzept, Realität, Umsetzung, Herausforderungen. In H. Heilmann, *Virtuelle Organisationen* (pp. 7-20). Heidelberg: dpunkt-Verlag.

Anderson, M. C. (2001). *Case Study on the Return on Investment of Executive Coaching.* MetrixGlobal, LLC.

Anderson, P. / Meyer, A. / Eisenhardt, K. / Carley, K. / Pettigrew, A. (1999). Introduction to the Special Issue: Applications of Complexity Theory to Organization Science. *Organization Science*, Vol. 10(3), pp. 233-236.

Argyris, C., & Schoen, D. (1978). *Organisational learning: a theory of action perspective.* New York: Addison-Wesley.

Atkinson, P. E. (2012). Return on investment in executive coaching: effective organisational change. *Management Services (Spring 2012)*, pp. 20-23.

Baker, W. E., & Sinkula, J. M. (2002). Market orientation, learning orientation and product innovation: delving into the organization's black box. *Journal of Market-Focussed Manageneg*, 5 (1), 5-23.

Baker, W. E., & Sinkula, J. M. (1999). The synergistic effect of market orientation and learning orientation on organizational performance. *Journal of the Academy of Marketing Science*, 27 (4), 411-427.

Baron, L., & Morin, L. (2009). The Coach-Coachee Relationship in Executive Coaching: A Field Study. *Human Ressource Development Quarterly, Spring Vol. 20/1*, pp. 85-106.

Barrett, P., & Sexton, M. (2006). Innovation in Small, Project-Based Construction Firms. *British Journal of Management, Vol. 17*, pp. 331-346.

Beeby, M., & Booth, C. (2000). Networks and interorganizational learning: A critical review. *The Learning Organization*, 7 (2), 75-88.

Bekkers, V. (2003). E-government and the emerge of virtual organizations in the public sector. *Information Polity, Vol. 8*, pp. 89-101.

Bens, D. A. / Monahan, S. J. (2004). Disclosure Quality and the Excess Value of Diversification. *Journal of Accounting Research*, pp. Vol.42(4), pp. 691-730.

Berger, M. (1996). Making the virtual offica a reality. *Sales & Marketing Management, Vol. 6* , pp. 18-22.

Bierly, P., & Chakrabarti, A. (1996). Generic knowledge strategies in the US pharmaceutical industry. *Strategy Management Journal , 17*, 123-135.

Billet, M. T. / Chen, C./ Martin, X. / Wang, X. (2013). Internal Information Asymmetry, Internal Capital Markets, and Firm Value . URL: https://www2.bc.edu/~pontiff/Conference%20Papers/BCMW_11212013.pdf, accessed [03/18/2014].

Bleecker, S. E. (1994, March-April). The Virtual Organization. *The Futurist* , pp. 9-14.

Bluckert, P. (2005). The foundations of a psychological approach to executive coaching. *Industial and Commercial Training, Vol.37/4* , pp. 171-178.

Boisot, M. (2003). *Is There a Complexity Beyond the Reach of Strategy?* In: Mitleton-Kelly, E. (Ed.): Complex Systems and Evolutionary Perspectives on Organisations. The Application of Complexity Theory to Organisations, Bringley, UK: (Emerald), 2003, p. 185-202.

Bontis, N., Crossan, M. M., & Hulland, J. (2002). Managing an organizational learning system by aligning stocks and flows. *Journals of Management Studies , 39* (4), 437-469.

Bortolot, J. (2014, March). The un-office: New workplace trends include movable walls, outdoor spaces and sometimes no office at all. *Entrepreneur* , pp. 20-21.

Bozarth, C. C. / Warsing, D. P. / Flynn, B. B. / Flynn, E. J. (2009). The impact of supply chain complexity on manufacturing plant performance. *Journal of Operations Management* , Vol. 27(1), pp. 78-93.

Bozer, G. (2013). The role of coachee characteristics in executive coaching for effective sustainability. *Journal of Management Development, Vol. 32/3* , pp. 277-294.

Bozer, G., & Sarros, J. C. (2012, February). Examining the Effectiveness of Executive Coaching on Coachees' Performance in the Israeli Context. *International Journal of Evidence Based Coaching and Mentoring; 10(1)* , pp. 14-32.

Brady, D. (2010, April 25). CAN GE STILL MANAGE? *BusinessWeek* .

Breu, K., & Hemingway, C. (2004). Making organizations virtual: The hidden cost of distributed teams. *Journal of Information Technology, Vol. 3* , pp. 191-202.

Browde, B. (2011). Coaching Political Leaders: Can Coaching Be Used To Improve The Quality Of Executive-Level Government? *Journal of Leadership Studies, Vol. 5/1* , pp. 71-75.

Burnes, B. . (2005). Complexity Theories and Organizational Change. *International Journal of Management Reviews* , Vol. 7(2), pp. 73-90.

Bushman, R. / Chen, Q. / Engel, E. / Smith, A. (2004). Financial accounting information, organizational complexity and corporate governance systems. *Journal of Accounting and Economics* , pp. Vol. 37 (2), pp. 167-201.

Camarinha-Matos, L. M., & Afsarmanesh, H. (2007). A framework for virtual organization creation in a breeding enviroment. *Annual Reviews in Control, Vol. 31* , pp. 119-135.

Camelot Management Consultants . (2012). Survey "Mastering Complexity": Most European companies are afraid of losing control over rising complexity. *Press Release* , URL: http://www.camelot-mc.com/en/press/press-releases/press-archive-2012/survey-mastering-complexity-most-european-companies-are-afraid-of-losing-control-over-rising-complexity/, accessed [03/08/2014].

Cangelosi, V. E., & Dill, W. R. (1965). Organizational Learning: Obersavtions toward a theory. *Administrative Science Quarterly , 10* (2), 175-203.

Carillo, P. M. / Kopelman, R. E. (1991). Organization Structure and Productivity: Effects of Subunit Size, Vertical Complexity, and Administrative Intensity on Operating Efficiency. *Group Organization Management* , Vol.16(1), pp. 44-59.

Choi, T. Y. / Krause, D. R. (2006). The supply base and its complexity: Implications for transaction costs, risks, responsiveness, and innovation. *Journal of Operations Management* , Vol. 24(5), pp. 637-652.

Choo, C. W., & Bontis, N. (2002). *The strategic management of intellectual capital and organizational knowledge.* Oxford: Oxford University Press.

Christie, P. M., & Levary, R. R. (1998). Virtual corporations: Recipe for success. *Industrial Management, Vol. 4* , pp. 7-11.

Cohen, M. . (1999). Commentary on the Organization Science Special Issue on Complexity. *Organization Science* , Vol. 10(3), pp. 373-376.

Cohen, M., & Sproul, L. (1991). Editors introduction. *Organization Science - Special Issue on Organisational Learning , 2* (1), 1-3.

Coyle, J., & Schnarr, N. (1995). The Soft-Side Challenges of the "Virtual Corporation". *Human Resource Planning, Vol. 1* , pp. 41-42.

Crossan, M. M., Lane, H. W., & White, R. (1999). Organizational learning framework: from intuition to institution. *Academy of Management Review , 3* (24), 522-537.

Crossan, M., & Berdrow, I. (2003). Organizational learning and strategic renewal. *Strategic Management Journal , 24* (1), 1087-1105.

Crossan, M., & Guatto, T. (1996). Organizational Learning Profile. *Journal of Organizational Change Management , 9* (1), 107-122.

Cyert, R., & March, J. (1963). *A behavioral theory of the firm* (2nd Edition ed.). Malden, MA, USA: Blackwell.

Davenport, T. H., & Pearlson, K. (1998). Two cheers for the virtual office. *Sloan Management Review, Vol. 4* , pp. 51-65.

de Haan, E. (2011). Executive coaching in practice: what determines helpfulness for clients of coaching? *Personnel Review, Vol. 40/1* , pp. 24-44.

Decarolis, D. M., & Deeds, D. L. (1999). The impact of stocks and flows of organizational knowledge on firm performance: an empirical investigation of the bio-technology industry. *Strategy Management Journal , 20*, 953-968.

Demanpour, F. (1996). Organizational Complexity and Innovation: Developing and Testing Multiple Contingency Models. *Management Science* , Vol. 42.(5), pp. 693-716.

Demirkan, S./ Radhakrishnan, S. / Urcan, O. (2011). Discretionary Accruals Quality, Cost of Capital, and Diversification. *Journal of Accounting, Auditing & Finance* , pp. Vol. 27(4), pp. 496–526.

Denning, Steve. (2014). Can A Big Old Hierarchical Bureaucracy Become A 21st Century Network? *Forbes*, URL: http://www.forbes.com/sites/stevedenning/2014/03/21/can-a-big-old-hierarchical-bureaucracy-become-a-21st-century-network/, accessed [03/24/14].

Dervitsiotis, K. N. (2012). An innovation-based approach for coping with increasing complexity in the global economy. *Total Quality Management*, Vol. 23(9), pp. 997- 1011.

Dodgson, M. (1993). Organizational Learning: A Review of Some Literatures. *Organization Studies*, *14* (3), 375-394.

Douglas, C. A., & Morley, W. H. (2000). *Executive coaching: An annotated Bibliography.* North Carolina: Center for Creative Leadership.

Drucker, P. F. (1998, October 5). Management's new paradigms. *Forbes*, pp. 152-177.

Dumitraşcu, V. / Dumitraşcu, R. A. (2011). Approach to the Organisational Complexity in Terms of Network and Intellectual Capital Concepts. *Romanian Journal of Economics*, Vol. 32(1), pp. 191-215.

Duru, A. / Reeb, D. M. (2002). International Diversification and Analysts' Forecast Accuracy and Bias. *The Accounting Review*, pp. Vol. 77(2), pp. 415-433.

Economist Intelligence Unit. (2011). The Complexity Challenge: How businesss are bearing up. *The Economist*, URL: http://mib.rbs.com/docs/MIB/Insight/Simplifying-complexity/EIU_report-The_Complexity_Challenge.pdf, pp. 1-32, accessed [03/16/2014].

Edmonds, B. (1999). *What is Complexity? - The philosophy of complexity per se with application to some examples in evolution.* In Heylighen, F. and Aerts, D. (Eds.); Dordrecht: (Kluwer), pp. 1-18.

Enescu, C., & Popescu, D. M. (2012, July). Executive Coaching - Instrument for Implementing Organizational Change. *Review of International Comparative Management, Vol. 13/3*, pp. 378-386.

Ennis, S. A. (2012). *The Executive Coaching Handbook.* Retrieved März 10, 2014, from http://www.executivecoachingforum.com/

Espejo, R. (2003). *Social Systems and the Embodiment of Organisational Learning.* In: Mitleton-Kelly, E. (Ed.): Complex Systems and Evolutionary Perspectives on Organisations. The Application of Complexity Theory to Organisations, Bringley, UK: (Emerald), 2003, p. 53-70.

Fabac, R. (2010). Complexity in Organizations and Environment - Adaptive Changes and Adaptive Decision-Making. *Interdisciplinary Description of Complex Systems - scientific journal*, Vol. 8(1), pp. 34-48.

Fawcett, S. E. / Waller, M. A. (2011). Making sense out of chaos: Why Theory is Relevant to Supply Chain Research. *Journal of Business Logistics*, Vol. 32(1), pp. 1-5.

Feldman, D. C., & Lankau, M. J. (2005, November). Executive Coaching: A Review and Agenda for Future Research. *Journal of Management*, pp. 828-848.

Field, L. (1997). Impediments to empowerment and learning within organisations. *The Learning Organisation*, *4* (4), 149-158.

Finger, M., & Buergin, S. (1998). *The concept of the "Leaning Organization" applied to the transformation of the public sector: Conceptual contributions for theory development.* . London: Sage.

Firescu, V., Filip, D., & Vlad, R. (2013, March). The virtual factory in supply chains management. *Review of Management & Economic Engineering* , pp. 33-40.

Fitzgerald, L., & Van Eijnatten, F. M. (2002). Chaos speak: a glossary of chaordic terms and phrases. *Journal of Organizational Change Management , 15* (4), 412-423.

Fontaine, D., & Schmidt, G. F. (2009). The Practice of Executive Coaching Requires Practice: A Clarification and Challenge to Our Field. *Industrial and Organizational Psychology, Vol. 2* , pp. 277-279.

Franke, U. J. (1999). The virtual web as a new entrepreneurial approach to network organizations. *Entrepreneurship and regional development, Vol. 11* , pp. 203-229.

Friedlander, F. (1983). *Patterns of Individual and Organizational Learning.* San Francisco: Jossey-Bass.

Gökmen, A. (2012, March). Virtual business operations, e-commerce & its significanc and the case of Turkey: current situation and its potential. *Electronic Commer Research, Vol. 12, Issue 1* , pp. 31-51.

Gøtzsche, N. / Klausen, M. K. . (2014). The Optimal Response Strategy for MNCs in a Complex Environment: An Economic Approach . pp. 1-128.

Garvin, D. (1993, July/August). Building a learning organization. *Harvard Business Review* , 78-91.

Gemmil, G. / Smith, C. . (1985). A Dissipative Structure Model of Organization Transformation. *Human Relations* , Vol. 38(8), pp. 751-766.

Gerschberger, M. / Engelhardt-Nowitzki, C. / Kummer, S. / Staberhofer, F. (2012). A model to determine complexity in supply networks . *Journal of Manufacturing Technology Management* , Vol. 23(8), pp. 1015-1037.

Gerschberger, M. / Staberhofer, F. / Engelhardt-Nowitzki, C. (2011). Complexity Parameters in Supply Networks– an extensive Literature Review. URL: http://www.agtil.at/uploads/images/PDFs/final_fullpaper_Supply%20Chain%20Complexity%20Parameters_ICLS_final.pdf, accessed [03/21/2014].

Ghoshal, S. / Nohria, N. (1993). Horses for Courses: Organizational Forms for Multinational Corporations. *Sloan Management Review* , Vol. 34(2), pp. 23-35.

Gibson, C. B., & Birkinshaw, J. (2004). The antecedents consequences, and mediating role of organizational ambidexterity. *Academy of Management Journal , 47* (1), 209-226.

Gilson, C., Dunleavy, P., & Tinkler, J. (2009). *Organizational Learning in Goverment Sector Organizations: Literature Review.* London School of Economics Public Policy Group. London: LSE Public Policy Group.

Glen, S. S. / Malott, M. E. (2004). Complexity and selection: Implications for organizational change. *Behavior and Social Issues* , Vol. 13(2), pp. 89-106.

Goldstein, J. (1999). Emergence as a Construct: History and Issues . *Emergence* , Vol. 1(1), pp. 49-72.

Good, D. (2010). Cognitive Behavioral Executive Coaching. A Structure for Increasing Leader Flexibility. *OD Practitioner, Vol. 42/3* , pp. 18-23.

Goodrick, E. / Reay, T. (2011). Constellations of Institutional Logics: Changes in the Professional Work of Pharmacists. *Work and Occupations* , Vol. 38(3), pp. 372–416.

Gorelick, C. (2005). Organizational learning vs the learning organization: a conversation with a practionier. *The Learning Organization*, 12 (4), 383-388.

Größler, A. / Grübner, A. / Milling, P. M. (2006). Organisational adaptation processes to external complexity. *International Journal of Operations & Production Management*, Vol. 26(3), pp. 254-281.

Graham, W. (2008). Towards Executive Change: A psychodynamic group coaching model for short executive programmes. *International Journal of Evidence Based Coaching and Mentoring, Vol. 6/1*, pp. 67-78.

Gray, D. E. (2006). Executive Coaching: Towards a Dynamic Alliance of Psychotherapy and Transformative Learning Processes. *Management Learning, Vol. 37/4*, pp. 475-497.

Greenwood, R. / Raynard, M. / Kodeih, F. / Micelotta, E. R. / Lounsbury, M. (2011). Institutional Complexity and Organizational Responses. *The Academy of Management Annals*, Vol. 5(1), pp. 317-371.

Greve, H. R. (2003). *Organizational Learning from Performance Feedback: A Behavioural Perspective on Innovation and Change.* Cambridge: Cambridge University Press.

Grobman, G. M. (2006). Complexity Theory: A new way to look at organizational change. *Public Administration Quarterly*, Vol. 29, (3/4), pp. 350-382.

Hannafey, F. T., & Vitulano, L. A. (2013). Ethics and Executive Coaching: An Agency Theory Appproach. *Journal of Business Ethics*, pp. 599-603.

Hashemi, A. / Butcher, T. / Chhetri, P. (2013). A modeling framework for the analysis of supply chain complexity using product design and demand characteristics. *International Journal of Engineering, Science and Technology*, Vol. 5(2), pp. 150-164.

Hernez-Broome, G., & Boyce, L. A. (2011). *Advancing Executive Coaching.* San Francisco: Jossey-Bass a Willey Imprint.

Hooley, G. / Beracs, J. . (1997). Marketing strategies for the 21st Century: lessons from the top Hungarian companies. *Journal of Strategic Marketing*, Vol. 5(3), pp. 143-165.

Huber, G. (1991). Organizational Learning: The Contributing Processes and the Literatures. *Organization Science*, 1 (2), 88-115.

Hurley, R. E., & Hult, G. T. (1998). Innovation, market orientation and organizational learning: an integration and empirical examination. *Journal of Marketing*, 62, 42-54.

Ikehara, H. (1999). Implications of Gestalt theory and practice for the learning organisation. *The Learning Organisation*, 2 (6), 63-69.

Introna, L. D. (2003). *Complexity Theory and Organisational Intervention ? Dealing with (in)commensurability.* In: Mitleton-Kelly, E. (Ed.): Complex Systems and Evolutionary Perspectives on Organisations. The Application of Complexity Theory to Organisations, Bringley, UK: (Emerald), 2003, pp. 205-219.

Jerez-Gomez, P., Lorente, J., & Valle-Cabrera, R. (2005). Organizational learning capability: a proposal of measurement. *Journal of Business Research* (58), 715-725.

Jia, X. (2010). Complex Organizational Structure and Chinese Firm Value. *Wharton Research Scholars Journal*, Vol. 10, pp. 1-30.

Jimenez, D., & Sanz-Valle, R. (2011). Innovation, organizational learning and Performance. *journal of Business Research* (64).

Joo, B.-K. e. (2012, Spring). Multiple Faces of Coaching: Manager-as-coach, Executive Coaching, and Formal Mentoring. *Organization Development Journal Vol. 30/1* , pp. 19-38.

Junior, V. M. / Pascucci, L. / Murphy, J. P. (2012). Implementing Strategies in Complex Systems: Lessons from Brazilian Hospitals. *BAR Brazilian Administration Review* , Vol. 9(2), pp. 19-37.

Kürümlüoglu, M., Nostdal, R., & Karvonen, I. (2005). Base concepts. In L. M. Camarinha-Matos, H. Afsarmanesh, & O. Martin, *Virtual Organizations Systems and Practices.* New York: Springer.

Kampa-Kokesch, S., & Anderson, M. Z. (2008). Executive coaching: A comprehensive review of the literature. In R. R. Kilburg, & R. C. Diedrich, *The Wisdom of Coaching. Essential Papers in Consulting Psychology for a World of Change* (pp. 39-59). Washington: American Psychological Association.

Kasper-Fuehrer, E. C., & Ashkansasy, N. M. (2001). Communicating trustworthiness and building trust in interorganizational virtual organizations. *Journal of Management, Vol. 27* , pp. 235-254.

Kenny, J. (2006). "Strategy and the learning organisation: a maturity model for the formation of strategy". *The Learning Organization* , 13 (4), 353-368.

Keskin, H. (2006). Market orientation, learning orientation, and innovation capabilities in SMEs. *European Journal of Innovation Management* , 9 (4), 396-417.

Kilburg, R. R. (2008). Toward a conceptual understanding and definition of executive coaching. In R. R. Kilburg, & R. C. Diedrich, *The Wisdom of Coaching. Essential Papers in Consulting Psychology for a World of Change* (pp. 21-30). Washington: American Psychological Association.

Kock, N. (2000). Benefits for virtual organizations from distributed groups. *Communication of the ACM, Vol. 11* , pp. 107-112.

Koonce, R. (2010, September/October). Narrative 360° Assessment and Stakeholder Analysis: How a Powerful Tool Drives Executive Coaching Engagements. *Global Business and Organizational Excellence* , pp. 25-37.

Larsen, K. R., & McInerey, C. R. (2002). Preparing to work in the virtual organization. *Information & Management, Vol. 39* , pp. 445-456.

Latheemaki, S., Toivonen, J., & Mattila, M. (2001). Critical aspects of organizational learning research and proposals for its measurement. *British Journal of Management* , 12 (2), 113-129.

Lawton, T. C., & Michaels, K. P. (2001). Advancing to the virtual value chain: Learning from the DELL model. *Irish Journal of Management, Vol. 22* , pp. 91-112.

Lewin, A. Y., Long, C. P., & Carroll, T. (1999). The co-evolution of new organizational forms. *Organization Science* , 10 (1), 535-550.

Lieberman, M. (1987). The Learning Curve, Diffusion, And Competitive Strategy. *Strategic Management Journal* , 8, 441-452.

Lin, L.-H., & Lu, I.-Y. (2005). Adoption of virtual organization by Taiwanese electronic firms: An empirical study of organization structure innovation. *Journal of Organizational Change*, pp. 184-200.

Lipnack, J., & Stamps, J. (2000). *Virtual Teams: People Working Across Boundaries With Technology.* New York: John Wiley & Sons.

Liston, P., Byrne, J., Heavey, C., & Byrne, P. J. (2008, March). Discrete-event simulation for evaluating virtual organizations. *International Journal of Production Research, Vol. 46, No. 5* , pp. 1335-1356.

Liu, C. L. / Lai, S. H. (2012). Organizational Complexity and Auditor Quality. *Corporate Governance: An International Review* , pp. Vol. 20(4), pp. 352–368.

Lloria, B., & Moreno-Luzon, M. (2013). Organizational learning: Proposal of an integrative scale and research instrument. *Journal of Business Research* (67), 692-697.

Mackie, D. (2007, December). Evaluating the effectiveness of executive coaching: Where are we now and where do we need to be? *Australian Psychologist; 42(4)* , pp. 310-318.

Maden, C. (2012). Transforming Public Organizations into Learning Organizations: A Conceptual Model. *Public Organization Review* (12), 71-84.

Malott, M. E. / Martinez, W. S. (2006). Addressing organizational complexity: A behavioural systems analysis application to higher education. *Pschology Press* , Vol 41(6), pp. 559-570.

Manconi, A. / Massa, M. . (2010). Modigliani and Miller Meet Chandler: Organizational Complexity, Capital Structure, and Firm Value. *Social Science Research Network* , URL: http://faculty.insead.edu/massa/Research/org_structure.pdf, accessed [03/20/2014].

Manson, S. M. (2001). Simplifying Complexity: A Review of Complexity Theory. *Geoforum* , Vol. 32(3), pp. 405-415.

March, J. G. (1991). Exploration and exploitation in organizational learning. *Organization Science , 2* (1), 71-87.

March, J., & Levitt, B. (1988). Organisational learning. *Annual Review of Sociology , 14*, 319-340.

March, J., & Olsen, J. (1975). The uncertainty of the past: Organizational learning under ambiguity. *European Journal of Political Research* (3), 147-171.

Mason, R. B. (2013). Distribution tactics for success in turbulent versus stable environments: A complexity theory approach. *Journal of Transport and Supply Chain Management* , Vol. 7(1), pp. 1-9.

Maznevski, M. / Steger, U. / Amann, W. (2007). *Managing Complexity in Global Organizations as the Meta-challenge.* In: Maznevski, M. / Steger, U. / Amann, W. (Ed.): Managing Complexity in Global Organizations, Chichester: (Wiley), 2007, pp. 3-14.

McAdam, S. (2005). *Executive Coaching: How to choose, use and maximize value for yourself and your team.* London: Thorogood Publishing Limited .

McKenna, D. D., & Davis, S. L. (2009). Hidden in Plain Sight: The Active Ingredients of Executive Coaching. *Industrial and Organizational Psychology, Vol.2* , pp. 244-260.

Meyer, M. W. / Lu, X. . (2004). Managing Indefinite Boundaries: The Strategy and Structure of a Chinese Business Firm. *Management and Organization Review* , Vol. 1(1), pp. 57–86.

Mitleton-Kelly, E. (n.y.). Complexity Lexicon. *London School of Economics and Political Science (LSE)* , http://www.lse.ac.uk/researchAndExpertise/units/complexity/lexicon.aspx, accessed [03/21/2014].

Mitleton-Kelly, E. (2003). *Ten Principles of Complexity and Enabling Infrastructures.* In: Mitleton-Kelly, E. (Ed.): Complex Systems and Evolutionary Perspectives on Organisations. The Application of Complexity Theory to Organisations, Bringley, UK: (Emerald), 2003, p. 23-50.

Moen, F., & Skaalvik, E. (2009). The Effect from Executive Coaching on Performance Psychology. *International Journal of Evidence Based Coaching and Mentoring, Vol. 7/2*, pp. 31-49.

Moldoveanu, M. (2004). An intersubjective measure of organizational complexity: A new approach to the study of complexity in organizations. *Emergence: Complexity & Organization*, Vol. 6(3), pp. 9-26.

Moller, C. (1997, April). The virtual organisation. *Automation in Construction, Vol. 6, Issue 1*, pp. 39-43.

Morecroft, J. W., & Sterman, J. D. (1994). *Modeling for learning organizations.* Portland, USA: Productivity Press.

Morin, E. (2005). Restricted complexity, general complexity. Paper presented at the: . *Colloquium 'Intelligence de la complexite: epistemologie et pragmatique'*, URL: http://cogprints.org/5217/1/Morin.pdf, accessed [03/10/2014].

Mowshowitz, A. (1997). On the Theory of Virtual Organizations. *Syst. Res. Behav. Sci., Vol. 14*, pp. 373-384.

Mowshowitz, A. (1997, September). Virtual Organization: A virtually organized company links its business goals with the procedures needed to achieve them. *Communications of the ACM, Vol. 40, No. 9*, pp. 30-37.

Mowshowitz, A. (1994, May). Virtual organization: A vision of management in the information age. *The Information Society, Vol. 10, Issue 4*, pp. 267-288.

Msanjila, S. S., & Afsarmanesh, H. (2008, March). Trust analysis and assessment in virtual organization breeding environments. *International Journal of Production Research, Vol. 46, No. 5*, pp. 1253-1295.

Mun, J., Shin, M., & Jung, M. (2011, May). A goal-oriented trust model for virtual organization creation. *Journal of Intelligent Manufacturing, Vol. 22*, pp. 345-354.

Murphy, S. A. (2004, November). Recourse to executive coaching: the mediating role of human resources. *International Journal of Police Science & Management*, pp. 175-186.

Natale, S. M., & Diamante, T. (2005). The Five Stages of Executive Coaching: Better Process Makes Better Practice. *Journal of Business Ethics, Vol. 59*, pp. 361-374.

Naveen, L. (2006). Organizational Complexity and Succession Planning. *Journal of Financial & Quantitative Analysis*, Vo. 41 (3), pp. 661-683.

Nedopil, C. / Steger, U. / Amann, W. (2011). *Managing Complexity in Organizations: Text and Cases.* Houndmills: (Palgrave Macmillan), 2011, pp. 3-22.

Nobre, F. S. / Tobias, A. M. / Walker, D. S. (2010). A New Contingency View of the Organization: Mananging Complexity and Uncertainty Through Cognition. *BAR - Brazilian Administration Review*, Vol. 7(4), pp. 379-396.

Nobre, F. S. / Tobias, A. M. / Walker, D. S. (2008). *Organizational and Technological Implications of Cognitive Machines: Designing Future Information Management Systems.* Hershey, PA: (Information Science), 2008.

Nocks, J. (2007, April). Executive Coaching - Who Needs It? *The Physician Executive* , pp. 46-48.

Nonaka, I. (1994). A dynamic theory of organizational knowledge creation. *Organization Science , 5* (1), 14-37.

Nonaka, I., & Takeuchi, H. (1995). *The knowledge-creating company: How Japanese companies create the dynamics of innovation.* New York-Oxfrod: Oxford University Press.

Orenstein, R. L. (2006, Spring). Measuring Executive Coaching Efficacy? The Answer Was Here All the Time. *Consulting Psychology Journal: Practice and Research, Vol 58/2* , pp. 106-116.

Pache, A. C. / Santos, F. (2010). When worlds collide: The internal dynamics of organizational responses to conflicting institutional demands. *Academy of Management Review* , Vol. 35(3), pp. 455-476.

Pangil, F., & Chan, J. M. (2014). The mediating effect of knowledge sharing on the relationship between trust and virtual team effectiveness. *Journal of Knowledge Management, Vol. 18* , pp. 92-106.

Pedler, M., Burgoyne, J., & Boydell, T. (1991). *The Learning Company.* New York: McGraw-Hil.

Peltier, B. (2001). *The Psychology of Executive Coaching: Theory and Application.* New York: Taylor & Francis.

Plumlee, M. A. (2003). The effect of information complexity on analysts' use of that information. *The Accounting Review* , Vol. 78(1), pp. 275-296.

Plump, C. M., & Ketchen, D. J. (2013). Navigating the possible legal pitfalls of virtual teams. *Journal of Organizational Design, Vol. 2* , pp. 51-55.

Poorzamani, Z. / Razmpou, A. . (2013). Quality Grade of Information Asymmetry and Firms' Cash Flow Values. *Technical Journal of Engineering and Applied Sciences* , Vol. 22(3), pp. 3177-3184.

Preece, A. (2001, March). Supportin Virtual Organizations Through Constraing Fusion. *International Journal of Intelligent Systems in Accounting Finance & Management, Vol. 10, Issue 1* , pp. 25-37.

Pun, K. F., & Nathai-Balkissoon, M. (2011). Integrating knowledge management into organisational learning. *The Learning Organization , 18* (3), 203-223.

Randall, W. (2013). Are the Performance Based Logistics Prophets Using Science or Alchemy to Create Life-Cycle Affordability? *Defence Aquisition Journal , 20* (3), 325-348.

Reeves, W. B. (2006, December). The Value Proposition For Executive Coaching. *Financial Executive* , pp. 48-49.

Reinicke, B. (2011, April). Creating a Framework for Research on Virtual Organizations. *Journal of Information Systems Applied Research, Vol. 4, No. 1* , pp. 49-56.

Reynolds, R., & Ablett, A. (1998). Transforming the rhetoric of organisational learning to the reality of the learning organisation. *The Learning Organization , 5* (1), 24-35.

Rezgui, Y., & Wilson, I. (2005). Socio-organizational issues. In L. Camarninha-Matos, A. Hamideh, & M. Ollus, *Virtual Organizations Systems and Practice.* New York: Springer.

Riddle, D., Zan, L., & Kuzmycz, D. (2009). Five Myth About Executive Coaching. *Leadership In Action: Issues & Observations, Vol. 29/5* , pp. 19-21.

Riemer, K., & Vehring, N. (2012). Virtual or vague? A literature review exposing conceptual differences in defining virtual organizations in IS research. *Electron Markets* , pp. 267-282.

Robertson, D. A. (2004). The Complexity of the Corporation. *Human Systems Management* , Vol. 23(2), pp. 71-78.

Sanson, M. (2006). *Executive Coaching: An international analysis of the supply of executive coaching services [Dissertation]*. St. Gallen: University of St. Gallen.

Scholz, C. (1996). Virtuelle Organisation: Konzeption und Realisation. *Zeitschrift Führung und Organisation, Jg. 65* , pp. 204-2010.

Schwandt, A. . (2009). Measuring organizational complexity and its impact on organizational performance – A comprehensive conceptual model and empirical study. *(Diss., Technischen Universität Berlin)* .

Schwandt, A. / Franklin, J. R. (Ed.). (2010). *Logistics: The Backbone for Managing Complex Organizations.* Bern: (Haupt), 2010, pp. 19ff.

Senge, P. (1990). *The fifth discipline. The art and practice of the learning organization.* New York, New York, USA: Doubleday.

Shao, Y. P., Liao, S. Y., & Wang, H. Q. (1998, October). A model of virtual organisations. *Journal of Information Science, Vol. 24* , pp. 305-312.

Shelbourn, M., Hassan, T., & Carter, C. (2005). Legal and contractual framework for the VO. In L. M. Camarhinha-Matos, H. Afsarmanesh, & M. Ollus, *Virtual Organizations Systems and Practices* (pp. 167-176). New York: Springer.

Sherman, S., & Alyssa, F. (2004, November). The Wild West of Executive Coaching. *Harvard Business Review* , pp. 82-90.

Skiffington, S., & Zeus, P. (2003). *Behavioral Coaching: How To Build Sustainable Personal And Organizational Strength.* New South Wales: McGraw Hill.

Slater, S. F., & Narver, J. C. (1994). Market Oriented Isn't Enough: Build a Learning Organization. *Marketing Science Institute* , 94-103.

Smith, A. C. T. . (2005). Complexity theory for organisational futures studies. *foresight* , Vol. 7(3), pp. 22-30.

Smither, J. W. (2011). Can Psychotherapy Research Serve as a Guide for Research About Executive Coaching? An Agenda for the Next Decade. *Journal of Business Psychology, Vol. 26* , pp. 135-145.

Spector, J., & Davidsen, P. (2005). *How can organizational learning be modeled and measured?* Florida State University ; University of Bergen. Amsterdam: Elsevier.

Stapleton, D. / Hanna, J. B. / Ross, J. R. (2006). Enhancing supply chain solutions with the application of chaos theory. *Supply Chain Management: An International Journal* , Vol. 11 (2), pp. 108-114.

Stern, L. R. (2009). Challenging Some Bsic Assumptions About Psychology and Executive Coaching: Who Knows Best, Who Is the Client, and What Are the Goals of Executive Coaching . *Industrial and Organizational Psychology, Vol. 2* , pp. 268-271.

Stoica, M., & Ghillic-Micu, B. (2009, May). Virtual organization - cybernetic economic system. modeling partner selection process. *Economic Computation & Economic Cybernetics Studies & Research, Vol 34, Issue 2* , pp. 1-11.

Stomski, L. e. (2011). Coaching Programs: Moving beyond the One-on-One. In G. Hernez-Broome, & L. A. Boyce, *Advancing Executive Coaching. Setting the Course for Successful Leadership Coaching* (pp. 177-204). San Francisco: Jossey-Bass.

Sturmberg, J. P. / Martin, C. M. / Katerndahl, D. A. (2014). Systems and Complexity Thinking in the General Practice: Literature: An Integrative, Historical Narrative Review. *Annals of Family Medicine* , Vol. 12(1), 66-74.

Sun, H. C. (2003). Conceptual clarifications for organizational learning, learning organization and a learning organization. *Human Resource Development International , 6* (2), 153-166.

Swart, J., & Harcup, J. (2012). 'If I learn do we learn?': The link between executive coaching and organizational learning. *Management Learning, Vol. 44/4* , pp. 337-354.

The Boston Consulting Group. (1973). *The Experience Curve- Reviewed.* (T. B. Group, Producer) Retrieved 3 20, 2014, from bcg perspectives: www.bcgperspectives.com/content/classics/corporate_finance_corporate_strategy_portfolio _management_the_experience_curve_reviewed_history/

Torbert, W. R. (1999). The distinctive questions developmental action inquiry asks. *Management Learning , 30* (2), 189-206.

Tsoukas, H. / Dooley, K. J. . (2011). Introduction to the Special: Towards the Ecological Style: Embracing Complexity in Organizational Research. *Organization Studies* , Vol. 32(6) 729–735.

Tucker, B. / Furness, C. / Olsen, J. / McGuirl, J. / Oztas, N. / Millhiser, W. . (2003). Complex Social Systems: Rising Complexity in Business Environments. *New England Complex Systems Institute* , pp. 1-8.

Turoff, M. (1985). Information, value, and the internal marketplace. *Technological Forecasting Society Change, Vol. 27* , pp. 357-373.

Unland, R., & Tianfield, H. (2003). IT enabling: Essence of virtual organizations. *International Journal of Information Technology and decision making* , pp. 367-370.

Valaski, J., Malucelli, S., & Reinehr, S. (2012). Ontologies application in organizational learning. A literature Review. *Expert Systems with Applications* (39), 7555-7561.

Villani, E. / Philipps, N. W. . (2013). Beyond Institutional Complexity: The Case of Different Organizational Successes in Confronting Multiple Institutional Logics. Paper presented at: . *35th DRUID Celebration Conference 2013, Barcelona* , pp. 1-40.

Wade, M. . (2013). ORGANIZATIONAL COMPLEXITY: THE HIDDEN KILLER. *International Institute for Management Development* , URL: http://www.imd.org/research/challenges/TC084-13-organizational-complexity-michael-wade.cfm, accessed [03/12/2014].

Walczak, S. (2008). Knowledge management and organizational learning. *The Learning Organization , 15* (6), 486-494.

Wang, C. L., & Ahmed, P. K. (2003). Organisational learning: a critical review. *The Learning Organization , 10* (1), 8-17.

Wang, C., & Ahmed, P. (2002). *A Review of the Concept of Organisational Learning.* Wolverhampton Business School, Management Research Centre. Wolverhampton: University of Wolverhampton.

Washylyshyn, K. M. (2008). Executive Coachin: An Outcome Study. In R. R. Kilburg, & R. C. Diedrich, *The Wisddom of Coaching. Essential Papers in Consulting Psychology for a World of Change* (pp. 79-89). Washington: American Psychological Association.

Werther, W. B. (1999). Structure-Driven Strategy and Virtual Organization Design. *Business Horizons, Vol. 42* , pp. 13-18.

Workman, M., Kahnweiler, W., & Bommer, W. (2003). The effects of cognitive style and media richness on commitment to telework and virtual teams. *Journal of Vocational Behaviour, Vol 63* , pp. 199-219.

Xing, J. / Manning, C. A. (2005). Complexity and Automation Displays of Air Traffic Control: Literature Review and Analysis. *Final Report* , pp, 1-20.

Team-based Organization

Maximilian Geißinger, Jana Krennmayer

Abstract. *"Coming together is a beginning; keeping together is progress; working together is success."* Henry Ford's quote on teamwork reinforces the significance of teams in the business world. Until this day, the benefit of team-based working is undisputed. In a dynamic, ever-changing and globalized business environment, team-based work is vital for organizations. This paper provides a concise overview of literature concerning team-based organizations and identifies current research gaps

Keywords: Teams, organization, corporation, allocation, resources, dynamic environment, flexibility

1 Introduction

Henry Ford's quote on teamwork reinforces the significance of teams in the business world. Ever since, the benefit of team-based ways of working has been undisputed. In a dynamic, ever-changing and globalized business environment, team-based work is vital for organizations, or to put in other words: "individualism is out, teamwork is in" (Parker 2003). It is no secret that team-based working positively impacts organizations' effectiveness and productivity (Griener 2010, Bishop and Mahajan 2005, Gibson and Kirkman 1999). As explained later on in this article, the transition to team-based organizational structures can be mostly explained by environmental changes forcing organizations adapting accordingly (Mohrman and Quam 1999).

The purpose of this article is to provide a concise overview of literature concerning team-based organizations. Such a literature review is useful in order to outline the status quo of the topic, to initiate future research by working out current research gaps and to facilitate the practical application of theoretical concepts.

The contribution is subdivided into four parts. The first section provides a definitional as well as a historical view of teams which is essential to comprehend the principle of team-based organizations. The second section illustrates the main factors impacting team effectiveness, which are agreed upon by the majority of academics. In the second step of this part, team-based organizational structures and team effectiveness is commented on. Contrasting attitudes help to figure out the strengths, weaknesses, opportunities and threats of team-based organizations. The third section goes more into detail when it comes to research gaps of the topic. Outlining research gaps is vital in order to advance and improve team-based work. The last section summarizes the previous parts and presents the key findings of this literature review.

2   Definition and Historical Development

According to Katzenbach and Smith (1993), a team consists of people having complementary capabilities, using them with the same goal or purpose and holding each other responsible for their actions. Bengtsson and Niss (2000) follow a similar approach whereas Cohen and Bailey (1997) add a social perspective. They describe a team as a social entity which is integrated in a bigger social system. Additionally, they state that there is no concise distinction of the terms team and group, both are used interchangeably. Ba-Banutu (2012) describes a team as two or more people who interact to reach a common goal and therefore positively influence each other. This definition adds the aspect of team members impacting each other, which is vital as can be seen later on in the context of social loafing or free riding. Another aspect that has to be taken into account is the variety of teams. According to Forrester and Drexler (1999) the term team-based can have several meanings. Teams can be permanent, temporary, cross-functional or functional, for example.

The literature initially mentions teams in 1951 when examining the psychological situation of work groups in relation to the social structure of work systems (Trist and Bamforth 1951). According to Gibson and Kirkman (1999), Procter and Gamble was the first US corporation which introduced work teams in the 1960s. Especially in the automotive industry, companies such as Volvo and Toyota initiated team-based organizational structures in the 1970s (Harvey et al. 1998). Emery (1980) coined the term self-managing groups based on the production of the Volvo Kalmar for example. In the 1990s, 93% of Fortune 1000 companies used problem-solving groups (Devine et al. 1999). The fact that over 85% of Fortune 1000 companies included some team-based compensation in 2005 (HBR 2008), reinforces that team-based work still expands its position, even in the 21st century.

What explains the triumph of teams? First of all, a great number of scientists argue that the ever-increasing necessity for teams can be mostly explained by globalization (Roufaiel and Meissner 1995; Heap 1996). Globalization increased the overall level of competitiveness. Consequently, companies had to adapt accordingly to compete on price, quality and innovation (Harvey 1998). Another reason explaining the need for teams is the discrepancy between managers and employee activities. It was sheer impossible for managers to handle all employee activities on a daily basis (Gibson and Kirkman 1999). Team-based working was a solution in order to stay competitive and to manage the mass of employees and their activities. It was found that team-based organizational structures increase overall organizational performance (Hill 1982; West 2002; Timothy et al. 2010, Griener 2010). Teams improve organizational learning (Wageman 1997), increase individuals' productivity (Katzenbach and Smith 1993) and make it easier for organizations to make use of their employees' skills and knowledge. Finally one can argue that the success of organizations mainly depends on the effectiveness of teams (Rico et al. 2011).

3 Team Effectiveness and Critical Review of Team-Based Organizational Structures

Initiating teams could result in strong a competitive advantage because team-based structures can increase quality and customer service, enhance productivity and decrease costs (DDI 2013). External economic conditions mentioned in the previous part force corporations to switch to a team-based organization. This means to move from a traditional functional structure relying on the individual as a performing unit to a less hierarchical team-based structure (Mohrman and Quam 1999). This change is necessary due to the fact that teams will not survive in an organization characterized by traditional hierarchical structures (Mohrman and Quam 1999). According to Guzzo and Dickson (1999) the social system in which teams operate defines the context of team performance. In other words, when talking about team-based organizations the organization itself and its context have to be considered. Teams need to be integrated in their organizations (Mickan and Rodger 2000), simultaneously the organizational context has a significant impact on the team's effectiveness (Rico et al. 2011). Team effectiveness is a key to success for team-based organizations (Wuchty et al. 2007). It is no wonder that there are plenty of academic and scientific papers concerning this topic. But what makes a team effective? The majority of authors agree upon several pivotal factors necessary for team effectiveness:

Team autonomy is one of the most discussed factors. According to Rico et al. (2011) increased team autonomy is directly related to team performance. The positive impact of team autonomy as a vital factor for team creativity, innovation and performance, which is supported by a great number of scientists (Haas 2010; Harvey et al. 1998; Cohen and Bailey 1997; Ancona 1990). Nevertheless, there are some critical voices challenging team autonomy's positive association on effectiveness. Locke and Schweiger (1979) found that autonomy increased team satisfaction but not performance. Perlow (1999) argues that highly autonomous teams are reluctant when it comes to the input and ideas of externals. This reasoning is supported by Katz and Allen (1982) as well. As one can see, autonomy is a factor about which there are opposing opinions.

Leadership is another key element impacting team effectiveness. Team leadership is mainly about enabling teams to optimally exploit team knowledge, experience and skills (West and Markiewicz 2004). According to Mickan and Rodger (2000) the need for an appropriate team leader increases with task complexity. Boni and Weingart (2012) described principled team leadership as a foundation for team effectiveness. Guzzo and Dickson (1996) found that leaders with high expectations or outstanding tactical skills and team performance are positively related. Gilstrap (2013) focuses more on the challenges of leadership and emphasizes on the defined supervisory distribution of roles. He states that, the concepts of leadership as a shared experience and individual accountability when it comes to team-based decision making, are entirely new to today's corporations. The importance of effective team leadership is reinforced when comparing the traditional management position and a team manager. Miller (2005) illustrates the difference as follows (Figure 1):

The Traditional Manager	The Team Manager / Coach
1. Direct to work 2. Decide how to fix problems 3. Hire and fire 4. Know the score 5. Catch and control mistakes 6. Know and answer 7. Pride in personal achievement	1. Assign process responsibility 2. Develop problem solving skills and encourage 3. Develop and encourage individuals and teams 4. Assure information flow to teams 5. Reward continuous improvement 6. Create collective wisdom 7. Pride in ream achievement

Figure 1: The traditional manager vs. the team manager / coach (Miller, 2005)

However, one should keep in mind that team leadership can negatively influence team effectiveness as well. Team leadership is completely different from usual supervising activities. A high level of team leader dominance can lead to reduced team communication and thus to poor team performance (Tost et al. 2013).

Diversification can be seen as an asset which increases overall team effectiveness (Ba Banutu 2012). According to the majority of experts, heterogeneous team structures foster teams' creativity and decision-making effectiveness (Guzzo and Dickson 1996).Furthermore, it was found that team diversity has a positive influence on team members' innovativeness which is beneficial for team effectiveness (Vegt and Janssen 2003). Nevertheless, it is vital to differentiate between surface-level diversity, based on demographics and deep-level diversity, based on attitudes and values (Harrison et al. 1998). Team structures which are based on superficial diversity can barely be used for representative statements and hardly have explanatory power (Ilgen et al. 2005).

Communication is the last key element presented in this review. This element has a central position concerning team effectiveness and performance. Especially when it comes to team based structures, communication is one of the key issues. Based on a survey of Blanchard (2006) ineffective communication between team members is the main reason for poor team performance. This fact illustrates that effective and efficient communication amongst team members is pivotal. Team performance is dependent on the effectiveness of team communication since it is vital for feedback, problem and conflict solving (Myrtle 2012, Guzzo and Dickson 1996, Daft 2007). Of course there are many more factors impacting team effectiveness. However, the previously mentioned factors are mentioned most frequently in literature.

Team effectiveness is vital for team-based organizations, but what about the organization itself? According to Beyerlein and Harris (2003) team-based organizing is not about the team, it is about the organization. The organization has to be aligned accordingly to allow for team-based collaboration (team work must fit the organizational internal and external environment). There is a clear need for integrating teams within the organizational culture (Pearce and Ravlin 1987). The context of the organization as organizational systems, processes and management structures for example (Mohrman and Quam 1999) plays a decisive role as well (Rico et al. 2011). The organizational culture must support team-based strategies and make team work a subject of discussion (Syrus 2012, DDI 2013). According to West and Markiewicz (2008) a team-based work system has to be implemented in six steps (Figure 2):

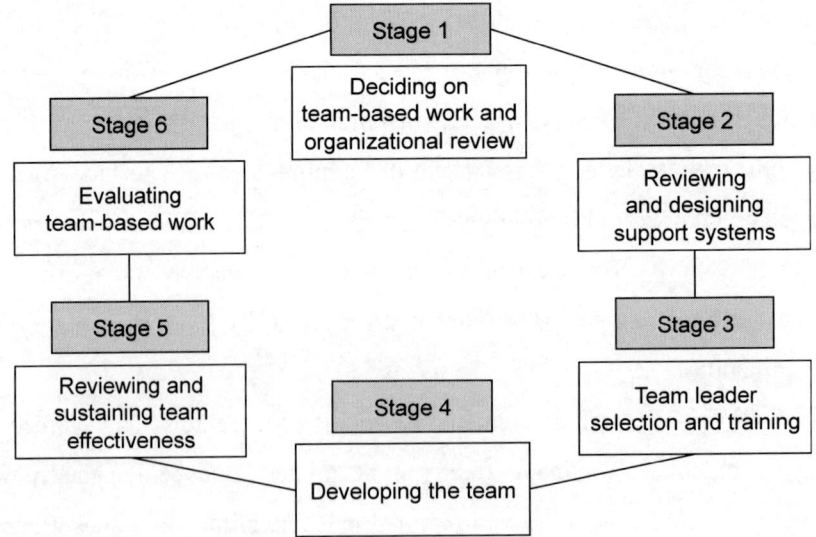

Figure 2: The six stage model of TBW (West & Markiewicz 2008)

Furthermore, the aforementioned authors introduced a table, which is illustrated below. The table is intended to help companies follow a time frame to which point in time each given milestone could have been reached during the TBW implementation phase (Figure 3).

Target activity	Target date
Senior management commitment	1 month
Team-based working goals agreed	6 weeks
Implementation steering group appointed	6 weeks
Reviewing activity completed	2 months
New team structure designed	4 months
Support system review completed	4 months
Team leader / member selection criteria agreed	4 months
Initial team leader training completed	6 months
Team leader learning sets established	7 months
Development plans in place	7 months
Support systems changes completed	9 months
Initial team performance evaluations completed	15 months
Evaluation completed	18 months

Figure 3: Key milestones in the TBW process (West & Markiewicz 2008)

Although the team-based approach seems to continue its triumph, it does not mean that team-based organizing has no downsides.. According to Harvey et al. (1998), throwing together individuals, who are not familiar with each other can result in employee resistance against team work and other team members. Furthermore, the empowerment of individuals does not necessarily mean that they are able to cope with their new responsibility. Some might be just overwhelmed by this new situation causing job dissatisfaction. Effectively differentiating between empowerment and team self-management is another issue of team-based organizations triggering tensions between the top management and teams (Mohrman and Quam 1999). Moreover, the focus on team-based performance means that individuals' performance is less noted. Experts speak about depreciating individuals' contribution (Mohrmann and Quam 1999).

In the contect of teams, organizational anomalies are mainly elicited because of missing congruence between organizational structures and team structures, this can result in team isolation and organizational barriers when it comes to team work (Forrester and Drexler 1999). Besides, another problem is the dependency on team success when implementing a team-based structure. Team members have to make sacrifices for the benefit of the whole team (Ba Banutu 2012). Different work ethics exacerbates this dependency even more and increase the overall complexity of team-based structures. Dependency also creates other issues such as social loafing and free riding. According to Scott and Einstein (2001) the effort and capability of each team member greatly varies which fosters social loafing. Additionally, the authors state that missing recognition or evaluation of individual efforts is the main reason for social loafing. Team work can sap the motivation of individuals, leading to social loafing (Williams and Karau 1991). This again results in a greater workload for the rest of the team provoking dissatisfaction amongst team members (Karau und Williams 1993).

Though literature describes heterogeneity as an element fostering team performance, it is a trouble spot for team conflict (Hogg and Terry 2000). Team conflict is one of the major issues when considering team-based organizations. It is sheer impossible to maintain a conflict free organizational environment or team environment. Team conflict can be destructive or productive (Global Knowledge 2006). What is made of it depends on the conflict solving abilities of top management and team leaders (Global Knowledge 2006) and on internal systems fostering interteam cooperation and support (West and Markiewicz 2008). Finally, one should keep in mind that team-based working is not always the most efficient way of tackling a task. Inappropriate teams are time consuming, challenging to create and to manage (Myrtle 2012). Team failures are costly and include opportunity costs, organizational inefficiencies, loss of customer goodwill and an aggravating employee-management relationship (Bishop and Mahajan 2005).

4   Research Gaps in the Field of Team-Based Organizing

So far, plenty of research has been conducted on team-based structures as well as on team effectiveness. Nevertheless, team-based organizations find themselves in a highly dynamic and ever-changing environment, meaning that the demands for team-based structures change as well. This of course, stimulates further in depth research within this field. According to Guzzo and Dickson (1996), there is not only a need for conducting research on effectiveness but in fact a greater need to research on how teams as part of a social system impact overall system effectiveness. To date, there just has been marginal research in this topic. Another aspect that has not been focused on so far is culture. Of course, the cultural aspect came up when it comes to diversified teams, but there is a clear need for research on how culture and different cultural settings impact teams (Rico et al. 2011). Gong et al. (2013) stress the importance of further investigating team creativity in general and the relationship between team learning and creativity in particular. Finally, since the power of team leaders can have negative impacts on team performance, it is of great interest how the subjective experience of power impacts the behavior of individual team members (Tost et al. 2013).

5 Conclusion

In summary, it can be stated that the topic of team-based organization is steadily gaining popularity in research. Team-based organizational structures did not appear out of thin air, the concept has evolved over decades. Nowadays it is a well-established approach in the business world. This literature review has shown that there are several pivotal factors and elements concerning the external and internal setting of corporations fostering team effectiveness as the key component of team-based organizations. Organizations, as well as researchers definitely clarified that team effectiveness is key to success when it comes to team-based organizations. There are elements, such as autonomy, leadership, diversification and communication on which the majority of researchers and experts agree upon. Nevertheless, it should be clear that team-based organizing is no panacea for all kinds of business related issues. The concept is a powerful tool, which has to be applied carefully. Team-based organizing only works when internal and external factors are adapted for this approach, provided that management is really willing to implement such a concept. The literature suggests that the implementation of team-based organizing is difficult, time and cost consuming and triggers considerable expenses when not initiated, performed and monitored appropriately. It is vital to understand that team-based organizing does not fit all organizations or business units, nor is it a guarantee for success.

Exemplary studies from Devine et al. (1999), Guzzo and Dickson (1996) and Tost et al. (2013) have helped define the status quo of team-based organization. Additionally, they provide pivotal insides and point out directions for research.

References

Ancona, D. (1990). *Outward bound: strategies for team survival in an organization.* [online].Available at: http://www.jstor.org/discover/10.2307/256328?uid=3737864&uid=2129&uid=2&uid=70&uid=4&sid=21103629491797 [Accessed: 02/03/2014].

Ba Banutu, G. (2012). *The importance of effective and efficient team work in an organization.* [online].Available at: http://ideas.repec.org/a/mgn/journl/v5y2012i3a4.html [Accessed: 01/03/2014].

Bengtsson, L. and Niss, C. (2000). *Control in team-based organisations – a case study.* [online]. Available at: http://www.hig.se/download/18.4a72647f12120571ab080001104/1353629703783/BengtssonNissNEW.pdf [Accessed: 02/03/2014].

Beyerlein, M. and Harris, C. (2003). *Critical success factors in team-based organizing.* [online].Available at: http://www.google.de/url?sa=t&rct=j&q=&esrc=s&source=web&cd=2&cad=rja&uact=8&ved=0CEAQFjAB&url=http%3A%2F%2Fmedia [Accessed: 01/03/2014].

Bishop, W. and Mahajan, A. (2005). *The use of teams in organizations: when a good idea isn't and when a good idea goes bad.* [online]. Available at: http://labmed.ascpjournals.org/content/36/5/281.full.pdf [Accessed: 02/03/2014].

Blenchard. (2006). *The critical role of teams.* [online]. Available at: http://www.kenblanchard.com/Leading-Research/Research/The-Critical-Role-of-Teams [Accessed: 01/03/2014].

Boni, A. and Weingart, L. (2012). *Building teams in entrepreneurial companies.* [online].Available at: http://connection.ebscohost.com/c/articles/84497033/building-teams-entrepreneurial-companies [Accessed: 01/03/2014].

Cohen, S. and Bailey, D. (1997). *What make teams work: Group effectiveness research from the shop floor to the executive suite.* [online]. Available at: http://www-leland.stanford.edu/group/wto/cgi-bin/docs/Cohen_Bailey_97.pdf [Accessed: 02/03/2014].

Daft, R. (2007). *Organization theory and design.* Mason: South-Western Cengage Leaning.

DDI. (2013). *Best practices of team-based organizations.* [online]. Available at: http://www.camcinstitute.org/university/pages/toolkit/0407/ddi_bestpracticesteambasedorganizations_wp.pdf [Accessed: 02/03/2014].

Devine, D. et al. (1999). *Teams in organizations: prevalence, characteristics and effectiveness.* [online].Available at: http://sgr.sagepub.com/content/30/6/678.abstract [Accessed: 02/03/2014].

Emery, F. (1980). *Designing socio-technical systems for greenfield sites.* [online]. Available at: http://moderntimesworkplace.com/archives/ericsess/sessvol2/10EMDESI.pdf [Accessed: 02/03/2014].

Forrester, R. and Drexler, B. (1999). A model for team-based organization performance. [online]. Available at: http://www.jstor.org/discover/10.2307/a4165563?uid=3737864&uid=2129&uid=2&uid=70&uid=4&sid=21103629008497 [Accessed: 02/03/2014].

Gibson, C. and Kirkman, B. (1999). *Our past present future in teams: The role of human resource professionals in managing team performance.* [online]. Available at: http://web.merage.uci.edu/~cgibson/Publication%20files/Book%20Chapters/Our%20Past%20Present%20and%20Future.pdf[Accessed: 02/03/2014].

Gilstrap, D. (2013). *Leadership and decision-making in team-based organizations: a model bounded chaotic cycling in emerging system states.* [online].Available at: http://soar.wichita.edu/handle/10057/6632 [Accessed: 01/03/2014].

Global Knowledge (2006). *Effectively managing team conflict.* [online].Available at: http://gclearningservices.com/assets/Managing_Conflict.pdf [Accessed: 01/03/2014].

Gong, Y. et al. (2013). *A multilevel model of team goal orientation, information exchange, and creativity.* [online]. Available at: http://amj.aom.org/content/56/3/827.abstract [Accessed: 01/03/2014].

Griener, J. (2010). *Team-Based Organizational Structure.* [online]. Available at: http://dtpr.lib.athabascau.ca/action/download.php?filename=mba-09/open/grienerjoanne.pdf [Accessed: 02/03/2014].

Guzzo, R. and Dickson, M. (1996). *Teams in organizations: recent research on performance and effectiveness.* [online].Available at: http://www.ncbi.nlm.nih.gov/pubmed/15012484[Accessed: 02/03/2014].

Haas, M. (2010). *The doubled-edged sword of autonomy and external knowledge: analyzing team effectiveness in a multinational organization.* [online].Available at: https://mgmt.wharton.upenn.edu/files/?whdmsaction=public:main.file&fileID=3889 [Accessed: 02/03/2014].

Harrison, D., Price, K. and Myrtle, B. (1998). *Beyond rational demography: time and the effects of surface- and deep-level diversity on work group cohesion.* [online].Available at: http://amj.aom.org/content/41/1/96.abstract [Accessed: 01/03/2014].

Harvey, S., Millet, B. and Smith, D. (1998). *Developing successful teams in organisations.* [online]. Available at: http://eprints.usq.edu.au/13737/ [Accessed: 02/03/2014].

HBR. (2008). *Low-trust teams prefer individualized pay.* [online].Available at: http://www.researchgate.net/publication/234137540_Low-trust_teams_prefer_individualized_pay/file/79e4151276a590e6b6.pdf [Accessed: 02/03/2014].

Heap, N. (1996). *Building the organizational team.* [online].Available at: http://www.emeraldinsight.com/journals.htm?articleid=838077 [Accessed: 02/03/2014].

Hill, W. (1982). *Group versus individual performance.* [online].Available at: http://www.ee.oulu.fi/~vassilis/courses/socialweb10F/reading_material/7/Hill82.pdf [Accessed: 02/03/2014].

Hogg, M. and Terry, D. (2000). *Social identity and self-categorization processes in organizational contexts.* [online].Available at: http://amr.aom.org/content/25/1/121.abstract [Accessed: 01/03/2014].

Ilgen, D. et al. (2005). *Teams in organizations: from input-process-output models to IMOI models.* [online].Available at: http://www.annualreviews.org/doi/abs/10.1146/annurev.psych.56.091103.070250 [Accessed: 01/03/2014].

Karau, S. and Williams, K. (1993). *Social loafing: a meta analytical review and theoretical integration.* [online].Available at: http://doi.apa.org/journals/psp/65/4/681.pdf [Accessed: 01/03/2014].

Katz, R. and Allen, T. (1982). *Investigating the not invented here syndrome.* [online].Available at: http://onlinelibrary.wiley.com/doi/10.1111/j.1467-9310.1982.tb00478.x/abstract [Accessed: 02/03/2014].

Katzenbach, J. and Smith, D. (1993). *The discipline of teams.* [online]. Available at: http://hbr.org/2005/07/the-discipline-of-teams/ar/1 [Accessed: 02/03/2014].

Locke, E. and Schweiger, D. (1979). *Participation in decision-making: one more look.* In: Research in organizational behavior. Greenwich: JAI press.

Mickan, R. and Rodger, S. (2000). *Characteristics of effective teams: a literature review.* [online].Available at: http://www.researchgate.net/publication/12145106_Characteristics_of_effective_teams_a_literature_review/file/9fcfd50f5894593069.pdf [Accessed: 02/03/2014].

Miller, L. M. (2005*). Lean Teams: Developing the Team-Based Organization; The Skills and Practices of High Performance Business Teams.* Miller Management Press, LLC.

Mohrman, S and Quam, K. (1999). *Consulting to team based organizations: An organizational design and learning approach.* [online]. Available at: http://ceo.usc.edu/pdf/g99_9.pdf [Accessed: 02/03/2014].

Myrtle, R. (2012). *Creating and managing high performance teams.* [online]. Available at: http://www.nacs.gov.tw/NcsiWebFileDocuments/37e73ad5123369ce8adc644aa11612cf.pdf[Accessed: 01/03/2014].

Parker, G. (2003). *Cross-functional Teams: Working with allies, enemies and other strangers.* San Francisco: Jossey-Bass.

Pearce, J. and Ravlin, E. (1987). *The design and activation of self-regulating work groups.* [online].Available at: http://hum.sagepub.com/content/40/11/751.abstract [Accessed: 01/03/2014].

Perlow, L. (1999). *The time famine: toward a sociology of work time.* [online].Available at: http://www.interruptions.net/literature/Perlow-ASQ99.pdf [Accessed: 02/03/2014].

Rico, R., Alcover de la Hera, C. and Tabernero, C. (2011). *Work team effectiveness, a review of research from last decade.* [online]. Available at: http://www.psychologyinspain.com/content/full/2011/15006.pdf [Accessed: 02/03/2014].

Roufaiel, N. and Meissner, M. (1995). *Self-managing teams: a pipeline to quality and technology management.* [online]. Available at: http://www.emeraldinsight.com/journals.htm?articleid=842894 [Accessed: 02/03/2014].

Scott, S. and Einstein, W. (2001). *Strategic performance appraisal in team-based organizations: one size does not fit all.* [online].Available at: https://www.tamu.edu/faculty/payne/PA/Scott%20&%20Einstein%202001.pdf [Accessed: 01/03/2014].

Syrus, P. (2012). *Team-based performance evaluation.* [online].Available at: http://www.tpogassociates.com/HealthCareTeamBook/ch11.pdf [Accessed: 01/03/2014].

Timothy, T., West, A. and Dawson, J. (2010). *Team-based working and employee well-being.* [online]. Available at: http://eprints.lancs.ac.uk/53136/1/Mike_West_Team_Based_Working_and_Employee_Well_Being.pdf [Accessed: 02/03/2014].

Tost, L., Gino, F. and Larrick, R. (2013). *When power makes others speechless: the negative impact of leader power on team performance.* [online].Available at: http://dash.harvard.edu/handle/1/10996804 [Accessed: 01/03/2014].

Trist, E. and Bamforth, K. (1951). *Some social and psychological consequences of the longwall method of coal-getting.* [online]. Available at: http://www.uv.es/gonzalev/PSI%20ORG%2006-07/ARTICULOS%20RRHH%20SOCIOTEC/Trist%20Long%20Wall%20Method%20HR%201951.pdf[Accessed: 02/03/2014].

Van der Vegt, G. and Jannsen, O. (2003). *Joint impact of interdependence and group diversity on innovation.* [online].Available at: http://jom.sagepub.com/content/29/5/729.abstract [Accessed: 01/03/2014].

Wageman, R. (1997). *Critical success factors for creating superb self-managing teams.* [online].Available at: http://faculty.haas.berkeley.edu/kurkoski/BA105/Readings/Wagemen%20-%20self-managing%20teams.pdf [Accessed: 02/03/2014].

West, M. (2002). *Sparkling fountains or stagnant ponds.* [online].Available at: http://onlinelibrary.wiley.com/doi/10.1111/1464-0597.00951/abstract [Accessed: 02/03/2014].

West, M. and Markiewicz, L. (2004). *Building team-based working. A practical guide to organizational transformation.* Oxford, UK: Blackwell.

West, M. and Markiewicz, L. (2008). *Introduction to Team-Based Organizations, in Building Team-Based Working: A Practical Guide to Organizational Transformation.* Oxford, UK: Blackwell Publishing Ltd.

Wuchty, S., Jones, B. and Uzzi, B. (2007). *The increasing dominance of teams in production of knowledge.* [online].Available at: http://www.kellogg.northwestern.edu/faculty/jones-ben/htm/Teams.ScienceExpress.pdf [Accessed: 02/03/2014].

Section II: Organizational Properties

Organizational Identity

Philipp Aich, Alexander Antusch

Abstract. The concept of organizational identity has received considerable attention in organization and management research over more than two decades, as, it turned into a key element for understanding organizations and their interactions with the environment. This contribution shows that organizational identity is a rich field for researchers with considerable potential for investigation. While this domain has already been explored, there are still opportunities for further research.

Keywords: Organization, organizational identity, interaction with organizational environment, change management

1 Introduction

1.1 The concept of Organizational Identity

Since its introduction by Albert and Whetten in 1985, the concept of organizational identity (OI) has become an important concept informing organization and management research over more than two decades. It turned in to a key element in the understanding of organizations and their interactions with the environment. Due to the richness of the concept and the opportunity that it provides for investigation, interest has increased for theoretical and empirical identity research within organizational settings. Research in this domain extends several levels of analysis, ranging from individual or personal to organizational. Personal identity usually draws on unique individual characteristics that do not stem from group membership (Alvesson et al. 2008). Social identity – in contrast to personal identity – applies to the perceptoin of a person, arising from the person's membership in a social group (Tajfel & Turner 1979). By contrast, organizational identity is generally understood as the characteristics that are implied to be central, distinctive and enduring in an organization (Albert & Whetten 1985; Dutton et al. 1994). Looking at the majority of theoretical and empirical accounts of OI, it becomes obvious that organizational identity is positioned as a deep cultural phenomenon of an organization (Gioia et al. 2000). This phenomenon resides in interpretive schemes that organizational members mutually compile in order to allocate significance to their shared history, experiences and activities (Gioia 1998; Ravasi & Schultz 2006).

The growing interest in identity issues emphasizes the importance and practical relevance of the OI concept to a number of organizational areas such as strategy (Dutton, 1997), management and leadership (Gioia & Chittipeddi 1991; Pratt and Foreman 2000), inter-organizational collaboration (Beech & Huxham 2004) and corporate communication (Cheney & Christensen 2001; Schultz et al. 2000).

1.2 Approach

Against this background, this article exhibits the following structure. At first, different authors' views on OI are analyzed while areas of disagreement are exposed, before three dominant perspectives are identified. From there, potential future research is discussed. In a final step, the literature findings will be summarized.

2 Analysis of Organizational Identity

2.1 Different authors' perceptions of Organizational Identity

The concept of OI has already interested philosophers for many years and therefore meanwhile became a highly important research topic for scholars (Brown 2006; Corley et. al. 2006) and also an object of inquiry for managers (Cheney 1991). Ashforth and Mael (1996) have described the concept to be a "more or less internally consistent system of pivotal beliefs, values and norms, typically anchored in the organizational mission that informs sensemaking and action". Thus the concept of OI strongly helps to understand internal conflicts (Humphreys & Brown, 2002), decision-making (Riantoputra 2010), strategic change (Ravasi & Philips 2011) and issue interpretation and response (Dutton & Dukerich 1991; Gioia & Thomas 1996). Ashfort and Mael (1996) state that an organization members' understandings of the pronounced character defining identity at various organizational levels are most of the times formed by means of comparison with the leading competitors. Some scholars have suggested to distinguish between and link various levels of analysis, connecting micro and macro level structures, thereby creating diverse lines of OI research (Ashforth & Mael 1996; Polzer 2000).

With repect to organizational members, OI can be, according to Elsbach and Kramer (1996), composed as their cognitive conception or perception of their organization's central and distinctive characteristics. From a practical point of view, OI tasks "function as organizational identity referents for members when they are acting or speaking on behalf of their organization" (Whetten 2006). Thus OI is addresses the matter of "who we are as an organization", meaning that OI is supposed to be a "self-reflective question" (Whetten 2006). According to Albert and Whetten (1985) and Gioia (1998), OI is a central concept that is able to deliver a practical framework to understand activities within organizations. Hence, OI can strain, allocate and form the interpretations and activities of organizational members at the same time (Dutton & Dukerich 1991; Gioia 1998; Whetten 2006).

The original concept of Albert and Whetten (1985) encouraged many researchers to investigate OI. Albert and Whetten argued that the identity of an organization was distinguished by several propositions regarding the central, distinctive and enduring characteristics, which was widely acknowledged in the research. However, over subsequent decades, certain criticism regarding the OI concept appeared. For instance, Gioia and Thomas (1996), Gioia (1998) and Fombrun (1996) have considered distinctiveness from a different angle than did researchers before. They challenged the notion of distinctiveness, given considerable similarities among organizations. On the other hand, they found it very difficult to describe enduringness as a characteristic, since today's business world is changing very fast. Accordingly, it seems to be obvious that concepts, structures, processes etc. within organizations cannot be hidden from changes nowadays.

2.2 Research perspectives

Organizational identity has formerly been categorized into at least three philosophical perspectives (Alvesson et al. 2008): functional, interpretive and post-modern perspectives. Based on this classification, different theoretical fields can be described and further research opportunities identified.

2.2.1 Functionalist perspectives

The functionalist perspective assumes that organizational identities consist of essential, objective and tangible features (Elsbach & Kramer 1996). They dominate research on OI in organizational fields of study as well as in associated areas such as marketing and strategy (Balmer & Greyer 2006; Brown et al. 2006; Corley & Gioia 2004; Cornelissen et al. 2007; Fombrun & Shanley 1990; He 2012; He & Balmer 2007; He & Murkherjee 2009; Martin et al. 2011). According to Olins (1989) and van Riel and Balmer (1997), in marketing and brand management, OI is usually linked to physical characteristics of companies, corporate logos, corporate identity, company his-tory and documentation. One very typical example for this point of view is the identity change at France Telecom including a new logo and visual identity program (Brun 2000). Functionalist perspectives often try to classify the identity of an organization and responses of identity to environmental appeals (Rao et al. 2003; Smith 2011).

Whetten and Mackey (2002) try to discuss a perspective of organizations as social actors with legal status. Their identities are supposed to be distinguished via the rallied entity-level obligations and actions. According to these authors, such a concept has construct validity, which is suitable for model building, hypothesis testing and empirical measurement. Furthermore, according to Whetten Mackey, the concept objectifies organizations, and provides them with an objective position. The belief in a functionalist perspective holds that OI can be summarized as a social fact that is manipulable and observable (Gioia 1998) Corley et al. (2006), however, warms about the restriction of "exercises in positivist epistemology".

2.2.2 Interpretive perspectives

In the second perspective, the interpretive or social constructionist perspective, scholars investigated how we jointly establish who we are. Therefore in this case the definition slightly deviates from the functionalist perspective (Pratt & Rafaeli 1997).

The interpretive perspective sees OI as the socially achieved result of certain dependencies between socially classified individual cognitions, always reflecting the question of "who the organization is" (Corley et al. 2006, Dutton et al. 1994; Harquail & King 2003). As already mentioned before, in the vast majority of research, OI corresponds to rather shared opinions regarding the characteristics that are implied to be central, distinctive and enduring in an organization. That way the work experience of organizational members receives significance, whereas the opinions are constructed through interactions among several participants across professional divisions and hierarchical levels (Glynn 2000; Harrison 2000; Kjaergaard & Ravasi 2011). Pratt (2003) identifies two possible perspectives. On the one hand, he distinguishes between an "aggregate" view, which is therefore recognized as an addition of individual perspectives. On the other hand, he characterizes a "gestalt" view, suggesting mutual identities are located in relationships that unite cognitive people. The interpretive perspective generally proceeds in a very ductile way, which is accessible to political influence at several levels and more equivocal than a functionalist perspective. Conceptual psychological phenomena like beliefs, values and assumptions have been an important premise for researchers in order to analyze organizations' identities. Recently, researchers argued that social cognition and the use of language are supposed to be "embodied" (Harquail & King 2003). They proposed the recognition of this embodiment in order to unwrap how characters compose organizations' identities. This in turn implies concentrating on people's "bodily-kinesthetic, visual-spatial, temporal-aural and emotional experiences in their organizations" in or-der to interpret "what is central, distinctive and enduring about an organization". This requires more substantial analysis with a variety of information (Harquail & King 2003).

2.2.3 Post-modern perspectives

In the post-modern perspective, OI is defined as temporary and separated reflections about what organizations are. Post-modern perspective scholars consider that organizational identity is "impermanent and subject to a continuous deconstruction and reconstruction" (Hatch & Schultz 1997).According to Dunn (1998), the concept of post-modern perspectives descends from "a growing sense of the problematization of identity". Traditional surveys, by contrst, are generally connected with questioning, challenge, indeterminacy, fragmentation and difference (Rosenau 1992). Other researchers define OI at different organization levels as a myth or illusion (Baudrillard 1998). Coupland and Brown (2004) have investigated, in a case study of Royal Dutch Shell, the characteristics of identities within an organization. They analyzed dialogues between "insiders" and "outsiders" and reasoned that the development of identities is based on on-going arguments.

The vast majority of scholars, who conduct research beyond the main perspective, have identified OI as content created through narrative lecture (Brown & Humphreys 2006; Chreim 2005; Czarniawska-Joerges 1994; Humphreys & Brown 2002). According to Czarniawska-Joerges (1994), OI is composed of ongoing developments of narration "...where both the narrator and the audience formulate, edit, applaud and refuse various elements of the ever-produced narrative". Fruthermore, OI has been described as the collectivity of narratives related to identity that organizational members compose in their dialogues, stories or papers (Brown 2006). These members aspire to realign the thoughts on issues of power, reflexivity, voice, plurivocity, temporality and fictionality (Brown et al. 2005).

3 Research Gap

OI has appealed to a high number of researchers over the last few decades. Even though the literature on OI is already exceptionally rich, there is still room for further investigation and research. For instance, one significant open research issue is the relevance of OI in crisis situations (Reger 1998; Davies et al. 2003). Furthermore, according to Brown (2001), the consideration of identities within organizations could support empirical as well as theoretical examination of the relationship between organization and environment. Another interesting idea that should be further analyzed is the comprehension of OI as a valuable and socially complex source that could be the origin of competitive advantage. That would also include the connection of OI to the strategy of an organization. (Hamel & Prahalad 1994; Stimpert et al. 1998; Barney et al. 1998; Whetten & Mackey 2002). Furthremore, the interdependence between the identity and the image of an organization requires a deeper exploration, e.g. how changes in one of them affect the other (Ravasi & Phillips 2011).

Overall, several scholars revealed that research on OI should generally turn more attention to investigating concretely organizational identity in place of examining self-identity in an organizational context (Gioia et al. 2000).

4 Conclusion

In this article, an overview of the different views on OI has been given, confirming that OI has become a highly significant concept in regarding organization research. The concept achieved to be a subject of quite intensive organizational study. The concept's practical relevance at several levels of and its ability to include analytical cognitions at the micro- and macro-levels clearly emphasizes its potential. OI research has helped gain insight into the character and behavior of organizations and their members.

The main three different perspectives, the functionalist, intepretivist and postmoden approaches, led to a variety in opinions regarding the origin of OI and its strategic importance for organizational. The functionalist view regards identity as a main characteristic of the organization remaining long-term persistent and being shared by organizational members (Hatch and Schultz 1997). The interpretive view on the other hand, has continuously questioned this opinion (Gioia 1998). Overall, on can say that OI is a very rich field for researchers with great potential for investigation. While already been explored, there are still enough opportunities for further research.

References

Albert, S. & Whetten, D.A. (1985): Organizational identity, Research in organizational behavior, Vol. 7, p. 263-295.

Alvesson, M., K.L. Ashcraft, & R. Thomas. (2008): Identity Matters: Reflections on the Construction of Identity Scholarship in Organization Studies. Organization, 15(1), p. 5-28.

Ashforth, B.E., & Mael, F.A. (1996): Organizational identity and strategy as a context for the individual. Advances in Strategic Management, 13, p. 17-64.

Balmer, J.M.T., & Greyser, S. A. (2006): Corporate marketing: Integrating corporate identity, corporate branding, corporate communications, corporate image and corporate reputation. European Journal of Marketing, 40(7/8), p. 730 - 741.

Barney, J.B., Bunderson S., Foreman, P., Gustafson, L.T., Huff, A.S., Martins, L.L. Reger, R.K., Sarason, Y. & Stimpert J.L. (1998): A Strategy Conversation on the topic of Organization Identity, in Whetten, A.D. & Godfrey, P.C. (Eds.), Identity in Organizations. Building Theory Through Conversations, Sage Publications, United States of America, p. 99–168.

Brown, A.D. (2001): Organization Studies and identity: Towards a research agenda, Human Relations, Vol 54. Iss.1.

Brown, A.D. (2006): A narrative approach to collective identities. Journal of Management Studies, 43, p. 731-753.

Brown, T.J., Dacin, P.A., Pratt, M.G., & Whetten, D.A. (2006): Identity, Intended Image, Construed Image, and Reputation: An Interdisciplinary Framework and Suggested Terminology. Journal of the Academy of Marketing Science, 34(2), p. 99-106.

Brown, S.L. & Eisenhardt, K.M. (1997): The art of continuous change: Linking complexity theory and time-paced evolution in relentlessly shifting organizations, Administrative Science Quarterly, Vol. 42, p. 1-34.

Brown, A.D. & Humphreys, M. (2006): Organizational identity and place: A discursive exploration of hegemony and resistance. Journal of Management Studies, 43, p. 231-257.

Brown, A.D., Humphreys, M. & Gurney, P.M. (2005): Narrative, Identity and Change: A case study of Laskarina Holidays. Journal of Organizational Change Management, 18, p. 312-326.

Bru, M. (2002): Creating a new identity for France Telecom: Beyond a visual exercise. In B. Moingeon & G. Soenen (eds.), Corporate and organizational identities: Integrating strategy, marketing, communication, and organizational perspectives. London: Routledge, p. 133-155.

Cheney, G. (1991): Rhetoric in an organizational society, managing multiple identities. Columbia, SC: University of South Carolina Press, p. 201.

Chreim, S. (2005): The continuity-change duality in narrative texts of organizational identity. Journal of Management Studies, 42, p. 567-593.

Corley, K.G. & Gioia, D.A. (2004): Identity ambiguity and change in the wake of a corporate spin-off. Administrative Science Quarterly, 49, p. 173-208.

Corley, K.G., Harquail, C.V., Pratt, M.G., Glynn, M.A., Fiol, M., & Hatch, M.J. (2006): Guiding organizational identity through aged adolescence. Journal of Management Inquiry, 15, p. 85-99.

Cornelissen, J.P., Haslam, S. A., & Balmer, J.M.T. (2007): Social Identity, Organizational Identity and Corporate Identity: Towards an Integrated Understanding of Processes, Patternings and Products. British Journal of Management, 18, p. 1-16.

Coupland, C. & Brown, A.D. (2004): Constructing organizational identities on the Web: A case study of Royal Dutch Shell. Journal of Management Studies, 41, p. 1323-1347.

Czarniawska-Joerges, B. (1994): Narratives of individual and organizational identities. In S. Deetz (ed.), Communicaton Yearbook. Newbury Park, CA: Sage, p. 193-221.

Davies, G., Chun, R., Vinhas da Silva, R. & Roper, S. (2003): Corporate Reputation and competitiveness, Routledge, London and New York.

Dunn, R.G. (1998): Identity crises, a social critique of postmodernity. Minneapolis: University of Minnesota Press.

Dutton, J., & Dukerich, J. (1991): Keeping an eye on the mirror: Image and identity in organizational adaptation. Academy of Management Journal, 34, p. 517-554.

Dutton, J.E., Dukerich, J. M., & Harquail, C. V. (1994): Organizational images and member identification. Administrative Science Quarterly, 39, p. 239-263.

Elsbach, K.D. & Kramer, R.M. (1996): Members' responses to organizational identity threats: Encountering and countering the Business Week rankings, Administrative Science Quarterly, Vol. 41, p. 442-476.

Empson, L. (2004): Organizational identity change: Managerial regulation and member identification in an accounting firm acquisition, Accounting, Organizations and Society, Vol. 29, p. 759-781.

Fombrun, C.J. (1996): Reputation: Realizing value from the corporate image. Boston: Harvard Business School Press.

Fombrun, C. & Shanley, M. (1990): What's in a name? Reputation building and corporate strategy. Academy of Management Journal, 33, p. 233-258.

Giddens, A. (1991): Modernity and self-identity. Self and society in the late modern age. Cambridge: Polity Press.

Gioia, D.A. (1998): From individual to organizational identity. In D. A. Whetten & P.C. Godfrey (Eds.), Identity in organizations, building theory through conversations. Thousand Oaks, CA: Sage, p. 17-31.

Gioia, D.A., & Thomas, J.B. (1996): Identity, image, and issue interpretation: Sensemaking during strategic change in academia. Administrative Science Quarterly, 41, p. 370-403.

Gioia, D.A., Majken, S. & Corley, K.G. (2000): Organizational identity, image, and adaptive instability, The Academy of Management Review, Vol. 25 Iss. 1, p. 63–81.

Glynn, M.A. (2000): When cymbals become symbols: Conflict over organizational identity within a symphony orchestra. Organization Science, 11, p. 285-298.

Gustafson, L.T. & Reger, R.K. (1995): Using organizational identity to achieve stability and change in high velocity environments, Academy of Management Proceedings, p. 464-468.

Hamel, G. & Prahalad, C.K. (1994): Competing for the future, Harward Business School Press, USA.

Harquail, C.V., & King, A.W. (2003): Construing organizational identity: The role of embodied cognition. Organization Studies, 31, p. 1619-1648.

Harrison, J.D. (2000): Multiple imaginings of institutional identity. Journal of Applied Behavioral Science, 36, p. 425-455.

Hatch, M.J., & Schultz, M. (1997): Relations between organization culture, identity and image. European Journal of Marketing, 31, p. 356-365.

He, H. (2012): Corporate identity anchors: A managerial cognition perspective. European Journal of Marketing, 46(5), 609-625.

He, H., & Balmer, J.M.T. (2007): Identity Studies: Multiple Perspectives and Implications for Corporate-level Marketing. European Journal of Marketing, 41(7/8), p. 765-785.

He, H., & Baruch, Y. (2010): Organizational identity and legitimacy under major environmental changes: Tales of two UK building societies. British Journal of Management, 21, p. 44-62.

He, H., & Mukherjee, A. (2009): Corporate identity and consumer marketing: A process model and research agenda. Journal of Marketing Communications, 15(1), p. 1-16.

Hogg, M.A. & Terry, D.J. (2000): Social identity and self-categorization processes in organizational contexts, Academy of Management Review, Vol. 25 Iss. 1, p. 121-141.

Humphreys, M. & Brown, A.D. (2002): Narratives of organizational identity and identification: A case study of hegemony and resistance. Organization Studies, 23, p. 421-447.

Kjaergaard, Morsing, M., & Ravasi, D. (2011): Mediating identity: A study of media influence on organizational identity construction in a celebrity firm. Journal of Management Studies, 48, p. 514-543.

Lakoff, G. & Johonson, M. (1999): Philosophy in the flesh: The embodied mind and its challenge to western thought. New York: Basic Books.

Martin, K.D., Johnson, J.L., & French, J.J. (2011): Institutional pressures and marketing ethics initiatives: the focal role of organizational identity. Journal of the Academy of Marketing Science, 39, p. 574-591.

Olins, W. (1989): Corporate identity: Making business strategy visible through design. Boston: Harvard Business School Press.

Polzer, J.T. (2000): Identity in organizations: Building theory through conversations. Whetten, D.A. & Godfrey, P.C. (Eds.), Thousand Oaks, CA: Sage. Book review. Administrative Science Quarterly, p. 625-628.

Pratt, M.G. (2003): Disentangling collective identity. In J. T. Polzer, E. Mannix, & M. A. Neale (Eds.), Research on managing groups and teams. Vol. 5. Greenwich, CT: JAI, p. 161-188.

Pratt, M & Rafaeli, A. (1997): Organisational dress as a symbol of multilayered social identities, Academy of Management Journal, 40(4), p. 862-898.

Ran, B. & Duimering, P.R. (2007): Imaging the organization: Language use in organizational identity claims. Journal of Business and technical Communication, 21, p. 155-187.

Rao, H., Monin, P., & Durand, R. (2003): Institutional change in Toque Ville: Nouvelle cuisine as an identity movement in French gastronomy. American Journal of Sociology, 108, p. 795-843.

Ravasi, D. & Phillips, N. (2011): Strategies of alignment: organizational identity management and strategic change at Bang & Olufsen. Strategic Organization, 9, p. 103-135.

Reger, R.K. (1998): A Strategy conversation on the topic of organizational identity, in Whetten, A.D. and Godfrey, P.C. (Eds.), Identity in Organizations. Building Theory Through Conversations, Sage Publications, United States of America, p. 99-170.

Riantoputra, C.D. (2010): Know thyself: Examining factors that influence the activation of organizational identity concepts in top managers' minds. Group & Organization Management, 35, p. 8-38.

Rosenau, P.M. (1992): Post-modernism and the social sciences: insights, inroads and intrusions. Princeton: Princeton University Press.

Sillince, J.A.A. & Brown, A.D. (2009): Multiple Organizational Identities and Legitimacy: The Rhetoric of Police Websites, Human Relations, 62, p. 1829-1856.

Stimpert, J.L., Gustafson, L.T. & Sarason, Y. (1998): Organizational identity within the strategic management conversation: Contributions and assumptions, in Whetten, A.D. & Godfrey, P.C. (Eds.), Identity in Organizations. Building Theory Through Conversations, Sage Publications, United States of America, p. 83-98.

Van Riel, C.B. & Balmer, J.M.T. (1997): Corporate identity: The concept, its measurement, and management. European Journal of Marketing, 31, p. 341-355.

Whetten, D.A (2006): Albert & Whetten Revised. Strengthening the Concept of Organizational Identity, Journal of Management Inquiry, Vol. 15 No.3, p. 219-234.

Whetten, A.D. & Godfrey, P.C. (1998): Identity in Organizations. Building Theory Through Conversations, Sage Publications, United States of America.

Whetten, D.A., & Mackey, A. (2002): A social actor conception of organizational identity and its implications for the study of organizational reputation. Business & Society, 41, p. 393-414.

Organizational Complexity

Fabio Kledt, Philippe Evers, Debora Benson

Abstract. The world is becoming more and more complex. Because of this the business environment and the way business is being done is also becoming more complex. In order to withstand this, organizational adaptation is required. In an attempt to cope with this increasing complexity, a growing number of researchers have closely examined the topic of complexity in combination with organizations. The objective of this article is to examine the status quo of research on organizational complexity and critically review publications of the last decades to provide an updated paper on this topic. Furthermore, two current research gaps are presented to clarify where future research needs to be done. The paper ends with a brief conclusion.

Keywords: Complexity, organization, complexity, adaptation, organizational complexity, corporate complexity.

1 Introduction

Complexity has become a crucial feature of modern reality with huge power to change our way of thinking and seeing the world. Although globalization has created new markets and expanded supply chains, it has also contributed to an increase in complexity (Maznevski et al. 2007). Nowadays, management has to manage structures and processes dominated by an increased degree of complexity (Mitleton-Kelly 2003; Dumitraşcu & Dumitraşcu 2011). A global survey of the Economist Intelligence Unit (2011) points out that many executives of various industries see organizational complexity as one of the key business challenges of the coming years. Out of the 300 participants, 57 % think that their organizational structure is adding to complexity. Whenever organizations have to handle the different interests, goals and practices - arising from multiple institutional logics - they experience institutional complexity (Greenwood et al. 2011).

Based on this situation, Camelot Management Consultants (2012) carried out a further survey among more than 150 leading companies in different industries. In this context, 83% claim that the current degree of complexity in their company is too high, while 76% believe that it will increase even further. Just 6% of all interviewed companies have already applied appropriate instruments to handle it. Based on this result, it is clear that the study of organizational complexity has become a subject for organizational research (Anderson et al. 1999).

The aim of this paper is to examine the status quo of research on organizational complexity and review publications of the last decades to provide an updated account of this topic. The methodology is based on secondary research with a focus on organizations, and relating to business issues.

The structure of the article is as follows: First a conceptual framework is provided to obtain a better understanding of the issue. Then, different and similar authors' views are presented. Afterwards two current research gaps clarify where future research needs to be done. Finally, a conclusion summarizes the main results.

2 Conceptual Framework

When dealing with complexity, specifically organizational complexity, it is good to create a general understanding of the terms involved, because of its theoretical and subjective nature. Before presenting the fundamentals and the definition of complexity, the following subsection deals with complexity theory - a frequently used term in this context.

2.1 Complexity Theory

The emergence of complex systems theories is affiliated to the second half of the 19th century as physicists, mathematicians, chemists and others strived for superior explanatory models to describe and predict the behavior of these phenomena (Sturmberg et al. 2014). The beginnings of complexity theory are closely related to chaos and systems theory (Smith 2005). A significant contribution to the research on complexity theory derives from the Sante Fe Institute (SFI) in New Mexico, a focal point for those studying complexity theory (Mitleton-Kelly 2003).

Looking at the literature of different scholars, the term "Complexity Theory" can be generally defined as a generic term for numerous theories and ideas that are derived from various scientific disciplines (Goldstein 1999; Manson 2001; Burnes 2005).

Because of the changes in the organizational environment – in particular caused by advances in technology, more liberal trade regulations or the intensification of competitive pressure - the environment has become more chaotic, unpredictable, fragmented, uncertain, risky, complex and turbulent (Hooley & Beracs 1997; Stapleton et al. 2006; Fabac 2010; Fawcett & Waller 2011; Dervitsiotis 2012; Hashemi et al. 2013). Fawcett & Waller (2011) suggest that such problems need to be examined through "new lenses".

In an ever-changing environment, organizations want to be more adaptable and better able to learn from experience, in order to redesign themselves in consideration of these new demands (Cohen 1999).

Moreover, it has been shown, that complexity theory offers an interesting and persuasive account of certain natural phenomena such as chemical transformations, turbulence, the evolution of biological structures and so forth (Introna 2003; Mason 2013). Thus, there is a growing interest in applying complexity theory to organizations (Gemmil & Smith 1985; Anderson et al. 1999; Introna 2003; Smith 2005; Grobman 2006; Sturmberg et al. 2014). Why should complexity theory not provide sophisticated answers to randomness and instability for social systems - like organizations - as is the case for mathematical and physical systems (Introna 2003)?

2.2 Complexity: Fundamentals and Definition

The term complexity emerged in the field of natural sciences (Robertson 2004). Owing to the interdisciplinary investigation of the phenomenon the various authors offer different perspectives and views on complexity, which explains the many definitions of the term.

Mitleton-Kelly (2003) for example focuses on "objective complexity" by explaining how complexity emerges through connectivity and the inter-relationships of individual elements, while Boisot (2003) examines whether complexity can be reduced or whether it has to be absorbed by raising the issue of "subjectively experienced complexity". In addition, Espejo (2003) identifies the notion of "individual" and "social complexity" which refers to resources (human and others) and their connections within organizations.

However, Morin (2005) divides complexity into "generalized complexity" and "restricted complexity". Whereas "generalized complexity" - as an onto-epistemological template - considers all systems as complex, "restricted complexity" - as a more technical notion of complexity - defines particular mathematical techniques for modeling dynamic systems (Tsoukas & Dooley 2011).

Nonetheless, up to recent years no consensus on a comprehensive definition of the term has been reached (e.g. Edmonds 1999; Choi & Krause 2006; Bozarth et al. 2010; Fabac 2010; Tsoukas & Dooley 2011). The difficulty exists because complexity depends on which aspect you are concerned with (Edmonds 1999). Several theories arise from various scientists in the fields of physics, chemistry, biology, economics and mathematics, as well as evolution (Mitleton-Kelly 2003). Table 1 provides an overview of definitions from several types of studies.

Source	Definition
General understanding	Combination of size, variety and rules.
Complexity by Drozdz et al. (2002)	A trinity, comprising coherence, chaos and a gap between them.
Effective Measure Complexity (Grassberger 1986)	The amount of information that must be stored in order to make an optimal prediction about the next symbol to the level of granularity.
Topological complexity (Crutchfield & Young 1989)	The minimal size of the automaton that can statistically reproduce the observed data within a specified tolerance.
Cyclomatic complexity (McCabe 1976)	Difference between the total number of transitions and the total number of states.
Edmonds complexity (Edmonds 1999)	The difficulty of formulating an overall behavior with given atomic components and their inter-relations.
Relational complexity (Halford et al. 1998)	The number of interacting variables that must be presented in parallel to perform a process entailed in a task.
Kauffman's complexity (Kauffman 1993)	Number of conflicting constraints.

Table 1: Definitions of complexity (Xing & Manning 2005)

Although each definition focuses on a different aspect, there are considerable overlaps among them. Every definition is either entirely or partly concerned with three basic aspects of complexity: size, variety, and rules (Xing & Manning 2005). Overall, each definition of complexity reflects the perspective brought to bear upon it.

For the purposes of this article, complexity is defined as organizational complexity and is associated with *"[...] the intricate inter-relationships of individuals, of individuals with artifacts (such as IT), and with the effects of inter-actions within the organization and between organizations and their 'environment' which includes related businesses"* (Mitleton-Kelly 2013, no page reference). This definition focuses on interactions among individuals in the organizational context and therefore provides an appropriate definition for the remaining part of this paper.

3 Authors' Views: Differences and Similarities

The characteristics of complexity are ever more evident in modern organizations and in the environments in which they operate (Fabac 2010).

In the view of various authors there are four main drivers which are responsible for organizational complexity: diversity, interdependence, ambiguity and flux (Maznevski et al. 2007; Schwandt & Franklin 2010; Alfadly 2011; Nedopil et al. 2011). According to Moldoveanu (2004, p. 9), investigating organizational complexity is important in order to *"[...] confront and ultimately resolve, dissolve or capitulate to the difficulties of defining the property of complexity of an organizational phenomenon and [...] defining and defending a complexity measure for organizational phenomena, which allows one to declare one phenomenon more complex than another."*

Looking at prior studies, three major conceptualizations for institutional complexity have been recognized; "dominant logic", "competition", and "ongoing coexistence". Each of them analyzes a different degree of balance between logics (Pache & Santos 2010; Goodrick & Reay 2011). Villani & Philipps (2013) however go beyond by identifying that there is a dependency between the degree of success achieved by the organization in facing institutional complexity and the strategies an organization uses to handle multiple logics.

On the other hand, Glen & Malott (2004) classify three types of organizational complexity: environmental, component, and hierarchical complexities. Having done so, they then analyze these three types of complexity and their implications for organizational effectiveness. Based on this, it can be derived that complexity cannot be eliminated but managed. In order to survive and develop, it is becoming increasingly evident that organizations are forced to adapt their internal complexity according to the level of the environment's (external) complexity (Größler et al. 2006). *"Organizational complexity is costly and difficult to manage, and simplicity, wherever possible, is a virtue"* (Ghoshal & Nohria 1993, p. 24).

Regarding this, Ashkenas et al. (2013) evaluate 1,400 responses to a proprietary organizational complexity survey. Thereby, they deduce that a lot of the inhibiting complexity in organizations is generated or intensified by managers' own behaviors. To be more effective, mangers need to understand the behavioral implications of the entire complexity of a system.

Therefore, Tucker et al. (2003) as well as Dumitraşcu & Dumitraşcu (2011) emphasize the increasing need to shift from hierarchical structures to networked structures in order to confront the rising complexity. In this context, Damanpour (1996) considers structural complexity and organizational size as the two major indicators of organizational complexity. Denning (2014) even points out, that turning a big old hierarchical bureaucracy into a nimble 21st century networked organization represents one of the most difficult management challenges these days.

Moreover, Malott & Martinez (2006) address the application of behavioral analysis to the organizational level, through their case study. Since changing the behavior of relatively complex entities - such as organizations and individuals - is a different issue, the analysis of organizational complexity is essential in planning change. It is helpful to identify targets that justify the use of resources, which influence the organization's competitiveness. According to them, managing complexity requires an ongoing evaluation and assessment, and continuous analysis, design, and implementation.

Furthermore, various researchers claim that organizational complexity is associated with greater information asymmetry (Duru & Reeb 2002; Bens & Monahan 2004; Bushman et al. 2004; Demirkan et al. 2011). Looking at the influence of organizational complexity on a firm's value, previous literature proposes firm efficiency and information asymmetry as the two key drivers (Carillo & Kopelman 1991; Plumlee 2003; Meyer & Lu 2004; Manconi & Massa 2010; Poorzamani & Razmpou 2013; Billet et al. 2013). In addition, Liu und Lai (2012) expand these perspectives by arguing that information asymmetry - arising from organizational complexity - influences the demand of complex firms for higher quality auditors.

While these studies reveal the negative effects of structural complexity, another scholar provides a study which indicates that the complexity of Chinese firms actually increases their values (Jia 2010).

Alternatively, Mena (2003) looks at the effects of complexity and reaches a more positive conclusion. For his research, he studied five companies and carried out several case studies. The result was the development of five generic strategies, which were transferred into a Complexity – Uncertainty Model (Figure 1).

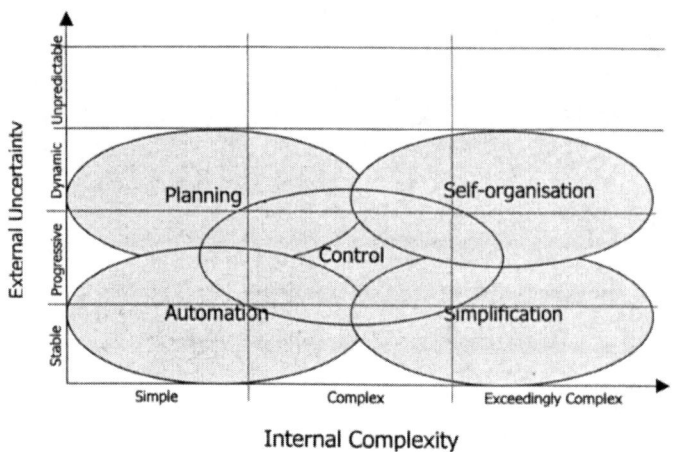

Figure 1: The Complexity-Uncertainty Model (Mena 2003)

"The model helped to show that Self-organization (a concept of complexity theory) is not only a concept that has potential benefits for organizations, but also one that

is essential for supporting organizations operating in uncertain and complex situations" (Mena 2003, p. 146). However, he himself states that it is difficult to assess the precise impact of each strategy on organizational performance. The same point of criticism is frequently heard when dealing with complexity.

By examining how human capital considerations affect the process of CEO succession, Naveen (2006) argues that operational complexity correlates with industry structure and firm size, as well as the degree of diversification. Taking this into account, Gøtzsche & Klausen (2014) provide an economic response strategy model to analyze the optimal response strategy for multinational corporations (MNC's) facing a high level of external complexity. The same basis is employed in an economic analysis of the direct effects of external complexity dimensions on the optimal level of integration. In this regard, Schwandt (2009) aims to resolve the theoretical discrepancy and to explain, as well as to empirically test, how organizations should respond to growing environmental complexity by developing a measurement model of organizational complexity.

Apart from this, Nobre et al. (2010) mention the importance of organizational cognition when it comes to the environmental complexity and uncertainty that the organization is faced with.

The authors Gerschberger et al. (2011) however refer to the importance of managing complexity in continuously growing supply chains. On the basis of existing literature they operationalize a generic set of parameters to determine the complexity within a supply network. Finally, the identification of the most relevant network segments is a critical success factor for a company's competitiveness.

4   Research Gaps

Finding a research gap turned out to be a very challenging task because only limited research has been carried out on the subject "organizational complexity" in general. Nevertheless, in the context of this article, the following two gaps can be derived.

The first research gap refers to the transformation of "new organizations" based on higher levels of automation. Whereas continuously developing and changing all the component features of an organization towards higher levels of cognition and complexity occurs, the aim of ensuring the existence of the organization however will remain the same and will not change in respect to, nor in the same proportions as its components. Consequently, it cannot be excluded that the degree of automation within a company may increase, whereby "new organizations" with more capabilities of computational capacity, including knowledge and uncertainty management, are required. These organizations will be able to operate more flexibly and manage higher levels of environmental complexity, as well as uncertainty, than organizations of today. However such transformations towards "new organizations" will have implications for society, and this has potential as a topic for further research (Nobre et al. 2008; Nobre et al. 2010).

Another gap is addressed by Villani and Philipps (2013) and concerns a more accurate analysis of the organizational decision-making process in order to successfully confront institutional complexity. There is already literature (e.g. Junior et al. 2012; Gøtzsche & Klausen 2013; Wade 2013) presenting response strategies dealing with such situations, but there is still a lack of knowledge of the whole process that leads an organization to strategically react in a specific way.

5 Conclusion

The previous sections have shown that there are different views and measures concerning the growing problems of complexity in combination with organizations.

Owing to the high dynamic, complex and fast changing environment, organizational adaptation - in the form of well designed and yet spontaneous changes of process, structure, and strategy - is required.

Clearly, the handling of the increasing complexity in a company is already a crucial factor in competition. This process needs to be controlled by the top management, but success requires the active engagement of all involved. Mastering and regulating the desired complexity, especially in products and processes is increasingly becoming a key success factor. Only those who have achieved transparency of the firm's operations are able to successfully survive in a rapidly changing industry. Since the characteristics of the external complexity drivers are difficult for the companies toinfluence, they have to respectively accept and adapt to those as far as possible. Within the scope of complexity management, a continuous examination of a firms' degree of complexity - as well as finding an optimal balance - is essential.

References

Abuelmaatti, A., & Rezgui, Y. (2008, January). Virtual Organizations in Practice: A European Perspective. *AMCIS 2008 Proceedings* , pp. 1-9.

Alfadly, A. A. (2011). Managing Complexity in Kuwaiti Organizations . *International Journal of Business and Management* , Vol. 6(3), pp. 142-145.

Alt, R., Legner, C., & Österle, H. (2005). Virtuelle Organistaionen: Virtuelle Organisation: Konzept, Realität, Umsetzung, Herausforderungen. In H. Heilmann, *Virtuelle Organisationen* (S. 7-20). Heidelberg: dpunkt-Verlag.

Anderson, M. C. (2001). *Case Study on the Return on Investment of Executive Coaching.* MetrixGlobal, LLC.

Anderson, P. / Meyer, A. / Eisenhardt, K. / Carley, K. / Pettigrew, A. (1999). Introduction to the Special Issue: Applications of Complexity Theory to Organization Science. *Organization Science* , Vol. 10(3), pp. 233-236.

Argyris, C., & Schoen, D. (1978). *Organisational learning: a theory of action perspective.* New York: Addison-Wesley.

Atkinson, P. E. (2012). Return on investment in executive coaching: effective organisational change. *Management Services (Spring 2012)* , S. 20-23.

Baker, W. E., & Sinkula, J. M. (2002). Market orientation, learning orientation and product innovation: delving into the organization's black box. *Journal of Market-Focussed Manageneg* , 5 (1), 5-23.

Baker, W. E., & Sinkula, J. M. (1999). The synergistic effect of market orientation and learning orientation on organizational performance. *Journal of the Academy of Marketing Science* , 27 (4), 411-427.

Baron, L., & Morin, L. (2009). The Coach-Coachee Relationship in Executive Coaching: A Field Study. *Human Ressource Development Quarterly, Spring Vol. 20/1* , S. 85-106.

Barrett, P., & Sexton, M. (2006). Innovation in Small, Project-Based Construction Firms. *British Journal of Management, Vol. 17* , pp. 331-346.

Beeby, M., & Booth, C. (2000). Networks and interorganizational learning: A critical review. *The Learning Organization* , 7 (2), 75-88.

Bekkers, V. (2003). E-government and the emerge of virtual organizations in the public sector. *Information Polity, Vol. 8* , S. 89-101.

Bens, D. A. / Monahan, S. J. (2004). Disclosure Quality and the Excess Value of Diversification. *Journal of Accounting Research* , pp. Vol.42(4), pp. 691-730.

Berger, M. (1996). Making the virtual offica a reality. *Sales & Marketing Management, Vol. 6* , S. 18-22.

Bierly, P., & Chakrabarti, A. (1996). Generic knowledge strategies in the US pharmaceutical industry. *Strategy Management Journal* , 17, 123-135.

Billet, M. T. / Chen, C./ Martin, X. / Wang, X. (2013). Internal Information Asymmetry, Internal Capital Markets, and Firm Value . URL: https://www2.bc.edu/~pontiff/Conference%20Papers/BCMW_11212013.pdf, accessed [03/18/2014].

Bleecker, S. E. (March-April 1994). The Virtual Organization. *The Futurist* , S. 9-14.

Bluckert, P. (2005). The foundations of a psychological approach to executive coaching. *Industial and Commercial Training, Vol.37/4*, S. 171-178.

Boisot, M. (2003). *Is There a Complexity Beyond the Reach of Strategy?* In: Mitleton-Kelly, E. (Ed.): Complex Systems and Evolutionary Perspectives on Organisations. The Application of Complexity Theory to Organisations, Bringley, UK: (Emerald), 2003, p. 185-202.

Bontis, N., Crossan, M. M., & Hulland, J. (2002). Managing an organizational learning system by aligning stocks and flows. *Journals of Management Studies, 39* (4), 437-469.

Bortolot, J. (March 2014). The un-office: New workplace trends include movable walls, outdoor spaces and sometimes no office at all. *Entrepreneur*, S. 20-21.

Bozarth, C. C. / Warsing, D. P. / Flynn, B. B. / Flynn, E. J. (2009). The impact of supply chain complexity on manufacturing plant performance. *Journal of Operations Management*, Vol. 27(1), pp. 78-93.

Bozer, G. (2013). The role of coachee characteristics in executive coaching for effective sustainability. *Journal of Management Development, Vol. 32/3*, S. 277-294.

Bozer, G., & Sarros, J. C. (February 2012). Examining the Effectiveness of Executive Coaching on Coachees' Performance in the Israeli Context. *International Journal of Evidence Based Coaching and Mentoring; 10(1)*, S. 14-32.

Brady, D. (25. April 2010). CAN GE STILL MANAGE? *BusinessWeek*.

Breu, K., & Hemingway, C. (2004). Making organizations virtual: The hidden cost of distributed teams. *Journal of Information Technology, Vol. 3*, S. 191-202.

Browde, B. (2011). Coaching Political Leaders: Can Coaching Be Used To Improve The Quality Of Executive-Level Government? *Journal of Leadership Studies, Vol. 5/1*, S. 71-75.

Burnes, B. . (2005). Complexity Theories and Organizational Change. *International Journal of Management Reviews*, Vol. 7(2), pp. 73-90.

Bushman, R. / Chen, Q. / Engel, E. / Smith, A. (2004). Financial accounting information, organizational complexity and corporate governance systems. *Journal of Accounting and Economics*, pp. Vol. 37 (2), pp. 167-201.

Camarinha-Matos, L. M., & Afsarmanesh, H. (2007). A framework for virtual organization creation in a breeding enviroment. *Annual Reviews in Control, Vol. 31*, S. 119-135.

Camelot Management Consultants . (2012). Survey "Mastering Complexity": Most European companies are afraid of losing control over rising complexity. *Press Release*, URL: http://www.camelot-mc.com/en/press/press-releases/press-archive-2012/survey-mastering-complexity-most-european-companies-are-afraid-of-losing-control-over-rising-complexity/, accessed [03/08/2014].

Cangelosi, V. E., & Dill, W. R. (1965). Organizational Learning: Obersavtions toward a theory. *Administrative Science Quarterly, 10* (2), 175-203.

Carillo, P. M. / Kopelman, R. E. (1991). Organization Structure and Productivity: Effects of Subunit Size, Vertical Complexity, and Administrative Intensity on Operating Efficiency. *Group Organization Management*, Vol.16(1), pp. 44-59.

Choi, T. Y. / Krause, D. R. (2006). The supply base and its complexity: Implications for transaction costs, risks, responsiveness, and innovation. *Journal of Operations Management*, Vol. 24(5), pp. 637-652.

Choo, C. W., & Bontis, N. (2002). *The strategic management of intellectual capital and organizational knowledge.* Oxford: Oxford University Press.

Christie, P. M., & Levary, R. R. (1998). Virtual corporations: Recipe for success. *Industrial Management, Vol. 4* , S. 7-11.

Cohen, M. . (1999). Commentary on the Organization Science Special Issue on Complexity. *Organization Science* , Vol. 10(3), pp. 373-376.

Cohen, M., & Sproul, L. (1991). Editors introduction. *Organization Science - Special Issue on Organisational Learning , 2* (1), 1-3.

Coyle, J., & Schnarr, N. (1995). The Soft-Side Challenges of the "Virtual Corporation". *Human Resource Planning, Vol. 1* , S. 41-42.

Crossan, M. M., Lane, H. W., & White, R. (1999). Organizational learning framework: from intuition to institution. *Academy of Management Review , 3* (24), 522-537.

Crossan, M., & Berdrow, I. (2003). Organizational learning and strategic renewal. *Strategic Management Journal , 24* (1), 1087-1105.

Crossan, M., & Guatto, T. (1996). Organizational Learning Profile. *Journal of Organizational Change Management , 9* (1), 107-122.

Cyert, R., & March, J. (1963). *A behavioral theory of the firm* (2nd Edition Ausg.). Malden, MA, USA: Blackwell.

Davenport, T. H., & Pearlson, K. (1998). Two cheers for the virtual office. *Sloan Management Review, Vol. 4* , S. 51-65.

de Haan, E. (2011). Executive coaching in practice: what determines helpfulness for clients of coaching? *Personnel Review, Vol. 40/1* , S. 24-44.

Decarolis, D. M., & Deeds, D. L. (1999). The impact of stocks and flows of organizational knowledge on firm performance: an empirical investigation of the bio-technology industry. *Strategy Management Journal , 20*, 953-968.

Demanpour, F. (1996). Organizational Complexity and Innovation: Developing and Testing Multiple Contingency Models. *Management Science* , Vol. 42.(5), pp. 693-716.

Demirkan, S./ Radhakrishnan, S. / Urcan, O. (2011). Discretionary Accruals Quality, Cost of Capital, and Diversification. *Journal of Accounting, Auditing & Finance* , pp. Vol. 27(4), pp. 496–526.

Denning, Steve. (2014). Can A Big Old Hierarchical Bureaucracy Become A 21st Century Network? *Forbes* , URL: http://www.forbes.com/sites/stevedenning/2014/03/21/can-a-big-old-hierarchical-bureaucracy-become-a-21st-century-network/, accessed [03/24/14].

Dervitsiotis, K. N. (2012). An innovation-based approach for coping with increasing complexity in the global economy. *Total Quality Management* , Vol. 23(9), pp. 997- 1011.

Dodgson, M. (1993). Organizational Learning: A Review of Some Literatures. *Organization Studies , 14* (3), 375-394.

Douglas, C. A., & Morley, W. H. (2000). *Executive coaching: An annotated Bibliography.* North Carolina: Center for Creative Leadership.

Drucker, P. F. (1998, October 5). Management's new paradigms. *Forbes* , pp. 152-177.

Dumitrașcu, V. / Dumitrașcu, R. A. (2011). Approach to the Organisational Complexity in Terms of Network and Intellectual Capital Concepts. *Romanian Journal of Economics*, Vol. 32(1), pp. 191-215.

Duru, A. / Reeb, D. M. (2002). International Diversification and Analysts' Forecast Accuracy and Bias. *The Accounting Review*, pp. Vol. 77(2), pp. 415-433.

Economist Intelligence Unit. (2011). The Complexity Challenge: How businesss are bearing up. *The Economist*, URL: http://mib.rbs.com/docs/MIB/Insight/Simplifying-complexity/EIU_report-The_Complexity_Challenge.pdf, pp. 1-32, accessed [03/16/2014].

Edmonds, B. (1999). *What is Complexity? - The philosophy of complexity per se with application to some examples in evolution.* In Heylighen, F. and Aerts, D. (Eds.); Dordrecht: (Kluwer), pp. 1-18.

Enescu, C., & Popescu, D. M. (July 2012). Executive Coaching - Instrument for Implementing Organizational Change. *Review of International Comparative Management, Vol. 13/3*, S. 378-386.

Ennis, S. A. (2012). *The Executive Coaching Handbook.* Abgerufen am 10. März 2014 von http://www.executivecoachingforum.com/

Espejo, R. (2003). *Social Systems and the Embodiment of Organisational Learning.* In: Mitleton-Kelly, E. (Ed.): Complex Systems and Evolutionary Perspectives on Organisations. The Application of Complexity Theory to Organisations, Bringley, UK: (Emerald), 2003, p. 53-70.

Fabac, R. (2010). Complexity in Organizations and Environment - Adaptive Changes and Adaptive Decision-Making. *Interdisciplinary Description of Complex Systems - scientific journal*, Vol. 8(1), pp. 34-48.

Fawcett, S. E. / Waller, M. A. (2011). Making sense out of chaos: Why Theory is Relevant to Supply Chain Research. *Journal of Business Logistics*, Vol. 32(1), pp. 1-5.

Feldman, D. C., & Lankau, M. J. (November 2005). Executive Coaching: A Review and Agenda for Future Research. *Journal of Management*, S. 828-848.

Field, L. (1997). Impediments to empowerment and learning within organisations. *The Learning Organisation*, 4 (4), 149-158.

Finger, M., & Buergin, S. (1998). *The concept of the "Leaning Organization" applied to the transformation of the public sector: Conceptual contributions for theory development. .* London: Sage.

Firescu, V., Filip, D., & Vlad, R. (March 2013). The virtual factory in supply chains management. *Review of Management & Economic Engineering*, S. 33-40.

Fitzgerald, L., & Van Eijnatten, F. M. (2002). Chaos speak: a glossary of chaordic terms and phrases. *Journal of Organizational Change Management*, 15 (4), 412-423.

Fontaine, D., & Schmidt, G. F. (2009). The Practice of Executive Coaching Requires Practice: A Clarification and Challenge to Our Field. *Industrial and Organizational Psychology, Vol. 2*, S. 277-279.

Franke, U. J. (1999). The virtual web as a new entrepreneurial approach to network organizations. *Entrepreneurship and regional development, Vol. 11*, S. 203-229.

Friedlander, F. (1983). *Patterns of Individual and Organizational Learning.* San Francisco: Jossey-Bass.

Gökmen, A. (March 2012). Virtual business operations, e-commerce & its significanc and the case of Turkey: current situation and its potential. *Electronic Commer Research, Vol. 12, Issue 1*, S. 31-51.

Gøtzsche, N. / Klausen, M. K. . (2014). The Optimal Response Strategy for MNCs in a Complex Environment: An Economic Approach. pp. 1-128.

Garvin, D. (July/August 1993). Building a learning organization. *Harvard Business Review*, 78-91.

Gemmil, G. / Smith, C. . (1985). A Dissipative Structure Model of Organization Transformation. *Human Relations*, Vol. 38(8), pp. 751-766.

Gerschberger, M. / Engelhardt-Nowitzki, C. / Kummer, S. / Staberhofer, F. (2012). A model to determine complexity in supply networks . *Journal of Manufacturing Technology Management*, Vol. 23(8), pp. 1015-1037.

Gerschberger, M. / Staberhofer, F. / Engelhardt-Nowitzki, C. (2011). Complexity Parameters in Supply Networks– an extensive Literature Review. URL: http://www.agtil.at/uploads/images/PDFs/final_fullpaper_Supply%20Chain%20Complexity%20Parameters_ICLS_final.pdf, accessed [03/21/2014].

Ghoshal, S. / Nohria, N. (1993). Horses for Courses: Organizational Forms for Multinational Corporations. *Sloan Management Review*, Vol. 34(2), pp. 23-35.

Gibson, C. B., & Birkinshaw, J. (2004). The antecedents consequences, and mediating role of organizational ambidexterity. *Academy of Management Journal*, 47 (1), 209-226.

Gilson, C., Dunleavy, P., & Tinkler, J. (2009). *Organizational Learning in Goverment Sector Organizations: Literature Review.* London School of Economics Public Policy Group. London: LSE Public Policy Group.

Glen, S. S. / Malott, M. E. (2004). Complexity and selection: Implications for organizational change. *Behavior and Social Issues*, Vol. 13(2), pp. 89-106.

Goldstein, J. (1999). Emergence as a Construct: History and Issues . *Emergence*, Vol. 1(1), pp. 49-72.

Good, D. (2010). Cognitive Behavioral Executive Coaching. A Structure for Increasing Leader Flexibility. *OD Practitioner, Vol. 42/3*, S. 18-23.

Goodrick, E. / Reay, T. (2011). Constellations of Institutional Logics: Changes in the Professional Work of Pharmacists. *Work and Occupations*, Vol. 38(3), pp. 372–416.

Gorelick, C. (2005). Organizational learning vs the learning organization: a conversation with a practionier. *The Learning Organization*, 12 (4), 383-388.

Größler, A. / Grübner, A. / Milling, P. M. (2006). Organisational adaptation processes to external complexity. *International Journal of Operations & Production Management*, Vol. 26(3), pp. 254-281.

Graham, W. (2008). Towards Executive Change: A psychodynamic group coaching model for short executive programmes. *International Journal of Evidence Based Coaching and Mentoring, Vol. 6/1*, S. 67-78.

Gray, D. E. (2006). Executive Coaching: Towards a Dynamic Alliance of Psychotherapy and Transformative Learning Processes. *Management Learning, Vol. 37/4*, S. 475-497.

Greenwood, R. / Raynard, M. / Kodeih, F. / Micelotta, E. R. / Lounsbury, M. (2011). Institutional Complexity and Organizational Responses. *The Academy of Management Annals*, Vol. 5(1), pp. 317-371.

Greve, H. R. (2003). *Organizational Learning from Performance Feedback: A Behavioural Perspective on Innovation and Change.* Cambridge: Cambridge University Press.

Grobman, G. M. (2006). Complexity Theory: A new way to look at organizational change. *Public Administration Quarterly*, Vol. 29, (3/4), pp. 350-382.

Hannafey, F. T., & Vitulano, L. A. (2013). Ethics and Executive Coaching: An Agency Theory Appproach. *Journal of Business Ethics*, S. 599-603.

Hashemi, A. / Butcher, T. / Chhetri, P. (2013). A modeling framework for the analysis of supply chain complexity using product design and demand characteristics. *International Journal of Engineering, Science and Technology*, Vol. 5(2), pp. 150-164.

Hernez-Broome, G., & Boyce, L. A. (2011). *Advancing Executive Coaching.* San Francisco: Jossey-Bass a Willey Imprint.

Hooley, G. / Beracs, J. . (1997). Marketing strategies for the 21st Century: lessons from the top Hungarian companies. *Journal of Strategic Marketing*, Vol. 5(3), pp. 143-165.

Huber, G. (1991). Organizational Learning: The Contributing Processes and the Literatures. *Organization Science*, *1* (2), 88-115.

Hurley, R. E., & Hult, G. T. (1998). Innovation, market orientation and organizational learning: an integration and empirical examination. *Journal of Marketing*, *62*, 42-54.

Ikehara, H. (1999). Implications of Gestalt theory and practice for the learning organisation. *The Learning Organisation*, *2* (6), 63-69.

Introna, L. D. (2003). *Complexity Theory and Organisational Intervention ? Dealing with (in)commensurability.* In: Mitleton-Kelly, E. (Ed.): Complex Systems and Evolutionary Perspectives on Organisations. The Application of Complexity Theory to Organisations, Bringley, UK: (Emerald), 2003, pp. 205-219.

Jerez-Gomez, P., Lorente, J., & Valle-Cabrera, R. (2005). Organizational learning capability: a proposal of measurement. *Journal of Business Research* (58), 715-725.

Jia, X. (2010). Complex Organizational Structure and Chinese Firm Value. *Wharton Research Scholars Journal*, Vol. 10, pp. 1-30.

Jimenez, D., & Sanz-Valle, R. (2011). Innovation, organizational learning and Performance. *journal of Business Research* (64).

Joo, B.-K. e. (Spring 2012). Multiple Faces of Coaching: Manager-as-coach, Executive Coaching, and Formal Mentoring. *Organization Development Journal Vol. 30/1* , S. 19-38.

Junior, V. M. / Pascucci, L. / Murphy, J. P. (2012). Implementing Strategies in Complex Systems: Lessons from Brazilian Hospitals. *BAR Brazilian Administration Review*, Vol. 9(2), pp. 19-37.

Kürümlüoglu, M., Nostdal, R., & Karvonen, I. (2005). Base concepts. In L. M. Camarinha-Matos, H. Afsarmanesh, & O. Martin, *Virtual Organizations Systems and Practices.* New York: Springer.

Kampa-Kokesch, S., & Anderson, M. Z. (2008). Executive coaching: A comprehensive review of the literature. In R. R. Kilburg, & R. C. Diedrich, *The Wisdom of Coaching. Essential Papers in Consulting Psychology for a World of Change* (S. 39-59). Washington: American Psychological Association.

Kasper-Fuehrer, E. C., & Ashkansasy, N. M. (2001). Communicating trustworthiness and building trust in interorganizational virtual organizations. *Journal of Management, Vol. 27*, S. 235-254.

Kenny, J. (2006). "Strategy and the learning organisation: a maturity model for the formation of strategy". *The Learning Organization, 13* (4), 353-368.

Keskin, H. (2006). Market orientation, learning orientation, and innovation capabilities in SMEs. *European Journal of Innovation Management, 9* (4), 396-417.

Kilburg, R. R. (2008). Toward a conceptual understanding and definition of executive coaching. In R. R. Kilburg, & R. C. Diedrich, *The Wisdom of Coaching. Essential Papers in Consulting Psychology for a World of Change* (S. 21-30). Washington: American Psychological Association.

Kock, N. (2000). Benefits for virtual organizations from distributed groups. *Communication of the ACM, Vol. 11*, S. 107-112.

Koonce, R. (September/October 2010). Narrative 360° Assessment and Stakeholder Analysis: How a Powerful Tool Drives Executive Coaching Engagements. *Global Business and Organizational Excellence*, S. 25-37.

Larsen, K. R., & McInerey, C. R. (2002). Preparing to work in the virtual organization. *Information & Management, Vol. 39*, S. 445-456.

Latheemaki, S., Toivonen, J., & Mattila, M. (2001). Critical aspects of organizational learning research and proposals for its measurement. *British Journal of Management, 12* (2), 113-129.

Lawton, T. C., & Michaels, K. P. (2001). Advancing to the virtual value chain: Learning from the DELL model. *Irish Journal of Management, Vol. 22*, S. 91-112.

Lewin, A. Y., Long, C. P., & Carroll, T. (1999). The co-evolution of new organizational forms. *Organization Science, 10* (1), 535-550.

Lieberman, M. (1987). The Learning Curve, Diffusion, And Competitive Strategy. *Strategic Management Journal, 8*, 441-452.

Lin, L.-H., & Lu, I.-Y. (2005). Adoption of virtual organization by Taiwanese electronic firms: An empirical study of organization structure innovation. *Journal of Organizational Change*, S. 184-200.

Lipnack, J., & Stamps, J. (2000). *Virtual Teams: People Working Across Boundaries With Technology.* New York: John Wiley & Sons.

Liston, P., Byrne, J., Heavey, C., & Byrne, P. J. (March 2008). Discrete-event simulation for evaluating virtual organizations. *International Journal of Production Research, Vol. 46, No. 5*, S. 1335-1356.

Liu, C. L. / Lai, S. H. (2012). Organizational Complexity and Auditor Quality. *Corporate Governance: An International Review*, pp. Vol. 20(4), pp. 352–368.

Lloria, B., & Moreno-Luzon, M. (2013). Organizational learning: Proposal of an integrative scale and research instrument. *Journal of Business Research* (67), 692-697.

Mackie, D. (December 2007). Evaluating the effectiveness of executive coaching: Where are we now and where do we need to be? *Australian Psychologist; 42(4)*, S. 310-318.

Maden, C. (2012). Transforming Public Organizations into Learning Organizations: A Conceptual Model. *Public Organization Review* (12), 71-84.

Malott, M. E. / Martinez, W. S. (2006). Addressing organizational complexity: A behavioural systems analysis application to higher education. *Pschology Press*, Vol 41(6), pp. 559-570.

Manconi, A. / Massa, M. . (2010). Modigliani and Miller Meet Chandler: Organizational Complexity, Capital Structure, and Firm Value. *Social Science Research Network*, URL: http://faculty.insead.edu/massa/Research/org_structure.pdf, accessed [03/20/2014].

Manson, S. M. (2001). Simplifying Complexity: A Review of Complexity Theory. *Geoforum*, Vol. 32(3), pp. 405-415.

March, J. G. (1991). Exploration and exploitation in organizational learning. *Organization Science*, 2 (1), 71-87.

March, J., & Levitt, B. (1988). Organisational learning. *Annual Review of Sociology*, 14, 319-340.

March, J., & Olsen, J. (1975). The uncertainty of the past: Organizational learning under ambiguity. *European Journal of Political Research* (3), 147-171.

Mason, R. B. (2013). Distribution tactics for success in turbulent versus stable environments: A complexity theory approach. *Journal of Transport and Supply Chain Management*, Vol. 7(1), pp. 1-9.

Maznevski, M. / Steger, U. / Amann, W. (2007). *Managing Complexity in Global Organizations as the Meta-challenge.* In: Maznevski, M. / Steger, U. / Amann, W. (Ed.): Managing Complexity in Global Organizations, Chichester: (Wiley), 2007, pp. 3-14.

McAdam, S. (2005). *Executive Coaching: How to choose, use and maximize value for yourself and your team.* London: Thorogood Publishing Limited .

McKenna, D. D., & Davis, S. L. (2009). Hidden in Plain Sight: The Active Ingredients of Executive Coaching. *Industrial and Organizational Psychology, Vol.2*, S. 244-260.

Meyer, M. W. / Lu, X. . (2004). Managing Indefinite Boundaries: The Strategy and Structure of a Chinese Business Firm. *Management and Organization Review*, Vol. 1(1), pp. 57–86.

Mitleton-Kelly, E. (n.y.). Complexity Lexicon. *London School of Economics and Political Science (LSE)*, http://www.lse.ac.uk/researchAndExpertise/units/complexity/lexicon.aspx, accessed [03/21/2014].

Mitleton-Kelly, E. (2003). *Ten Principles of Complexity and Enabling Infrastructures.* In: Mitleton-Kelly, E. (Ed.): Complex Systems and Evolutionary Perspectives on Organisations. The Application of Complexity Theory to Organisations, Bringley, UK: (Emerald), 2003, p. 23-50.

Moen, F., & Skaalvik, E. (2009). The Effect from Executive Coaching on Performance Psychology. *International Journal of Evidence Based Coaching and Mentoring, Vol. 7/2*, S. 31-49.

Moldoveanu, M. (2004). An intersubjective measure of organizational complexity: A new approach to the study of complexity in organizations. *Emergence: Complexity & Organization*, Vol. 6(3), pp. 9-26.

Moller, C. (April 1997). The virtual organisation . *Automation in Construction, Vol. 6, Issue 1* , S. 39-43.

Morecroft, J. W., & Sterman, J. D. (1994). *Modeling for learning organizations.* Portland, USA: Productivity Press.

Morin, E. (2005). Restricted complexity, general complexity. Paper presented at the: . *Colloquium 'Intelligence de la complexite: epistemologie et pragmatique'* , URL: http://cogprints.org/5217/1/Morin.pdf, accessed [03/10/2014].

Mowshowitz, A. (1997). On the Theory of Virtual Organizations. *Syst. Res. Behav. Sci., Vol. 14* , pp. 373-384.

Mowshowitz, A. (1997, September). Virtual Organization: A virtually organized company links its business goals with the procedures needed to achieve them. *Communications of the ACM, Vol. 40, No. 9* , pp. 30-37.

Mowshowitz, A. (1994, May). Virtual organization: A vision of management in the information age. *The Information Society, Vol. 10, Issue 4* , pp. 267-288.

Msanjila, S. S., & Afsarmanesh, H. (March 2008). Trust analysis and assessment in virtual organization breeding environments. *International Journal of Production Research, Vol. 46, No. 5* , S. 1253-1295.

Mun, J., Shin, M., & Jung, M. (May 2011). A goal-oriented trust model for virtual organization creation. *Journal of Intelligent Manufacturing, Vol. 22* , S. 345-354.

Murphy, S. A. (November 2004). Recourse to executive coaching: the mediating role of human resources. *International Journal of Police Science & Management* , S. 175-186.

Natale, S. M., & Diamante, T. (2005). The Five Stages of Executive Coaching: Better Process Makes Better Practice. *Journal of Business Ethics, Vol. 59* , S. 361-374.

Naveen, L. (2006). Organizational Complexity and Succession Planning. *Journal of Financial & Quantitative Analysis* , Vo. 41 (3), pp. 661-683.

Nedopil, C. / Steger, U. / Amann, W. (2011). *Managing Complexity in Organizations: Text and Cases.* Houndmills: (Palgrave Macmillan), 2011, pp. 3-22.

Nobre, F. S. / Tobias, A. M. / Walker, D. S. (2010). A New Contingency View of the Organization: Mananging Complexity and Uncertainty Through Cognition. *BAR - Brazilian Administration Review* , Vol. 7(4), pp. 379-396.

Nobre, F. S. / Tobias, A. M. / Walker, D. S. (2008). *Organizational and Technological Implications of Cognitive Machines: Designing Future Information Management Systems.* Hershey, PA: (Information Science), 2008.

Nocks, J. (April 2007). Executive Coaching - Who Needs It? *The Physician Executive* , S. 46-48.

Nonaka, I. (1994). A dynamic theory of organizational knowledge creation. *Organization Science* , 5 (1), 14-37.

Nonaka, I., & Takeuchi, H. (1995). *The knowledge-creating company: How Japanese companies create the dynamics of innovation.* New York-Oxfrod: Oxford University Press.

Orenstein, R. L. (Spring 2006). Measuring Executive Coaching Efficacy? The Answer Was Here All the Time. *Consulting Psychology Journal: Practice and Research, Vol 58/2* , S. 106-116.

Pache, A. C. / Santos, F. (2010). When worlds collide: The internal dynamics of organizational responses to conflicting institutional demands. *Academy of Management Review* , Vol. 35(3), pp. 455-476.

Pangil, F., & Chan, J. M. (2014). The mediating effect of knowledge sharing on the relationship between trust and virtual team effectiveness. *Journal of Knowledge Management, Vol. 18* , S. 92-106.

Pedler, M., Burgoyne, J., & Boydell, T. (1991). *The Learning Company.* New York: McGraw-Hil.

Peltier, B. (2001). *The Psychology of Executive Coaching: Theory and Application.* New York: Taylor & Francis.

Plumlee, M. A. (2003). The effect of information complexity on analysts' use of that information. *The Accounting Review* , Vol. 78(1), pp. 275-296.

Plump, C. M., & Ketchen, D. J. (2013). Navigating the possible legal pitfalls of virtual teams. *Journal of Organizational Design, Vol. 2* , pp. 51-55.

Poorzamani, Z. / Razmpou, A. . (2013). Quality Grade of Information Asymmetry and Firms' Cash Flow Values. *Technical Journal of Engineering and Applied Sciences* , Vol. 22(3), pp. 3177-3184.

Preece, A. (March 2001). Supportin Virtual Organizations Through Constraing Fusion. *International Journal of Intelligent Systems in Accounting Finance & Management, Vol. 10, Issue 1* , S. 25-37.

Pun, K. F., & Nathai-Balkissoon, M. (2011). Integrating knowledge management into organisational learning. *The Learning Organization , 18* (3), 203-223.

Randall, W. (2013). Are the Performance Based Logistics Prophets Using Science or Alchemy to Create Life-Cycle Affordability? *Defence Aquisition Journal , 20* (3), 325-348.

Reeves, W. B. (December 2006). The Value Proposition For Executive Coaching. *Financial Executive* , S. 48-49.

Reinicke, B. (2011, April). Creating a Framework for Research on Virtual Organizations. *Journal of Information Systems Applied Research, Vol. 4, No. 1* , pp. 49-56.

Reynolds, R., & Ablett, A. (1998). Transforming the rhetoric of organisational learning to the reality of the learning organisation. *The Learning Organization , 5* (1), 24-35.

Rezgui, Y., & Wilson, I. (2005). Socio-organizational issues. In L. Camarninha-Matos, A. Hamideh, & M. Ollus, *Virtual Organizations Systems and Practice.* New York: Springer.

Riddle, D., Zan, L., & Kuzmycz, D. (2009). Five Myth About Executive Coaching. *Leadership In Action: Issues & Observations, Vol. 29/5* , S. 19-21.

Riemer, K., & Vehring, N. (2012). Virtual or vague? A literature review exposing conceptual differences in defining virtual organizations in IS research. *Electron Markets* , pp. 267-282.

Robertson, D. A. (2004). The Complexity of the Corporation. *Human Systems Management* , Vol. 23(2), pp. 71-78.

Sanson, M. (2006). *Executive Coaching: An international analysis of the supply of executive coaching services [Dissertation].* St. Gallen: University of St. Gallen.

Scholz, C. (1996). Virtuelle Organisation: Konzeption und Realisation. *Zeitschrift Führung und Organisation, Jg. 65* , S. 204-2010.

Schwandt, A. . (2009). Measuring organizational complexity and its impact on organizational performance – A comprehensive conceptual model and empirical study. *(Diss., Technischen Universität Berlin)* .

Schwandt, A. / Franklin, J. R. (Ed.). (2010). *Logistics: The Backbone for Managing Complex Organizations.* Bern: (Haupt), 2010, pp. 19ff.

Senge, P. (1990). *The fifth discipline. The art and practice of the learning organization.* New York, New York, USA: Doubleday.

Shao, Y. P., Liao, S. Y., & Wang, H. Q. (1998, October). A model of virtual organisations. *Journal of Information Science, Vol. 24* , pp. 305-312.

Shelbourn, M., Hassan, T., & Carter, C. (2005). Legal and contractual framework for the VO. In L. M. Camarhinha-Matos, H. Afsarmanesh, & M. Ollus, *Virtual Organizations Systems and Practices* (pp. 167-176). New York: Springer.

Sherman, S., & Alyssa, F. (November 2004). The Wild West of Executive Coaching. *Harvard Business Review* , S. 82-90.

Skiffington, S., & Zeus, P. (2003). *Behavioral Coaching: How To Build Sustainable Personal And Organizational Strength.* New South Wales: McGraw Hill.

Slater, S. F., & Narver, J. C. (1994). Market Oriented Isn't Enough: Build a Learning Organization. *Marketing Science Institute* , 94-103.

Smith, A. C. T. . (2005). Complexity theory for organisational futures studies. *foresight* , Vol. 7(3), pp. 22-30.

Smither, J. W. (2011). Can Psychotherapy Research Serve as a Guide for Research About Executive Coaching? An Agenda for the Next Decade. *Journal of Business Psychology, Vol. 26* , S. 135-145.

Spector, J., & Davidsen, P. (2005). *How can organizational learning be modeled and measured?* Florida State University ; University of Bergen. Amsterdam: Elsevier.

Stapleton, D. / Hanna, J. B. / Ross, J. R. (2006). Enhancing supply chain solutions with the application of chaos theory. *Supply Chain Management: An International Journal* , Vol. 11 (2), pp. 108-114.

Stern, L. R. (2009). Challenging Some Bsic Assumptions About Psychology and Executive Coaching: Who Knows Best, Who Is the Client, and What Are the Goals of Executive Coaching . *Industrial and Organizational Psychology, Vol. 2* , S. 268-271.

Stoica, M., & Ghillic-Micu, B. (May 2009). Virtual organization - cybernetic economic system. modeling partner selection process. *Economic Computation & Economic Cybernetics Studies & Research, Vol 34, Issue 2* , S. 1-11.

Stomski, L. e. (2011). Coaching Programs: Moving beyond the One-on-One. In G. Hernez-Broome, & L. A. Boyce, *Advancing Executive Coaching. Setting the Course for Successful Leadership Coaching* (S. 177-204). San Francisco: Jossey-Bass.

Sturmberg, J. P. / Martin, C. M. / Katerndahl, D. A. (2014). Systems and Complexity Thinking in the General Practice: Literature: An Integrative, Historical Narrative Review. *Annals of Family Medicine* , Vol. 12(1), 66-74.

Sun, H. C. (2003). Conceptual clarifications for organizational learning, learning organization and a learning organization. *Human Resource Development International* , 6 (2), 153-166.

Swart, J., & Harcup, J. (2012). 'If I learn do we learn?': The link between executive coaching and organizational learning. *Management Learning, Vol. 44/4* , S. 337-354.

The Boston Consulting Group. (1973). *The Experience Curve- Reviewed.* (T. B. Group, Produzent) Abgerufen am 20. 3 2014 von bcg perspectives: www.bcgperspectives.com/content/classics/corporate_finance_corporate_strategy_portfolio_management_the_experience_curve_reviewed_history/

Torbert, W. R. (1999). The distinctive questions developmental action inquiry asks. *Management Learning , 30* (2), 189-206.

Tsoukas, H. / Dooley, K. J. . (2011). Introduction to the Special: Towards the Ecological Style: Embracing Complexity in Organizational Research. *Organization Studies* , Vol. 32(6) 729–735.

Tucker, B. / Furness, C. / Olsen, J. / McGuirl, J. / Oztas, N. / Millhiser, W. . (2003). Complex Social Systems: Rising Complexity in Business Environments. *New England Complex Systems Institute* , pp. 1-8.

Turoff, M. (1985). Information, value, and the internal marketplace. *Technological Forecasting Society Change, Vol. 27* , S. 357-373.

Unland, R., & Tianfield, H. (2003). IT enabling: Essence of virtual organizations. *International Journal of Information Technology and decision making* , S. 367-370.

Valaski, J., Malucelli, S., & Reinehr, S. (2012). Ontologies application in organizational learning. A literature Review. *Expert Systems with Applications* (39), 7555-7561.

Villani, E. / Philipps, N. W. . (2013). Beyond Institutional Complexity: The Case of Different Organizational Successes in Confronting Multiple Institutional Logics. Paper presented at: . *35th DRUID Celebration Conference 2013, Barcelona* , pp. 1-40.

Wade, M. . (2013). ORGANIZATIONAL COMPLEXITY: THE HIDDEN KILLER. *International Institute for Management Development* , URL: http://www.imd.org/research/challenges/TC084-13-organizational-complexity-michael-wade.cfm, accessed [03/12/2014].

Walczak, S. (2008). Knowledge management and organizational learning. *The Learning Organization , 15* (6), 486-494.

Wang, C. L., & Ahmed, P. K. (2003). Organisational learning: a critical review. *The Learning Organization , 10* (1), 8-17.

Wang, C., & Ahmed, P. (2002). *A Review of the Concept of Organisational Learning.* Wolverhampton Business School, Management Research Centre. Wolverhampton: University of Wolverhampton.

Washylyshyn, K. M. (2008). Executive Coachin: An Outcome Study. In R. R. Kilburg, & R. C. Diedrich, *The Wisddom of Coaching. Essential Papers in Consulting Psychology for a World of Change* (S. 79-89). Washington: American Psychological Association.

Werther, W. B. (1999). Structure-Driven Strategy and Virtual Organization Design. *Business Horizons, Vol. 42* , S. 13-18.

Workman, M., Kahnweiler, W., & Bommer, W. (2003). The effects of cognitive style and media richness on commitment to telework and virtual teams. *Journal of Vocational Behaviour, Vol 63* , S. 199-219.

Xing, J. / Manning, C. A. (2005). Complexity and Automation Displays of Air Traffic Control: Literature Review and Analysis. *Final Report* , pp, 1-20.

Organizational Agility

Patrick Fuchs, Timea Havar-Simonovich

Abstract. The only thing that is constant is change. What the ancient Greek philosopher Heraclitus already recognized during the 5th century BC is even truer nowadays. Indeed, a number of academic studies argue that volatility at the firm level has multiplied over the last decades. Organizations operating in highly competitive and turbulent business environments are forced not only to adapt to changes as they occur, but also to proactively predict changes before they affect their operations. Organizational agility – loosely defined as a combination of flexibility, nimbleness, and speed – is increasingly considered a source of competitive advantage.

Keywords: Flexibility, speed, agility, organization, enterprise, corporation, change management

1 Introduction

The only thing that is constant is change. What the ancient Greek philosopher Heraclitus already recognized during the 5th century BC is even truer nowadays. In fact, a number of academic studies came to the conclusion that volatility at the firm level increased somewhere between two- and fourfold from the 1970s to the 1990s (Comin & Philippon 2005; Baker & Kennedy 2002; Huyett & Viguerie 2005; Wiggins & Timothy 2005). Especially in the light of recent events like the financial and Eurozone crisis, it seems reasonable to assume that volatility has continued to increase. In this turbulent world, many organizations are facing fierce competition stimulated by technological innovations, changing market environments and changing customer demands (Yaghoubi & Dahmardeh 2010). These developments call for a need to develop and improve organizational flexibility and responsiveness. Organizational agility – loosely defined as a combination of flexibility, nimbleness, and speed – is increasingly considered a source of competitive advantage (Singh et al. 2013). As a result, interest in organizational agility has grown exponentially for practitioners and researchers (Tichy & Charan 1989; Tallon & Pinsonneault 2011). A McKinsey and Company survey found that nine out of ten executives ranked organizational agility as both critical to business success and growing in importance over time (Sull 2009). Another survey by the Economist Intelligence Unit (2009) indicated that nearly 90 percent of 349 executives around the world stated that agility is either extremely important or somewhat important. There is little disagreement that agile organizations effectively manage the challenges of continuous change (Adler, Goldoftas & Levine 1999; Sarker & Sarker 2009; Grewal & Tansuhaj 2001; Tallon & Pinsonneault 2011).

The research of this contribution is threefold. First, common themes on agile organizations are identified in order to derive a definition that incorporates common ground. Second, a classification of literature investigating the concept of agility is provided. Third, a summary of different scientific approaches on how to enhance a firm's agility is given.

2 Literature review on organizational agility

2.1 Commonalities and an emerging definition

There have been numerous attempts by researchers to define what organizational agility is. An excerpt is displayed in table 1. Despite lacking a widely accepted definition (Noaker 1994; Goldman et al. 1995; Richards 1996; Van Assen et al. 2001), the concept of agility exhibits four similar traits or commonalities: First, most authors refer to agility as a set of organizational sense-response actions, which are characteristic for organizations operating in turbulent markets (Singh et al. 2013). For instance, Nadkarni and Narayanan (2007: p. 245) define organizational sense-response actions as an ability to "precipitate intentional change" involving rapid shifts in "strategic actions, asset deployment, and investment strategies." Tallon and Pinsonneault (2011: p. 464) specify agility as an organizational ability to "detect and respond to [environmental] opportunities and threats with ease, speed, and dexterity." At its core, most studies specify agility as persistent, systematic variations in enterprises' outputs, structures or processes that are identified, planned, and then executed as a strategy in order to gain competitive advantage (Tallon & Pinsonneault 2011).

Second, the sense-response actions that are viewed agile can be specified through a bi-dimensional concept of magnitude of variety change (flexibility) and rate (speed) of generating variety change (Singh et al. 2013). The magnitude of variety change is described by the degree to which an enterprise is capable of changing the level of variety generation in its products, processes, services or practices. Apple, for example, improved iPhone 5's magnitude of variety in its product offering over iPhone 4's by increasing the display (3.5 to 5 inch), storage (32 to 64 GB) and camera quality (5 to 8 megapixels) (Singh et al. 2013). It can be derived from literature that most researchers presume a positive relation between magnitude of variety generation and agility. As a general rule, the greater a firm's magnitude of variety generation the more agile the firm is deemed to be. The variety itself can be influenced in many ways. To wit, the number of decision alternatives (Judge & Miler 1991), the variety of different strategies implemented (Evans, 1991; Volberda 1996; Nadkarni & Narayanan 2007; Conboy 2009), the introduction of new products or product lines (Sanchez 1995; Sanchez & Mahoney 1996), and the offering of product variations (Worren, Moore & Cardona 2002). The rate of variety change refers to the speed of change and is defined as the change in variety per unit of time (Singh et al. 2013). Roughly speaking, it is the time it takes from sensing to executing a change in the magnitude of variety. Analog, most definitions of agility associate higher rate with greater agility. In order to assess how agile an organization really is, it is not sufficient to consider an enterprise's magnitude of variety change only, but also how long it takes the firm to do so. Returning to the example of Apple, the iPhone 5 was released about 11 months after the release of the iPhone 4s, which is approximately four months less than it took Samsung to release its Galaxy S3 after the release of the Galaxy S2 smartphone (Singh et al. 2013).

Third, most studies regard agility as a relative concept, which is heavily dependent upon environmental (industry) conditions. To this effect, Smith and Zeimthal (1996) relate to "uncertain", Volberda (1996) to "high variety" and Grewal and Tansuhaj (2001) to "high risk" environments respectively. Agility is a relative construct as different environments are characterized by varying degrees of market turbulence, competitive intensity, and customer need heterogeneity, thus, necessitating to examine organizational agility by comparing similar companies within a specific industry or environment (Grewal & Tansuhaj 2001; Nadkarni & Narayanan 2007; Singh et al. 2013). This implies the need to identify an enterprise's relative position in a specific environment. The relative position is described by the firm's "ability to generate higher magnitude and rate of variety in its sense-response actions vis-à-vis its set of competitors and the characteristics of the environment." (Singh et al. 2013: p. 9).

Fourth, the impact of agility, that is, whether agility improves firm performance depends on the characteristics of the environment. The literature under consideration suggests that a positive effect of agility on financial or strategic performance is more likely in case of more volatile environments (Nadkarni & Narayanan 2007). While financial performance refers to indicators such as revenue growth and/or profitability, strategic performance relates to efficiency and/or innovation (Grewal & Tansuhaj 2001). Contrarily, in case of slow velocity (Nadkarni & Narayanan 2007) and high demand environments (Grewal & Tansuhaj 2001) agility is deemed to affect firm performance detrimentally.

To sum up, the above-discussed four points stipulate what the scientific consensus of agility says. On this basis Singh et al. (2013: p. 10) formally define organizational agility as "the ability of a firm to sense and respond to the environment by intentionally changing (1) magnitude of variety and/or (2) the rate at which it generates this variety relative to its competitors."

2.2 Major research fields

Despite being a relatively young field of research, scientific literature investigating the concept of agility is already broad (Bottani 2008). According to Yaghoubi & Dahmardeh (2010) it can be classified into four main categories: First, studies focusing on the main feature of agile organizations. This category contains the research of Goldman et al. (1995), Kidd (1996), Gunasekaran (1998), and Yusuf et al. (1999). Second, studies emphasizing on the enablers of agility. Gunasekaran

(1998) was one of the first to come up with seven enablers of agility before Sharp et al. (1999) expanded this approach by presenting 10 enablers in their research. Third, studies developing conceptual models for the implementation of agility. Again, Gunasekaran (1998) was one of the first to propose an integrated framework. Sharifi & Zhang (1999) and Sharifi & Zhang (2001) developed a three-step approach for the purpose of implementing agility within manufacturing companies. Another three-step model analyzing the agility of production systems was suggested by Jackson & Johansson (2003). Fourth, studies measuring or evaluating agility. This represents the newest field in agility research and is thus only partly explored. A few examples are studies of Yusuf et al. (2001), Van Hoek (2001), Yang & Li (2002), Tsourveloudis & Valavanis (2002), Lin et al. (2006), and Jain et al. (2008).

2.3 Drivers, capabilities and enablers

The objective of current research is to study the effective factors on organizational agility. These factors are typically classified into three sections namely drivers, capabilities and enablers of agility (Yaghoubi & Dahmardeh 2010). Agility drivers determine the degree to which an environment is changing and thereby constitute how agile an organization needs to be in order to be competitive in this particular environment. Different firms exhibit different characteristics and thus experience different changes that may even be unique to them. A specific change may be undesirable for company A, while company B might welcome it. For instance, e-commerce led to insolvency proceedings for Neckermann, whilst Zalando's growth has been skyrocketing ever since. There is no scientific consensus on how to categorize the extent of change. Agility drivers can be of both internal and external nature (Kinicki & Kreitner 2008). External drivers refer to the environment of an organization. One method using external drivers, for instance, consists of the following five dimensions. First, market change, which is determined by changes in market growth, the variation of customer group composition, changes in product lifetimes, etc. Second, change in competitive intensity, influenced by entry barriers, cost-cutting pressure, innovations, etc. Third, change in customer demands. This depends on quality expectations, delivery times, etc. Fourth, technological change. Fifth, changes in social factors as a result of varying legal, political, cultural, and environmental conditions (Yaghoubi & Dahmardeh 2010; Lin et al. 2006; Sharifi & Zhang 1999). By contrast, a method using internal drivers classifies agility drivers based on organizational activities that are influenced by the change. Three categories exist: First, how change influences the current activities, plans, and projects of a company. This usually concerns lower levels of the organization and includes changing orders, delivery times, product or service characteristics, etc. Second, how change influences strategic plans and objectives of a company. These changes might endanger a firm's position in specific markets. Third, how change influences the business strategy of a company. This includes new business opportunities, but also emerging threats such as new competitors (Yaghoubi & Dahmardeh 2010; Lin et al. 2006; Bandarian 2003; Sharifi & Zhang 1999). To sum up, the literature provides numerous attempts to categorize the main drivers behind organizational agility; scientific consensus, however, is still not on the horizon.

Agility capabilities are simply an organization's abilities to sense and respond to changes (Sharifi & Zhang 1999). Capabilities are viewed as "strategic weapons in coping with an unpredicted, hostile, and ever-changing business environment" (Almahamid 2013: p. 10). There are several frameworks and methodologies available in the literature. One prominent example goes back to Sharifi & Zhang (1999); Zhang & Sharifi (2000), who developed a methodology for achieving agile capabilities in manufacturing companies. The authors divided the agility capabilities into four categories: responsiveness, competency, flexibility, and speed and described them as follows: Responsiveness is the ability to identify changes and respond to them quickly, reactively or proactively, and also to recover from them. Competency is the ability to efficiently and effectively realize enterprise objectives. It is an extensive list of abilities providing a company with productivity, efficiency, and effectiveness in achieving its goals. Examples of these abilities are strategic vision, sufficient technological capability, and cost-effectiveness. Flexibility or adaptability is the ability to implement different processes and apply different facilities to achieve the same goals. Flexibility can refer to both product volume and people. Speed or quickness is the ability to complete an activity as quickly as possible. This can relate to quickness in new products time-to-market or quickness in product and service delivery. Goldman et al. (1995) pursued a different approach and identified four strategic dimensions of agile capabilities: enriching the customers; cooperating to enhance competitiveness; organizing to master changes; and leveraging the impact of people and information. Jackson & Johansson (2003) emphasized that agile capabilities are not a specific goal companies should achieve, but rather are a necessity to maintain competitiveness in a turbulent business environment. More recently, Sherehiy et al. (2007) pointed out the global characteristics (beyond manufacturing and work force related ones) that could be applied to all aspects of an organization such as flexibility, responsiveness, speed, culture of change, integration and low complexity, high quality, customized products, and mobilization of core competencies.

Enablers are the levers to build up agile capabilities. According to Ahmadia et al. (2012) agility enablers are elements, concepts and techniques, which help obtaining a desirable level of agile capabilities. As agility must be incorporated in all functional areas of the organization to respond effectively to changes, acquiring agility requires flexibility and sensitivity in strategies, technologies, systems and human resources (Ahmadia et al. 2012; Bharadwaj 2000; Yusuf et al. 1999).

3 Conclusion

Organizations operating in highly competitive and turbulent business environments are forced not only to adapt to changes as they occur, but also to proactively predict changes before they affect their operations. Agility is a firm's "ability to compete and thrive in an unstable business environment by quickly detecting and seizing (golden) opportunities and tackling threats" (Trinh et al. 2012: p. 168). Thus, organizational agility is considered being a key business factor and an enabler of competitiveness.

Given the importance of the phenomenon to organizations, a more coherent theory of agility is needed. It is still a rather young field of research. Despite substantial advances in recent studies, a consistent and widely accepted definition has still been lacking. This impedes further theory development and decelerates advances in operationalization as to truly understand the effects of agility on competition and firm performance (Singh et al. 2013). In short, the door for future research is wide open.

Authors	Definition of agility
Sharifi & Zhang (1999)	Agility is ability to sense respond to, and exploit anticipated or unexpected changes in the business environment. Such organization must be able to identify the environmental changes and regarding them as the growth factors.
Yusuf et al. (1999)	Successful exploration of competitive bases such as speed, flexibility, innovation, quality, and profitability through the integration of reconfigurable resources and best practices in a knowledge-rich environment to provide customer-driven product and services in a fast changing market environment.
Vokurka & Fliedner (1998)	Agility is the ability to market successfully low-cost, high quality products with short lead times and in varying volumes that provide enhanced value to customers through customization.
Katayama & Bennett (1999)	Cope with demand volatility by allowing changes to be made in an economically viable and timely manner; abilities for meeting widely varied customer requirements in terms of price, specification, quality, quantity and delivery.
Huang (1999)	Agility is a response to the challenges posed by a business environment dominated by change and uncertainty. It involves a new way of doing business. It reflects a new mind-set on making, selling, and buying, an openness to new forms of commercial relationship, and new measures for assessing the performance of companies and people.
Naylor et al. (1999)	Agility means using market knowledge and a virtual corporation to exploit profitable opportunities in a volatile market place.

Authors	Definition of agility
Kodish et al. (1995)	Agility is a firm's ability to generate the required information for management decision-making in a turbulent environment.
Goldman (1995)	Agility is a comprehensive, strategic response to fundamental and irreversible structural changes that are undermining the economic foundations of mass production-based competition.
Maskell (2001)	Agility is the ability to thrive and prosper in an environment of constant and unpredictable change. So, the organizations must not get afraid of the work environment changes and avoid them, but they have to mention it as an opportunity to reach competitive advantage in market.

Table 1: Excerpt of agility definitions. Source: Own illustration based on Yaghoubi & Dahmardeh 2010

References

Adler, P.S., Goldoftas, B., & Levine, D.I. (1999): Flexibility versus efficiency? A case study of model changeovers in the Toyota Production System, *Organization Science*, 10: 43-68.

Ahmadia, S. A., Fathizadeha, A., Sadeghib, J., Daryabeigib, M., Taherkhanic, L. (2012): A study on the relationship between organizational structure and organizational agility: A case study of insurance firm, *Management Science Letters*, Vol. 2, 2777-2788.

Almahamid, S. M. (2013): E-government system acceptance and organizational agility: theoretical framework and research agendas, *International Journal of Information, Business and Management*, Vol. 5 (1), 4-19.

Bandarian, R. (2003): Agility: Why and How, *Management International Conference*, Tehran.

Baker, G. P., Kennedy, R. E. (2002): Survivorship and the economic grim reaper, *Journal of Law, Economics, and Organization*, 2002, Volume 18, Number 2, pp. 324-61.

Bharadwaj, A. S. (2000): A resource-based perspective on information technology capability and firm performance: An empirical investigation, *Management Information Systems Quarterly*, Vol. 24 (1), 169-196.

Bottani, E., On the assessment of enterprise agility: issues from two case studies, *International Journal of logistics: Research and Applications*, Vol.00, No.0, PP.1-18, 2008.

Conboy, K. 2009. Agility from first principles: Reconstructing the concept of agility in information systems development. *Information Systems Research*, 20: 329-354.

Diego A. Comin and Thomas Philippon (2005): The rise in firm-level volatility: Causes and consequences, *NBER Macroeconomics Annual*, 2005, Vol. 20, 167-228.

Economist Intelligence Unit (2009): *Organisational agility: How business can survive and thrive in turbulent times*.

Evans, J.S. (1991): Strategic flexibility for high technology manoeuvers: A conceptual framework, *Journal of Management Studies*, Vol. 28 (1), 69-89.

Goldman, S. L., R. N. Nagel and K. Preiss (1995). *Agile Competitors and Virtual Organizations: Strategies for Enriching the Customer*, New York, NY: Van Nostrand Reinhold.

Grewal, R., Tansuhaj, P. (2001): Building organizational capabilities for managing economic crisis: The role of market orientation and strategic flexibility, *Journal of Marketing*, Vol. 65, 67-80.

Gunasekaran, A. (1998): Agile manufacturing: enablers and an implementation framework, *International Journal of Production Research*, Vol. 36 (5), 1223-1247.

Huang, C. Y., Nof, S. Y. (1999): Enterprise agility: a view from the PRISM lab, *International Journal of Agile Management Systems*, Vol. 1 (1), 51-59.

Huyett, W. I., Viguerie, S. P. (2005): Extreme competition, *The McKinsey Quarterly*, Vol. 1, 47-57.

Jackson, M., Johansson, C. (2003): An agility analysis from a production system perspective, *Integrated Manufacturing Systems*, Vol. 14 (6), 482-488.

Jain, V., Benyoucef, L., Deshmukh, S. G. (2008): A new approach for evaluating agility in supply chains using Fuzzy Association Rules Mining. *Engineering Applications of Artificial Intelligence*, Vol. 21, 367-85.

Judge, W. Q., Miller, A. (1991): Antecedents and outcomes of decision speed in different environmental contexts, *Academy of Management Journal*, Vol. 34, 449-463.

Katayama, H., Bennett, D. (1999): Agility, adaptability and leanness: A comparison of concepts and a study of practice, *International Journal of Production Economics*, Vol. 60-61, 43-51.

Kidd, P.T. (1996): Agile manufacturing: A strategy for the 21st century, *Institution of Electrical Engineers colloquium*, Vol. 74, 61 EE, England.

Kinicki, A., Kreitner, R. (2008): *Organizational Behavior*, New York, 3th ed.

Kodish, J.L., Gibson, D.V., Amos, J.W. (1995): The development and operation of 197 an agile manufacturing consortium: the case of AAMRC, in: *Proceedings of the Fourth Annual Conference on Models, Metrics and Pilots*, Vol. 2.

Lin, C., Chiu, H., Tseng, Y. (2006): Agility evaluation using fuzzy logic, *International Journal of Production Economics*, Vol. 101, 353-368.

Maskell, B. (2001): The age of agile manufacturing, *Supply Chain Management: An International Journal*, Vol. 6 (1), 5-11.

Nadkarni, S., Narayanan, V. K. (2007): Strategic schemas, strategic flexibility, and firm performance: The moderating role of industry clockspeed, *Strategic Management Journal*, Vol. 28, 243-270.

Naylor, J. B., Naim, M. M., Berry, D. (1999): Leagility: Integrating the lean and agile manufacturing paradigms in the total supply chain, *International Journal of Production Economics*, Vol. 62, 107-118.

Noaker, P. M. (1994): *The Search for Agile Manufacturing*, Manufacturing Engineering, 40-43.

Richards, C. (1996): Agile Manufacturing: Beyond Lean?, *Production and Inventory Management Journal*, Vol. 2, 60-64.

Sanchez, R. (1995): Strategic flexibility in product competition, *Strategic Management Journal*, Vol. 16, 135-159.

Sanchez, R., Mahoney, J. T. (1996): Modularity, flexibility, and knowledge management in product and organization design, *Strategic Management Journal*, Vol. 17, 63-76.

Sarker, S., Sarker, S. (2009): Exploring agility in distributed information systems development teams: An interpretive study in an offshoring context, *Information Systems Research*, Vol. 20, 440-461.

Sharifi, H., Zhang, Z. (1999): A methodology for achieving agility in manufacturing organizations: An introduction, *International Journal of Production Economics*, Vol. 62, 7-22.

Sharifi, H., Zhang, Z. (2001): Agile manufacturing in practice: Application of a methodology, *International Journal of Operations & Production Management*, Vol. 21 (5-6), 772-794.

Sharp, J. M., Irani, Z., Desai, S. (1999): Working towards agile manufacturing in the UK industry, *International Journal of Production Economics*, Vol. 62, 155-169.

Sherehiy, B., Karwowski, W., Layer, J. (2007): A review of enterprise agility: Concepts, frameworks, and attributesǀ, *International Journal of Industrial Ergonomics*, Vol. 37 (5), 445-460.

Singh, J., Sharma, G., Hill, J., Schnackenberg, A. (2013): Organizational agility: What it is, what it is not, and why it matters, Academy of Management, *Annual Meeting Proceedings*.

Smith, A.D., Zeithaml, C. (1996): Garbage cans and advancing hypercompetition: The creation and exploitation of new capabilities and strategic flexibility in two regional bell operating companies, *Organization Science*, Vol. 7, 388-399.

Sull, D. (2009): How to Thrive in Turbulent Market, *Harvard Business Review*, Vol. 87 (2), 78-88.

Tallon, P. P., Pinsonneault, A. (2011): Competing perspectives on the link between strategic information technology alignment and organizational agility: Insights from a mediation model, *MIS Quarterly*, Vol. 35, 463-486.

Tichy, N., Charan, R. (1989): Speed, simplicity, self-confidence: An interview with Jack Welch, *Harvard Business Review*, Vol. 67 (5), 112-120.

Trinh, T. P., Molla, A., Peszynski, K. (2012): Enterprise Systems and Organizational Agility: A Review of the Literature and Conceptual Framework, *Communications of the Association for Information Systems*, Vol. 31 (8).

Tsourveloudis, N. C., Valavanis, K. P. (2002): On the Measurement of Enterprise Agility, *Journal of Intelligent and Robotic Systems*, Vol. 33, 329-342.

Van Assen, M. F., Hans, E. W., Van De Velde (2001): An agile planning and control framework for customer-order driven discrete parts manufacturing environments, *International Journal of Agile management Systems*, Vol. 2 (1), 16-23.

Van Hoek, R. (2001): Moving forward with Agility, *International Journal of Physical Distribution and Logistics Management*, Vol. 31 (4).

Vokurka, R. J., Fliedner, G. (1998): The journey toward agility, *Industrial Management & Data Systems*, Vol. 98 (4), 165-171.

Volberda, H. W. (1996): Toward the flexible form: How to remain vital in hypercompetitive environments, *Organization Science*, Vol. 7, 359-374.

Wiggins, R. R., Ruefli, T. W. (2005): Schumpeter's ghost: Is hyper competition making the best of times shorter?, *Strategic Management Journal*, Vol. 26 (10), 887-911.

Worren, N., Moore, K., Cardona, P. (2002): Modularity, strategic flexibility, and firm performance: A study of the home appliance industry, *Strategic Management Journal*, Vol. 23, 1123-1140.

Yaghoubi, N. M., Dahmardeh, M. R. (2010): Analytical approach to effective factors on organizational agility, *Journal of Basic and Applied Scientific Research*, Vol. 1 (1), 76-87.

Yang, S., Li, T. (2002): Agility Evaluation of Mass Customization Product Manufacturing, *Journal of Materials processing Technology*, Vol. 41, 166.

Yusuf, Y.Y., Sarhadi, M., Gunasekaran, A. (1999): Agile manufacturing: The drivers, concepts and attributes, *International Journal of Production Economics*, Vol. 62, 33-43.

Yusuf, Y.Y., Burns, N. D., Ren, J. (2001): A method for evaluating enterprise agility: An empirical study, in *16th International Conference on Production Research*, Prague, Czech Republic.

Zhang, Z., Sharifi, H. (2000): A methodology for achieving agility in manufacturing organizations, *International Journal of Operations and Production Management*, Vol. 20 (4), 496-512.

Organizational Alignment

Timo Kallenbach, Hanna Epple

Abstract. The objective of this article is to examine the status quo of research on organizational alignment and to review academic publications in this field. Organizational alignment is a theoretical approach where the individual goals of employees or departments should be matched with the organization's strategic goals to build competitive advantage through synergies. This contribution tries to answer the question what research gaps exist in the field of organizational alignment. To do so, secondary research data was gathered and analyzed to compare and contrast authors' views on this issue. Moreover, similar opinions are outlined and explained. The outcome of this review shows that there is no common agreement about how to define organizational alignment and about where to set conceptual boundaries. Different authors have various opinions. In addition, it appears that the current state of the literature lacks holistic frameworks and contains limited treatment of the human resources domain.

Keywords: Organizational alignment, organization, alignment, strategic alignment, strategic goals, strategy, leadership, corporate culture, change management, transformation

1 Introduction

One of the enduring topics in the corporate world is organizational alignment. This process, often called strategic alignment, is commonly viewed as a desired factor in organizations (Middleton, Harper 2004). Imagine a rowing team where every athlete is off rhythm. The boat will move in circles and not getting closer to the finish line. The same can be applied to organizations that are off alignment. As employees or departments tend to pursue their own goals, they might not be aligned with the overall goals of the organization. This can lead to teams working against each other rather than pooling their strengths for common achievements. By ensuring that everyone's activities are aligned with the organizational goals, moving the company in one direction will become easier.

This article closely examines the existing literature on organizational alignment. It has four parts, as visualized in the figure below. The first section is focused on the literature analysis with an explanation of the methodology, the analytical approach and general findings. Hereafter, the second section is concerned with the definition and classification of organizational alignment. The third section examines the research gaps in the existing literature. This part is followed by the fourth section, which deals with a critical review.

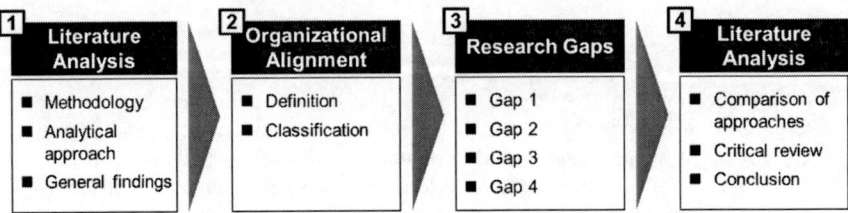

Figure 1: Structure of the article

2 Literature Analysis

The following section deals with the analysis of the reviewed literature. Therefore, it is divided into three subsections. The first one covers the methodological approach of this article, the second comprises the analytical approach while the third part highlights the general findings.

2.1 Methodology

The objective of this article is to review existing academic research literature concerning organizational alignment to define this specific term and to emphasize authors' views and concepts. A literature review of Middleton and Harper (2004) is used as a basis due to the fact that they followed a comparable objectives.

A literature review is an essential tool for the success of academic research, since it ensures the feasibility for future research. Moreover, literature reviews define the scope of investigations and can set a broad context of the respective study to enable an author to build a theory (Hart 1998).

2.2 Analytical Approach

Overall, contributions from peer-reviewed journals as well as from eleven books and one website have been analyzed under different aspects. Firstly, the analyses considered the main objective of the author(s). To classify the papers, authors' main approaches were divided into strategy, structure, culture and processes. This idea follows the St. Gallen Management Model (Ruegg-Stürm 2005). Secondly, the applied methodologies were identified - classified into theoretical models, case studies, surveys and models/frameworks. The third step was a distinction between a qualitative or quantitative approach (see Exhibit 1).

2.3 General Findings in the Literature

The analysis shows that literature about "organizational alignment" covers many different aspects, addressed by numerous authors. The majority of the reviewed literature is based on qualitative studies with the aim to derive theoretical models from the findings. Quantitative studies seem to play a subordinate role when it comes to "organizational alignment".

3 Terminology

Many academic papers and books have been published on the topic of organizational alignment over the last decades. To give an overview, the following two subchapters will firstly define the terms "organization" and "alignment" and then describe these words in a combined context.

3.1 Definition of "Organization" and "Alignment"

Despite the fact that most scholars do not give exact definitions of the term "organization", it will be used in this paper with the characteristics described by Frese, Graumann and Theuven (2012):

1. A number of persons and their activities are considered.
2. The persons and their actions have a common goal.

Thus, the action of one person in the system has potential influence on the action of other persons in the same system.

The term "alignment" covers a wide array of meanings and is used in many different backgrounds. It has its root in the Latin word *"lineare"*, later adopted by the French (*"aligner"*) and then transferred to the English language in the 18th century. The Oxford Dictionary (2014) describes it in different ways. The one which is most applicable in the context of this paper is *"a position of agreement or alliance"*.

3.2 Definition of "Organizational Alignment"

A vast variety of definitions referring to the term "organizational alignment" can be found in the reviewed literature. Tosti and Jackson (2003) stated that organizational alignment links strategy, processes, people, leadership, and culture to best accomplish the needs of an organization. Yu-Yuan Hung et al. (2007) defined an aligned organization as one, in which performance influences are mutually supportive and where every employee is focused on efficient and effective delivery of results. Leonard (2008) stressed that organizational alignment is the link of employees' interests with the ones of the organization. Robinson and Stern (1997) defined alignment in the following way: *"The degree to which the interests and actions of each employee support the organization's key goals."*

Since the late 1990s, various authors concentrate only on a fraction of the term organizational alignment. As a result; Cao, Baker and Hoffman (2010) attempted to categorize the existing literature into three different research fields: business alignment, structural alignment and strategic alignment.

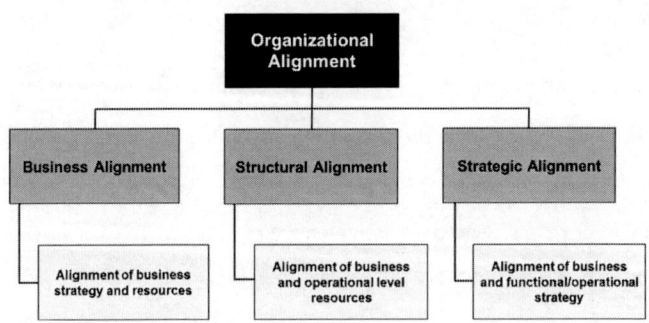

Figure 2: Research fields of organizational alignment (Based on Cao, Baker and Hoffman 2010)

The question that arises is why organizations should reach a certain level of alignment. Overall, it can be said that alignment is argued to be vital as it enables an organization to respond to its external environment and hence to perform effectively

(Parisi 2013). Tosti and Jackson (2003) highlighted that organizational alignment can lead to synergy effects because it occurs when strategic goals and cultural values are mutually supportive, and when organizational key components are linked and compatible with each other.

Nevertheless, Tosti and Jackson (2003) also state that only few organizations will achieve "complete" alignment – a condition that is not necessarily desirable. The goal should be to reach a degree of compatibility and consistency that allows employees to devote most of their energy towards accomplishing results – with a minimum of effort needed to overcome obstacles and within a reasonable amount of time. This would help organizations continue to grow and adapt.

Organizations are dynamic systems. And like any other system, they function best when all of their components are designed to work together in an efficient and smooth way. Any change that is introduced in an organization then must be aligned to fit into the existing process – or must adjust the system to accept the change (Furnham 2002).

Another question that arises is: who is responsible for organizational alignment? Middleton and Harper (2004) pointed out that organizational alignment is advocated by leading managers. To name just a few practitioners, Michael Dell (1999: 115), founder of the Dell Corporation, stated that *"you have to figure out how to align and blend everyone's talent to create value for your customers and shareholders. [...] profit sharing incentives encourage them to be productive as a team"*. The former CEO of General Electric, Jack Welch, added on this theory that *"by not aligning measurements and rewards, you often do not get what you are looking for"* (Welch 2001: 387). Louis Gestner, former CEO of IBM (2002: 100) supplemented that *"you can't transform institutions if the incentive programs are not aligned with your new strategy."* However, Macdonald (1994) argued that the majority of managers only react to changes when they are forced to, in response to a shift in business circumstances. Only few managers would decide changes in anticipation of arising crises. The idea of organizational alignment is to promote and support change processes originating from all departments of an organization. Middleton and Harper (2004) reasoned that relying on only a few creative or senior managers to guide the change is not sufficient and would probably lead to failure - without the acceptance by employees and management, implementations will be difficult.

According to Hansotia (2004), organizational alignment requires compatibility between strategy and culture. Day-to-day behavior should be consistent with stated values and the latter should be compatible with goals. Tosti and Jackson (2003) observe that most organizations interpret strategy as a considerable effort invested in the definition of strategic objectives and goals. According to them, while fewer organizations follow a cultural approach with clearly defined statements of values. Even fewer organisations make a consistent effort to ensure that these values are compatible with the organization's strategy.

Strategy is about matching internal capabilities with external opportunities to reach a superior performance (Porter 1998; Middleton, Harper 2004). In a contemporary business environment, in which organizations have to be more flexible and innovate as well as faster as their competitors, the complexity of strategy is mirrored in the concept of organizational alignment. The term "strategy" is no longer an unknown quantity for many corporations – more recently it is seen as an emergent (Abdel Al, McLellan 2013) and continuous practice based process (Jarzabkowski 2005). To round up the discussion, Faustenhammer and Ossler (2011) underlined that responsibility for organizational alignment addresses all corporate levels. It cannot be achieved without the commitment of the entire organization.

4 Research Gaps

The impact of organizational alignment on business performance has been studied for the past decades (Henderson, Venkatraman 1993; Luftman et al. 1993; Burn 1996; Luftman, Kempaiah 2007; Kearns, Lederer 2000; Sabherwal, Chan 2001; Beehr et al. 2009; Cao, Hoffman 2011; Heavin, Adam 2012). The retrieval of relevant databases for the search terms of "organizational alignment" and "strategic alignment" resulted in a total number of 58 academic papers. The result shows that many authors identified existing research gaps and complemented existing approaches.

4.1 Research Gap 1: Less publication about functions beyond HR

The first research gap, the lack of treatment of functions outside human resources has only been partly addressed (Middleton, Harper 2004). One research paper by Abdel Al and McLellan (2013) raised the issue of organizational alignment in the area of management accounting. Niven (2006) pursued an investigation from a supply-chain management perspective. The same direction was taken by Barney (1991), Powell (1992), Ward and Bickford (1996), Crotts and Ford (2008), Grant (2008) as well as by Lauver and Quinn Trank (2012). Some authors identified a connection of organizational alignment with IT functions and related implementation strategies (Baets 1992; Burn 1996; Davenport 1998; Ho et al. 2004; Sumner 2009; Baker et al. 2011). One author focused on organizational alignment from a marketing perspective (Steward 2005). Despite these efforts, the majority of journals, 20 in total, were dealing with HR and HR implementation strategies. Some of the scholars who focused on HR looked into motivation and loyalty (March 1991; Reichheld 1996; Kishore and McLean 2007). Montesino (2004) reviews organizational alignment from a reward system and training perspective. Several authors put their emphasis on corporate culture (Deal and Kennedy 1982; Kotter and Heskett 1992; Boswell, Boudreau 2001; Zachary, Fischler 2008; Goodman et al. 2011; Singh 2013). Thongpapanl et al. (2012) introduced a performance measurement tool. However, the majority of authors dealing with human resources in the context of organizational alignment focus on HR-strategies (Venkatraman, Camillus 1984; Roberts 1989; Woolfe 1993; Grant 1996; Kathuria 1997; Sabherwal et al. 2001; Sullivan et al. 2001; Fuller and Vassie 2002; Bergeron et al. 2004; Skaggs, Youndt 2004; Roberts et al. 2005; Yu-Yuan Hung et al. 2007; Yang, Hsu 2010; Andrews et al. 2011; Neubert et al. 2011; Wendt 2013).

4.2 Research Gap 2: Lack of quantitative data

Although there is a large body of research investigating organizational alignment, the largest share of reviewed literature is set up in a qualitative research context. The majority of scholars followed a qualitative approach. Only four authors (Simsek et al. 2009; Andrews, Beynon 2011; Cao, Hoffman 2011; Abdel Al, McLellan 2013) were identified to conduct surveys to gather quantitative data. However, while qualitative, longitudinal research allows it to capture development over time, quantitative research methods can usually encompass a larger sample group,

4.3 Research Gap 3: Lack of differentiation of strategy levels and their interactions

A differentiation of strategy levels (corporate, business and functional) and their interactions relating to organizational alignment has only been addressed by three papers (Galbraith, Nathanson 1978; Mintzberg 1978; Govindarajan 1988). A fourth source (Crittenden, Crittenden 2008: 303) stressed that *"successful strategy implementation, regardless of strategy levels, requires the input and cooperation of every member of a company's workforce"*. Other scholars share this view (Avison et al. 2004; Bergeron et al. 2004; Castro Christiansen 2008) and disregard any differentiation between strategic or organizational levels and instead conclude that successful organizational alignment has to comprise the entire workforce.

4.4 Research Gap 4: Lack of research on SMEs

The majority of the reviewed research papers considered organizational alignment at large organizations, mostly stock traded ones (Galbraith, Nathanson 1978; Macdonald 1994; Jarzabkowski 2003; Kearns, Sabherwal 2006; Andrews, Beynon 2011; Abdel Al, McLellan 2013; Parisi 2013). Only two sources investigated small and medium-sized enterprises (SMEs (Da Camara 2006; Dulipovici, Robey 2013). Cao and Hoffman (2011) considerd organizational alignment specifically for virtual enterprises (Cao, Hoffman 2011).

5 Conclusions

The previous sections have shown that organizational alignment plays an important role within organizations. Different researchers approached the topic from different perspectives. However, because of to the complexity of the topic and the recurring focus on HR related research, there currecntly exists no holistic model which comprises or structures all aspects of organizational alignment.

More research should be conducted in business areas outside the HR function in order to gain a more holistic picture and to identify similarities and differences. Since organizational alignment is dependent in many dynamic factors, both internally and externally, it is very difficult to find a one-fits-all approach for a successful action plan for organizational alignment. In general, organizational alignment is crucial for the success of organizations. In a today's globalized business world where people and companies are internationally connected, the success of organizations is based on the achievement of competitive advantage. Without a certain level of organizational alignment resulting from the cooperation of the workforce for achieving company's goals, a corporation will not be able to reach these advantages and be more likely to fail.

Appendix

Exhibit 1: Literature list with concepts and methodologies in terms of organizational alignment

			Main Emphasis				Methodology			Focus			Appr.	
			Strategy	Structure	Culture	Processes	Performance	Theory building	Case study	Survey	Model/ Framework	Organizational	Organizational & Individual	Individual	Quantitative	Qualitative
Author(s)	Year	Journal														
Abdel Al, S.F. et al.	2013	Journal of Accounting - Business & Management	X			X				X		X			X	
Andrews, R.A. et al.	2011	Public Organization Review	X						X	X	X				X	
Avison, D et al.	2004	The Journal of Strategic Information Systems	X							X		X				X
Baets, W.	1992	Journal of Strategic Information Systems	X	X				X								X
Baker, J. et al.	2011	Journal of the Association for Information Systems	X							X	X					X
Barney, J.	1991	Journal of Management Information Systems				X					X					X
Beehr, T.A. et al.	2009	Journal of Occupational and Organizational Psychology			X	X		X				X				X
Bergeron, F. et al.	2004	Information & Management	X	X						X	X					X
Cao, Q. et al.	2011	International Journal of Production Research				X		X	X		X			X	
Cao, Q. et al.	2012	International Journal of Production Research	X					X			X					X
Castro Christiansen, L.	2008	Journal of General Management			X			X				X				X
Crotts, J. C. et al.	2008	Business Communication Quarterly			X	X		X			X					X
Da Camara, N.	2006	Henley Manager Update	X	X						X						X
Deci, E.L.	1991	Journal of Personality and Social Psychology			X			X				X				X
Dulipovici, A. et al.	2013	Journal of Management Information Systems				X		X						X		X
Faustenhammer et al.	2011	Business Strategy Series	X	X	X			X				X				X
Fuller, C. W. et al.	2002	Employee Relations		X	X						X	X				X
Furnham, A.	2002	Journal of Change Management		X	X			X				X				X
Goodman, P. S. et al.	2011	Research in Organizational Behavior		X	X	X		X			X	X				X
Govindarajan, V.	1988	Academy of Management Journal	X			X		X				X				X
Grant, P.	1996	Strategic Management Journal		X	X	X					X	X				X
Grant, P.	2008	The International Journal of Clinical Leadership		X	X			X			X					X
Hamel, G. et al.	2003	Harvard Business Review	X	X	X				X	X		X				X
Hansotia, B.	2004	Database Marketing & Customer Strategy Management	X							X	X	X				X
Heavin, C. et al.	2012	Electronic Journal Information System Evaluation	X			X			X		X	X				X
Henderson, J. et al	1993	IBM Systems Journal	X	X				X			X	X				X
Jarzabkowski, P.	2003	Journal of Management Studies	X					X	X			X				X
Kearns, G. et al.	2000	Journal of Strategic Information Systems	X			X					X	X				X
Kearns, G. et al.	2006	Journal of Strategic Information Systems		X		X					X	X				X
Kishore, A.	2007	IEEE Transactions on Engineering Management	X	X		X					X	X				X
Kotter, J.P. et al.	1992	The Free Press			X				X				X			X
Lauver, K.J. et al.	2012	Journal of Business and Management		X		X				X		X				X
Leonard, J.	2008	ACIS 2008 Proceedings				X		X				X				X
Luftman, J. et al.	1993	IBM Systems Journal	X			X			X	X		X				X
Macdonald, K.H.	1994	Information Management & Computer Security		X						X		X	X			X
Middleton, P. et al.	2004	Journal of Change Management	X	X		X		X				X				X
Mintzberg, H.	1978	Management Science	X								X	X				X
Neubert, G. et al.	2011	International Journal of Computer Integrated Manufacturing				X			X		X	X				X
Parisi, C.	2013	Journal of Management & Governance			X	X	X	X	X		X				X	
Porter, M.E.	1998	The Free Press	X					X			X					X
Powell, T.C.	1992	Strategic Management Journal	X		X						X	X				X
Prieto Correia, V. et al.	2011	The Service Industries Journal	X	X					X		X					X
Roberts, M.L. et al.	2005	Database Marketing & Customer Strategy Management			X			X	X	X		X				X
Sabherwal, R. et al.	2001	Information Systems Research	X					X	X		X					X
Sabherwal, R. et al.	2001	Organization Science	X					X			X	X				X
Simsek, Z. et al.	2009	Journal of Management Studies			X	X		X	X	X			X		X	
Steward, H.	2005	Brand Management	X		X	X	X		X		X	X				X
Sullivan, W. et al.	2001	Journal of Change Management								X		X	X			X
Tallon, P.P.	2011	MIS Quarterly	X			X					X	X				X
Thongpapanl, N.T. et al.	2012	R&D Management	X			X			X	X		X				X
Tosti, D.T. et al.	2003	iChange World Consulting LLC	X	X	X	X		X	X		X			X		X
Wendt, R.	2013	Internet Document	X		X	X					X	X				X
Woolfe, R.	1993	Information Strategy	X					X				X				X
Yu-Yuan Hung, R. et al.	2007	Total Quality Management & Business Excellence	X			X			X	X		X				X

References

Olins, W. (1989): *Corporate identity: Making business strategy visible through design.* Boston: Harvard Business School Press.

Abdel Al, S.F.; McLellan, J.D. (2013): Strategy and Management Accounting Practices Alignment and its Effects on Organizational Performance. In *Journal of Accounting - Business & Management* 20 (1), pp. 1–27.

Andrews, R.A.; Beynon, M.J. (2011): Organizational Form and Strategic Alignment in a Local Authority: A Preliminary Exploration using Fuzzy Clustering. In *Public Organization Review* 2010 // 11 (3), pp. 201–218. DOI: 10.1007/s11115-010-0117-4.

Avison, D.; Jones, J.; Powell, P.; Wilson, D. (2004): Using and validating the strategic alignment model. In *The Journal of Strategic Information Systems* 13 (3), pp. 223–246. DOI: 10.1016/j.jsis.2004.08.002.

Baets, W. (1992): Aligning Information Systems with Business Strategy. In *Journal of Strategic Information Systems* 1 (4), pp. 205–213.

Baker, J.; Jones, D.R.; Qing, C.; Jaeki, S. (2011): Conceptualizing the Dynamic Strategic Alignment Competency. In *Journal of the Association for Information Systems* 12 (4), pp. 299–322.

Barney, J. (1991): Firm Resources and Sustained Competitive Advantage. In *Journal of Management Information Systems* 17 (1), pp. 99–120.

Beehr, T.A.; Glazer, S.; Fischer, R.; Linton, L.L.; Hansen, C.P. (2009): Antecedents for achievement of alignment in organizations. In *Journal of Occupational and Organizational Psychology* 82 (1), pp. 1–20. DOI: 10.1348/096317908X310247.

Bergeron, F.; Raymond, L.; Rivard, S. (2004): Ideal patterns of strategic alignment and business performance. In *Information & Management* (41), pp. 1003–1020.

Boswell, W.R.; Boudreau, J.W. (2001): How leading companies create, measure and achieve strategic results through "line of sight". In *Management Decision*, Vol. 39 (10), pp. 851-860.

Burn, J. (1996): IS Innovation and Organizational Alignment - A professional juggling act. In *Journal of Information Technology* 11 (1), pp. 3–12.

Cao Q., Baker J.; Hoffman J.J. (2010): The role of the competitive environment in studies of strategic alignment: a meta-analysis. In *International Journal of Production Research*, January 2012 Vol. 50 (2), pp. 567-580.

Cao, Q.; Hoffman, J.J. (2011): Alignment of virtual enterprise, information technology, and performance: an empirical study. In *International Journal of Production Research* 49 (4), pp. 1127–1149. DOI: 10.1080/00207540903555478.

Castro Christiansen, L. (2008): How the alignment of business strategy and HR strategy can impact performance: A practical insight for manager. In *Journal of General Management* 33 (4), pp. 13–33.

Crittenden, V.L.; Crittenden, W.F. (2008): Building capable organizations: The eight levers of strategy implementation. In *Business Horizons* (51), pp. 301–309.

Crotts, J. C.; Ford, R. C. (2008): Achieving Service Excellence by Design: The Organizational Alignment Audit. In *Business Communication Quarterly*, pp. 233–240. DOI: 10.1177/1080569908317319.

Da Camara, N. (2006): The relationship between internal and external stakeholders and organizational alignment. In *Henley Manager Update* 18 (1), pp. 41–52.

Davenport, H. (1998): Putting the enterprise into the enterprise system. In *Harvard Business Review*, Vol. 76 (4), pp. 121-31.

Deal, T.E.; Kennedy, A.A. (1982): Corporate Cultures. Boston, MA, United States of America: Addison-Wesley.

Dell, M. (1999): Direct from Dell: Strategies that revolutionized an industry. London, United Kingdom: HarperCollins.

Dulipovici, A.; Robey, D. (2013): Strategic Alignment and Misalignment of Knowledge Management Systems: A Social Representation Perspective. In *Journal of Management Information Systems* 29 (4), pp. 103–126. DOI: 10.2753/MIS0742-1222290404.

Faustenhammer, A.; Ossler, M. (2011): Preparing for the next crisis: what can organizations do to prepare managers for an uncertain future? In *Business Strategy Series* 12 (2), pp. 51–55.

Frese, E., Graumann, M.; Theuvsen, L. (2012): Grundlagen der Organisation: Organisation, Organisationstheorien und Organisationsgestaltung. Wiesbaden, Germany: Gabler Verlag.

Fuller, C. W.; Vassie, L. H. (2002): Assessing the maturity and alignment of organisational cultures in partnership arrangements. In *Employee Relations* 24 (5), pp. 540–555. DOI: 10.1108/01425450210443302.

Furnham, A. (2002): Managers as change agents. In *Journal of Change Management* 3 (1), pp. 21–29.

Galbraith, J. R.; Nathanson, D. A. (1978): Strategy Implementation: The Role of Structure and Process. New York, United States of America: West Publishing.

Gestner, L. (2002): Who Says Elephants Can't Dance: Inside IBM's historic turnaround. London, United Kingdom: HarperCollins.

Goodman, P. S.; Ramanujam, R.; Carroll, J. S.; Edmondson, A. C.; Hofmann; D. A.; Sutcliffe, K. M. (2011): Organizational errors: Directions for future research. In *Research in Organizational Behavior* (31), pp. 151–176.

Govindarajan, V. (1988): Contingency Approach to Strategy Implementation at a Business – Unit Level: Integrating Administrative Mechanism with Strategy. In *Academy of Management Journal* 31 (12), pp. 28–55.

Grant, P. (2008): The productive ward round: a critical analysis of organizational change. In *The International Journal of Clinical Leadership* (16), pp. 193–201.

Grant, R. (1996): Toward a knowledge-based theory of the firm. In *Strategic Management Journal* (17), pp. 109–122.

Hansotia, B. (2004): Customer metrics and organisational alignment for maximising customer equity. In *Database Marketing & Customer Strategy Management* 12 (1), pp. 1741–2439.

Hart, C. (1998): Doing a literature review. London, United Kingdom: Sage.

Heavin, C.; Adam, F. (2012): Exploring the Alignment of Organisational Goals with KM: Cases in Four Irish Software SMEs. In *Electronic Journal Information System Evaluation* 16 (3), pp. 25–36.

Henderson, J.; Venkatraman, N. (1993): Strategic Alignment: Leveraging information technology for transforming organizations. In *IBM Systems Journal* 32 (1), pp. 4–16.

Ho, C. F.; Wu, W.-H.; Tai Y.-M. (2004): Strategies for the adaptation of ERP systems. In *Industrial Management & Data Systems*, Vol. 104 (3), pp. 234 – 251

Jarzabkowski, P. (2003): Strategic Practices: An Activity Theory Perspective on Continuity and Change. In *Journal of Management Studies* 40 (1), pp. 23–55.

Jarzabkowski, P. (2005): Strategy as Practice: An Activity Based Approach. London, United Kingdom: Sage.

Kathuria, R.; Igbaria, M. (1997): Aligning IT applications with manufacturing flexibility. In *Journal of Operations Management*, Vol. 18 (1), pp. 611-629.

Kathuria, R.; Joshi, M.P.; Porth, S.J. (2007): Organizational alignment and performance: past, present and future. In *Management Decision*, Vol. 45 (3), pp. 503-517.

Kearns, G.; Lederer, A. (2000): The Effect of Strategic Alignment on the Use of IT-based Resources for Competitive Advantage. In *Journal of Strategic Information Systems*, pp. 265–293.

Kearns, G.; Sabherwal, R. (2006): Strategic Alignment between Business and Information Technology: A Knowledge-based View of Behaviours Outcomes and Consequences. In *Journal of Management Information Systems* 23 (3), pp. 129–162.

Kishore, A.; McLean, E. R. (2007): Re-conceptualizing Innovation Compatibility as Organizational Alignment in Secondary IT Adoption Contexts: An Investigation of Software Reuse Infusion. In *IEEE Transactions on Engineering Management* 54 (4), pp. 756–775. DOI: 10.1109/TEM.2007.906849.

Kotter, J.P.; Heskett, J.L. (1992): Corporate Culture and Performance. In The Free Press, New York, United States of America, 1992.

Krishnan, V.R. (2005): Transformational Leadership and outcomes: Role of relationship duration. In *Leadership & Organization Journal*, Vol. 26 (5/6), pp. 442-457.

Lauver, K.J.; Quinn Trank, C. (2012): Safety and Organizational Design Factors: Decentralization and Alignment. In *Journal of Business and Management* 18 (1), pp. 61–80.

Leonard, J. (2008): What are we Aligning? Implications of a Dynamic Approach to Alignment. In *ACIS 2008 Proceedings* (76).

Luftman, J.; Kempaiah, R. (2007): An Update on Business-IT Alignment: 'A Line' has been drawn. In *MIS Quarterly Executive* 6 (3), pp. 165–177.

Luftman, J.; Lewis, P.; Oldach, S. (1993): Transforming the Enterprise: The alignment of business and information technology strategies. In *IBM Systems Journal* 32 (1), pp. 198–221.

Macdonald, K.H. (1994): Organisational Transformation and Alignment: Misalignment as an Impediment. In *Information Management & Computer Security* 2 (4), pp. 16–29.

March, J. (1991): Exploration and Exploitation: Organizational Learning. In *Organization Science* 2 (1), pp. 71–87.

Middleton, P.; Harper, K. (2004): Organizational alignment: a precondition for information systems success? In *Journal of Change Management* 4 (4), pp. 327–338. DOI: 10.1080/146970104200030382.

Mintzberg, H. (1978): Patterns in Strategy Formation. In *Management Science* 24 (9), pp. 934–948.

Montesino, M. U. (2002): Strategic alignment of training, transfer-enhancing behaviours and training usage: a post training study. In *Human Resource Development Quarterly*, Vol. 13 (1), pp.89–108.

Neubert, G.; Dominguez, C.; Ageron, B. (2011): Inter-organisational alignment to enhance information technology (IT) driven services innovation in a supply chain: the case of radio frequency identification (RFID). In *International Journal of Computer Integrated Manufacturing* 24 (11), pp. 1058–1073. DOI: 10.1080/0951192X.2011.602363.

Niven, P.R. (2006): Balanced scorecard step-by-step. Maximizing performance and maintaining results. 2nd ed. Hoboken, N.J, United States of America: Wiley.

Ostroff, F.; Smith, D. (1992): The horizontal organization. In *The McKinsey Quarterly*, Vol. 1, pp. 148-167.

Parisi, C. (2013): The impact of organisational alignment on the effectiveness of firms' sustainability strategic performance measurement systems: an empirical analysis. In *Journal of Management & Governance* 17 (1), pp. 71–97. DOI: 10.1007/s10997-012-9219-4.

Pascale, R.T (1999): Surfing the edge of chaos. In *Sloan Management Review*, pp. 83-94.

Porter, M.E. (1996): What is Strategy? In *Harvard Business Review*, Vol. 74 (6), pp-61-78

Porter, M.E. (1998): Competitive strategy. Techniques for analyzing industries and competitors. New York, United States of America: The Free Press.

Powell, T.C. (1992): Organizational Alignment As Competitive Advantage. In *Strategic Management Journal* (13), pp. 119–134.

Reichheld, F. (1996): The Loyalty Effect: The Hidden Farce Behind Growth, Profits and Lasting Value. Boston, MA, United States of America: Harvard Business School Press.

Roberts, K. H. (1989): New challenges in organizational research: high reliability organizations. In *Organization & Environment* 3 (2), pp. 111–125.

Roberts, M.L.; Liu, R.R.; Hazard, K. (2005): Strategy, technology and organisational alignment: Key components of CRM success. In *Database Marketing & Customer Strategy Management* 12 (4), pp. 315–326.

Robinson, A.G.; Stern, S. (1997): Corporate Creativity - How Innovation and Improvement Actually Happen. San Francisco, CA, United States of America: Berrett-Koehler Publishers.

Ruegg-Stürm, J. (2005): The new St. Gallen management model. Hampshire, United Kingdom: Palgrave Macmillan.

Sabherwal, R.; Chan, Y. (2001): Alignment Between Business and IS Strategies: A Study of Prospectors Analyzers and Defenders. In *Information Systems Research* 12 (1), pp. 1–33.

Sabherwal, R.; Hirschheim, R.; Goles, T. (2001): The Dynamics of Alignment: Insights from a Punctuated Equilibrium Model. In *Organization Science* 12 (2), pp. 179–197.

Simsek, Z.; Heavey, C.; Veiga, J.F.; Souder, D. (2009): A Typology for Aligning Organizational Ambidexterity's Conceptualizations, Antecedents, and Outcomes. In *Journal of Management Studies* 46 (5), pp. 864–894. DOI: 10.1111/j.1467-6486.2009.00841.x.

Steward, H. (2005): Brand alignment across organisational boundaries. In *Brand Management* 13 (2), pp. 96–100.

Singh, A. (2013): A Study of Role of McKinsey's 7S Framework in achieving Organizational Excellence. In *Organization Development Journal*, Fall 2013, pp. 39-49.

Skaggs, B.; Youndt, M. (2004): Strategic Positioning, Human Capital, and Performance in service organizations: A Customer Interaction Approach. In *Strategic Management Journal*, Vol. 25, pp. 63-67.

Sullivan, W.; Sullivan, R.; Buflton, B. (2001): Aligning individual and organisaiionai values to support change. In *Journal of Change Management* 2 (3), pp. 247–254.

Sumner, M.R. (2009): How alignment strategies influence ERP project success. In *Enterprise Information System*, Vol. 3 (4), pp. 425-448.

Sun, H.; Hong, C. (2002): The alignment between manufacturing and business strategies: Its influence on business performance. In *Technovation*, Vol. 22 (11), pp. 699-705.

The Oxford Dictionary (2014): The Oxford Dictionary. Oxford University Press. Oxford, United Kingdom. Available online at http://www.oxforddictionaries.com/definition/english/alignment, checked on 3/20/2014.

Thongpapanl, N.T.; Clercq, D. de; Dimov, D. (2012): An investigation of the performance consequences of alignment and adaptability: contingency effects of decision autonomy and shared responsibility. In *R&D Management* 42 (1), pp. 14–30. DOI: 10.1111/j.1467-9310.2011.00666.x.

Tosti, D.T.; Jackson, S.F. (2003): Organizational Alignment. Edited by iChange World Consulting LLC. Novato, CA, United States of America.

Venkatraman, N.; Camillus, J. C. (1984): Exploring the concept of 'fit' in strategic management. In *Academy of Management Review* 9 (4), pp. 513–525.

Ward, P. T.; Bickford, D. J. (1996): Configurations of manufacturing strategy, business strategy, environment and structure. In *Journal of Management Information Systems* 22 (4), pp. 597–626.

Welch, J. (2001): Jack: What I've Learned Leading a Great Company and Great People. London, United Kingdom: Headline Book Publishing.

Wendt, R. (2013): The Importance of Driving Organizational Alignment. Boundless Network Inc. Austin, TX, United States of America. Available online at http://www.boundlessnetwork.com/the-importance-of-driving-organizational-alignment/, checked on 2/24/2014.

Woolfe, R. (1993): The Path to Strategic Alignment. In *Information Strategy* 9 (2), pp. 13–23.

Yang, Y.-C.; Hsu, J.-M. (2010): Organizational process alignment, culture and innovation. In *African Journal of Business Management*, Vol. 4 (11), pp.2231-2240.

Yu-Yuan Hung, R.; Chung, T.; Ya-Hui Lien, B. (2007): Organizational Process Alignment and Dynamic Capabilities in High-Tech Industry. In *Total Quality Management & Business Excellence* 18 (9), pp. 1023–1034. DOI: 10.1080/14783360701594154.

Zachary, L.J.; Fischler, L.A. (2008): Time to Check your Alignment?, In *LIA*, Vol. 28 (2), pp. 21-22.

Organizational Resilience

Gabriel Martin Böhm, Alexandre Dietz, Debora Benson

Abstract. Companies and organizations are faced with increasing uncertainty and a changing environment. Therefore, the term organizational resilience creates considerable interest among researchers. In the last few years several papers were published with the purpose of defining the term and investigating which characteristics an organization must have in order to become resilient. Drawing on several reviewed studies, this work tries to provide an overview of the different interpretations of organizational resilience and the related research fields. After analyzing the literature concerning the different research fields, it becomes obvious that much research still has to be done before the concept of organizational resilience is completely explored.

Keywords: Organizational resilience, resilience, organizations, threats, adaptation, dynamic environment, resilient organisations

1 Introduction

Nowadays the world is becoming more and more complex and dynamic. To withstand changes and uncertainty, companies have to build up capabilities and strategies to cope with those issues (Bhamra, Dani & Burnard 2011). This means that organizations do not just have to work efficiently, but must be able to anticipate and absorb external pressures (Fleming 2012) and turn threats into opportunities (Välinkangas & Romme 2012). This is where the terminology and concept of resilience comes into play.

While some literature reviews focus on the general description of the term resilience (Bahmra et al. 2011), this study describes research focused on organizational resilience. This work therefore follows a distinct structure. The first part describes the literature analysis, starting with the presentation of the review methodology and the analysis approach that were followed. At the end of this chapter, general findings are presented. Following on, the terms "organization" and "resilience" will be defined, as well as "organizational resilience". As derived from the analysis of the literature, five research fields of organizational resilience will be investigated:

Strategy, Structure & Organization, Culture, Processes and Performance & Measurement. Finally a critical review will be provided, as well as a further research fields.

2 Literature analysis

Starting by describing the review methodology, this part contains information on how the literature analysis was performed. Thereafter, the approachused to analyze the selected papers isdescribed. In conclusion, some general findings are provided.

2.1 Review methodology

The objective is to summarize the literature on academic research into organizational resilience, to define the term, and compare and contrast the various authors' concepts and views. A literature review of Bahmra et al. (2011) is taken as a basis since they followed a comparable objective and produced a literature review of the general term 'Resilience'. Nevertheless Bahmra et al. (2011) focused on the general term and understanding of 'Resilience', whereas this study focuses on "organizational resilience". Conducting a literature review is essential for the success of academic research because it ensures the research-abililty for future research (Hart, 1988). Furthermore, the literature review sets the broad context of the study, defines the scope of the investigations and justifies the decision determining that scope (Boote & Beile 2005). It thus leads towards theory development (Mccutcheon & Meredith 1993).

The literature collection process was carried out in two steps: First, the ten highest ranked Journals by "SCImago Journal & Country Rank" (Scimagojr.com 2014) were taken and searched for the keywords "organizational resilience" OR "resilient organizations" in title or abstract for the academic journals or proceeding paper collections within the period 1994-2014. All records were analyzed in the context of their relevance to the research subject and then considered together. Secondly, databases were searched for further paper and articles.

Using the collected papers, a deep literature investigation and analysis to find valuable information on organizational resilience can be performed for future research.

2.2 Analysis approach

In total, fifty articles were identified as being relevant for this work. Those articles were analyzed and compared from different perspectives. At first the analysis considered the main emphasis of each article's author. For example, the elements of an organization, according to Rüegg-Stürm (2005), namely strategy, structure/organization, culture and processes, serve as a basis. Secondly, performance/measurement is considered, to include benchmarks and literature focusing on the overall performance in relation to resilience. Furthermore, the methodologies followed by the authors are indicated. Papers are classified into the different aspects of theory building, case study, survey and model/framework description. Finally the distinction between quantitative and qualitative approaches is made.

2.3 General findings in the literature

The analysis shows that the literature on organizational resilience is quiet diverse and covers many different aspects. Moreover, the topic is addressed by numerous practitioners. Many of the journal articles found are qualitative studies which focus on theory building. Some case studies can be found, but the literature shows a lack of quantitative studies. However, it is obvious that without a common understanding or an integrated approach, it is difficult to apply quantitative research methods. Within the field of management and general organization, organizational resilience is not yet popular and is even less so in top journals (Figure 1 & 2).

3 Terminology

This part of the article deals with the terminology and introduces the terms organization and resilience, as well as the main subject of this work organizational resilience.

3.1 Definition Organization and Resilience

Even though most of the authors do not define the term "organization", it will be considered in this work as a system with two characteristics (Frese, Graumann & Theuvsen 2012):

- A number of people and their activities are involved.
- The people and their actions have a common goal; therefor the action of one person within the system has potential influence on the action of other persons.

Resilience covers a lot of different meanings and is used in different contexts. However, it has its roots in the Latin "resiliere" which means "to bounce back after a shock". Nowadays it is used in ecology, economics, child psychology, engineering and systems science (Sudmeier-Rieux 2014). At this point a definition of the general term resilience will not be derived, but instead it is discussed in an organizational context in the next chapter.

3.2   Defining Organizational Resilience

Within the literature there is a wide variety of definitions concerning the term "Organizational Resilience". Comparing the various authors' views, different components of organizational resilience can be identified (Figure 1 & 2).

A first question that arises is, when is resilience both evidenced and necessary. Most of the authors refer to external factors influencing the business and the performance of the organization. Starr, Newfrock & Delurey (2003) define those factors as systematic discontinuities. This definition is accepted by the following researchers: (Aleksic, Stefanovic, Arsovski & Tadic 2013) (Burnard & Bhamra 2011) (Gilly, Kechidi & Talbot 2013). Others specify the discontinuities and talk about "radical change" (Blohowiak 1996), "disaster event" (Comfort, Sungu, Yohnson & Dunn 2001) or "incident" (Elwood, 2009). Comparing the definitions, we can say that they do not differ significantly from each other, if we are talking about circumstances under which resilience is needed or evidenced.

Secondly, definitions of organizational resilience consider three different instances in which resilience is used as an ability of the organization to handle such discontinuities. Before the event takes place, organizations have to proactively build their resilience (Janellis 2013), are aware of possible scenarios (Faustenhammer & Gössler 2011) and anticipate changes (Gilly et al.). During discontinuity, resilient organizations have to be aware of their areas of vulnerability(Faustenhammer et al.

2011), must emphasize actions to address them (Goodman, Ramanujam, Caroll, Edmonson, Hofmann & Sutcliffe 2011) and have to be resistant (Elwood 2009). Finally, resilient organizations are able to return to the equilibrium point after the discontinuity occurs (Smith & Fischbacher 2009), work out positive solutions in favor of the organization (Tweedy 2009) and adapt to changes (Zhang & Liu 2012). Thirdly, organizational resilience addresses different corporate levels and aspects. Faustenhammer et al. identify components addressing strategic resilience (Faustenhammer et al. 2011) whereas others focus at the operational level (Janellis 2013). Starr et al. give an holistic view and include strategy, operations, management systems and governance structure, as well as decision-support capabilities (Starr et al. 2003).

In summary literature provides several definitions concerning organizational resilience. Whereas some authors focus on specific aspects, others provide a holistic concept of organizational resilience. A single, widely accepted definition is not available within the literature.

4 Research fields and related gaps within the field of organizational resilience

As stated before, the literature is analyzed in relation to each paper's main emphasis and research field: strategy, structure/organization, culture, processes and performance/measurement.

4.1 Strategy

Within the context of organizational resilience the strategy of organizations and enterprises is a highly discussed issue. It mainly can be subdivided into five fields of action, of which some are more inter-related than others.

At first authors discuss strategies on a more general level. They put emphasis on the overall importance of strategy but without further debate. Aleksic et al. (2013) consider an appropriate strategy to becritical in times of managing resilience, which must be aligned with the strategy of the overall organization. Starr et al. (2013) also mention the importance of aligning the strategy with the rest of the organization.

However, as well as Aleksic et al. (2013), they provide no explanation about how an alignment can be reached. Välinkangas et al. (2012) state that strategic resilience results if an organization quickly converts threats into opportunities and act effectively before their competition (Välinkangas 2012). In his definition the strategic resilience is a result of an action whereas Aleksic et al. (2013) consider strategy as a distinctive plan/target that can be followed in order to reach resilience.

A second topic within the literature, is the emphasis by some authors on the essential requirement of considering different scenarios, in order to achieve strategic resilience (Alesi 2008; Faustenhammer et al. 2011; Fleming 2012). Zhang et al. (2012) underline that from a strategic perspective, resilience is about the way of thinking about plans for future environmental changes. Companies must anticipate their evolving environment and must be prepared for the future (Bhamra et al. 2011).

The third topic is discussed by Janellis (2013), where it is stated that organizations have to consider a readiness strategy as well as a responsive strategy. This requires considering ways to minimize impact on people and the business through proactive preparation, on the one hand, and on the other, optimizing the performance of teams in crisis situations.

A fourth field of research is the relationship between experience and strategy. In the opinion of Crichton, Ramsay & Kelly (2009) it is very important to ensure that lessons learned are used in the strategic context. Furthermore, the frequency of strategic planning is considered an important aspect in achievingresilience. Neilson & Pasternack (2005) state that a rethink of organizational strategy is frequently required.

To summarize, the literature indicates strategies as an important issue inestablishing resilience. Organizations have to consider different future scenarios when they are setting up strategies. They must be able to anticipate, and be prepared, for the future. The work of Gibson & Tarrant (2010) should be highlighted here as they are providing four strategic options to reach resilience, namely a reliability, redundancy, flexibility or resistance strategy.

Within the research field relating to strategies most of the literature consists of qualitative research. Future research should contain quantitative studies as well. Furthermore, the inter-connectedness between an organization's strategy and its actual capabilities and resources is still at a conceptual level.However, one paper can be found which precisely describes distinct strategies towards organizational resilience (Gibson et al. 2010).

4.2 Structure and Organization

Authors also discuss the impact of the structure and organization when considering resilience. Analyzing the literature authors can be classified into two different groups. The first highlights the organization of the involved actors whereas the second also mention technical aspects.

To achieve resilience, people within the organization must be coordinated (Comfort et al. 2001; Horne & Orr 1997) and connected (Horne et al., 1998; Lee et al., 2013). A horizontal structure instead of a vertical organization should therefor be followed (Neilson et al. 2005) (Pellissier, 2011). A flexible (Pellissier 2011) as well as a self-organizing structure (Zhang et al., 2012) supports a horizontal collaboration within the organization whilst also fostering communication between different departments (Horne et al. 1997; Lee, Vargo & Seville 2013). Another important aspect, which is discussed in the literature, is the distribution and allocation of power. Dalziell & McManus (2004) argue that the ability to respond effectively towards changes in the environment is influenced by the level of centralization of decision-making (Starr et al. 2003; Lee at al. 2013; Paton, Smith & Violanti 2000).

Besides these structural aspects some authors also consider technical resources as a critical issue. Comfort et al. (2001) argue that information technology makes it possible to enable the necessary coordination and communication. Gibson et al. (2010) support this statement and state that resources and infrastructure capabilities are essential for organizational resilience.

In summary, the critical point of the organization is to secure overall coordination and communication. Therefor a flexible, horizontal structure is the focus for the authors. To be able to react rapidly, a decentralized decision-making is essential. Modern communication and IT tools, as well as other resources, providenecessary and successful support.

Future research needs to strengthen the focus on quantitative research, as the status quo remains on a very conceptual level and provides no recommendations for practice.

4.3 Culture

Cultural aspects are also considered important components of building resilience (Blohowiak 1996; Pulley 1997; Tweedy 2009; Ungericht & Wiesner 2011). Shared values allow a collective view of the environment (Horne et al. 1998), but organizational tolerance for uncertainty is fundamental to establishing resilience (Mallak 1998; Reilly 2006). To build up a culture that supports resilience, leadership is considered to be one of the most important factors (Cooper, Flint-Taylor & Pearn 2009; Everly, 2011; Faustenhammer et al. 2011; Kay, 2012; Paton et al., 2000; Stephenson et al., 2010). Resilient organizations therefor should invest in their leaders (Everly 2011) because as Stephenson, Seville, Vargo & Roger (2010) argue leadership maintains an adaptive capacity. To facilitate a resilient culture, learning and training for the members of the organization is necessary (Crichton et al. 2009; Elwood 2009; Horne et al. 1998). A good communication culture then allows a further dissemination of the organization's knowledge (Pulley 1997; Seville, Brunsdon Dantas, Le Masurier, Wilkinson & Vargo. 2007; Reilly 2006). While many authors just provide a general description of the culture Kay (2012), Legnick-Hall, Beck & Legnick-Hall (2011) and Robb (2000) define distinct elements and characteristics of a resilient culture.

4.4 Processes

In relation to the topic of organizational resilience, the literature discusses, on the one hand, characteristics that overall organizational processes must fulfill and, on the other hand, processes that need to be considered to build resilience.

On a generic level Burnard et al. (2011) state that operational resilience is achieved when resources are effectively linked with outcomes (Sutcliffe & Vogus, 2003). Robust processes (Lee et al. 2013; Stephenson et al. 2010) are considered to have a positive impact on organizational resilience (Elwood, 2009) and they enable organizations to successfully face uncertainty (Vogus & Sutcliffe 2007). To succeed, they must be "designed to ensure opportunities for on-going communication, agreement, alignment, and evaluation" (Mannen, Hinton, Kuijper & Porter 2012).

Overall, three distinct processes, that are important to reach organizational resilience, can be found in the literature. First, organizations need a robust and effective decision-making process (Burnard et al. 2011) (Fiksel 2003). Second, as was discussed within the research field of culture, organizations have to establish learning processes to draw the right conclusion and adapt their organization (Comfort et al. 2001) (Neilson et al. 2005). Nevertheless organizations have to set up a process to review, assess and adapt capabilities to address environmental changes (Elwood 2009) (Gibson et al. 2010).

To summarize, the literature defines different characteristics that have to be considered and ensured for processes to be effective. They have to be robust and serve as enablers to reach resilience. Furthermore, some specific processes can be indicated that substantively deal with resilience, for example an emergency-planning process. The literature remains, however, on a conceptual level and provides no detailed characteristics on how processes should be designed. In addition, an holistic view on how processes and the rest of an organization is linked is not provided.

Culture is an important issue that cannot be neglected by organizations. Important elements are common and shared values, as well as leadership. However, these characteristics have as yet received little attention. There is no common understanding of the specific indicators of a culture that facilitates resilience.Owing to that, there is apparently little quantitative research.

4.5 Performance & Measurement

Concerning the performance of the organization Sanchis & Poler (2013) provide a categorization framework of disruptions and uncertainties, and their influence on the enterprise resilience. The literature provides a number of works on factor categories and indicators. Although the categories defined by the authors differ, a lot of the factors are covered by all the authors, for example communication, resources, decision-making and planning (De Carvalho, De Souza & Gomes 2012; Janellis 2013; Lee et al. 2013; Mallak, 1998; McManus, Seville, Brunsdorn & Vargo 2007). Future research needs to focus on developing a standardized model, with well-defined criteria for identifying different scores for the factors. Furthermore studies have to be provided to determine whether a factor is important and which score, concerning the individual situation of an organization, should be applied.

5 Critical review & Conclusion

This article aims to provide deeper insights into the concept of "Organizational Resilience", as well as discuss the different aspects of the concept. However, this contribution has a certain limitation owing to the focus on 'organizational resilience' as the search criterion that was applied. The analyzed papers also identify relationships to other disciplines like risk management and business uncertainty.

Within the literature we can find a wide variety of definitions for organizational resilience. This article shows that authors focus on certain aspects and that an overall accepted definition is yet not available. As a first step future research has to close this gap and provide a common understanding of the term.

This paper follows the approach of classifying research results with the help of five different research fields: Strategy, Structure & Organization, Culture, Processes and Performance & Measurement. Looking at the years the papers were published, we can conclude that the topic of organizational resilience is becoming increasingly important. However, it still is not a topic found in top journals.

Future research is required to consider different aspects. Primarily, an holistic concept of organizational resilience needs to be developed. This article disclosed the diversity of factors currently related to organizational resilience. Furthermore, most of the research stays at a descriptive, general level with very few practical implications and direct measures for companies and organizations, although there are works that provide a model to benchmark and measure resilience. There remains, however, no holistic and standardized model, and there is, as yet, a lack of sufficient data.

Appendix

Concepts and methodologies in the organizational resilience literature

Author	Year	Journal	Strategy	Structure/ Organisation	Culture	Processes	Performance/ Measurement
Aleksic et al.	2013	Journal of Loss Prevention in the Process Industry	x				
Alesi	2008	Journal of Business Continuity & Emergency Planning	x				
Bhamra et al.	2011	International Journal of Production Research	x				
Blohowiak	1996	National Productivity Review			x		
Burnard et al.	2011	International Journal of Production Research				x	
Comfort et al.	2001	Journal of Contigencies and Crisis Management		x		x	
Cooper et al.	2009	Training Journal			x		
Crichton et al.	2009	Journal of Contigencies and Crisis Management	x		x		
Dalziell et al.	2004	International Forum for Engineering Decision Making		x			
De Carvalho	2012	Work: A Journal of Prevention, Assessment and Rehabilitation					x
Elwood	2009	Journal of Business Continuity & Emergency Planning			x	x	
Everly	2011	HBR Blog network			x		
Faustenhammer et al.	2011	Business Strategy Series	x		x		
Fiksel	2003	Environmental Science & Technology				x	
Fleming	2012	The Journal of Global Business Issues	x				
Gibson et al.	2010	The Australian Journal of Emergency Management	x	x		x	
Gilbert et al.	2012	Havard Business Review	x				
Gilly et al.	2013	European Management Journal	x	x	x		
Goodman et al.	2011	Research in Organizational Behavior					
Horne et al.	1998	Employment Relations Today	x	x	x		
Janellis Pty Ltd	2013	HBR submission	x				x
Kay et al.	2012	Keeping Good Companies			x		
Lee et al.	2013	Natural Hazards Review	x	x		x	x
Lengnick-Hall et al.	2011	Human Resource Management Review			x		
Mallak	1998	Health Manpower Management			x		
Mallak	1998	Industrial Management					x
Mannen et al.	2012	Journal of Leadership & Organizational Studies				x	
McCoy et al.	2009	Journal of Business Continuity & Emergency Planning			x		
McManus et al.	2007	Resilient Organisations Programme New Zealand					x
Neilson et al.	2005	Crown Business	x	x	x	x	
Paton et al.	2000	Disaster Prevention and Management			x	x	
Pellissier	2011	International Journal of Business and Management	x	x			
Pulley	1997	Leadership in Action			x		
Reilly	2006	American Management Association	x	x	x		
Robb	2000	OD Practitioner				x	
Sanchis et al.	2013	Proceedings of the 7th International Conference on Industrial Engineering and Industrial Management					x
Seville et al.	2007	Journal of Business Continuity & Emergency Planning	x	x	x		
Smith et al.	2009	Risk Management				x	
Starr et al.	2003	strategy+business	x	x			
Stephenson et al.	2010	Resilient Organisations Research Report 2010/03b	x	x		x	
Sudmeier-Rieux	2014	Disaster Prevention and Management	x				
Sullivan-Taylor et al.	2011	International Journal of Production Research		x			
Sutcliffe et al.	2003	Book: Positive Organizational Scholarship	x	x		x	
Trim et al.	2009	Journal of Business Continuity & Emergency Planning			x		
Tweedy	2009	human resources			x		
Ungericht et al.	2011	zfo				x	
Välikangas et al.	2012	Strategy and Leadership	x				
Vogus et al.	2007	IEEE International Conference on Systems, Man and Cybernetics, 2007				x	
Yamauchi et al.	2007	Journal of Advances in Management Research	x				
Zhang et al.	2012	International Conference on Enomics Marketing and Management	x	x			

Figure 1: Overview literature review part 1

Concepts and methodologies in the organizational resilience literature

Author	Year	Journal	Theory building	Case study	Survey	Model/ framework	Quantitative	Qualitative
Aleksic et al.	2013	Journal of Loss Prevention in the Process Industry		x		x	x	
Alesi	2008	Journal of Business Continuity & Emergency Planning	x					x
Bhamra et al.	2011	International Journal of Production Research	x					x
Blohowiak	1996	National Productivity Review	x					x
Burnard et al.	2011	International Journal of Production Research				x		x
Comfort et al.	2001	Journal of Contingencies and Crisis Management	x					x
Cooper et al.	2009	Training Journal	x					x
Crichton et al.	2009	Journal of Contingencies and Crisis Management	x	x				x
Dalziell et al.	2004	International Forum for Engineering Decision Making	x					x
De Carvalho	2012	Work: A Journal of Prevention, Assessment and Rehabilitation	x					x
Elwood	2009	Journal of Business Continuity & Emergency Planning				x		x
Everly	2011	HBR Blog network	x					x
Faustenhammer et al.	2011	Business Strategy Series	x					x
Fiksel	2003	Environmental Science & Technology	x					x
Fleming	2012	The Journal of Global Business Issues	x					x
Gibson et al.	2010	The Australian Journal of Emergency Management				x		x
Gilbert et al.	2012	Havard Business Review	x	x				x
Gilly et al.	2013	European Management Journal						x
Goodman et al.	2011	Research in Organizational Behavior	x	x				x
Horne et al.	1998	Employment Relations Today	x	x				x
Janellis Pty Ltd	2013	HBR submission		x	x		x	
Kay et al.	2012	Keeping Good Companies						x
Lee et al.	2013	Natural Hazards Review				x		x
Lengnick-Hall et al.	2011	Human Resource Management Review	x					x
Mallak	1998	Health Manpower Management	x		x			x
Mallak	1998	Industrial Management						x
Mannen et al.	2012	Journal of Leadership & Organizational Studies	x	x				x
McCoy et al.	2009	Journal of Business Continuity & Emergency Planning				x		x
McManus et al.	2007	Resilient Organisations Programme New Zealand		x		x		x
Neilson et al.	2005	Crown Business	x	x				x
Paton et al.	2000	Disaster Prevention and Management				x		x
Pellissier	2011	International Journal of Business and Management	x					x
Pulley	1997	Leadership in Action	x					x
Reilly	2006	American Management Association						x
Robb	2000	OD Practitioner	x					x
Sanchis et al.	2013	Proceedings of the 7th International Conference on Industrial Engineering and Industrial Management				x		x
Seville et al.	2007	Journal of Business Continuity & Emergency Planning	x					x
Smith et al.	2009	Risk Management	x					x
Starr et al.	2003	strategy+business				x		x
Stephenson et al.	2010	Resilient Organisations Research Report 2010/03b			x			x
Sudmeier-Rieux	2014	Disaster Prevention and Management	x					x
Sullivan-Taylor et al.	2011	International Journal of Production Research	x	x				x
Sutcliffe et al.	2003	Book: Positive Organizational Scholarship	x					x
Trim et al.	2009	Journal of Business Continuity & Emergency Planning	x					x
Tweedy	2009	human resources	x					x
Ungericht et al.	2011	zfo	x					x
Välikangas et al.	2012	Strategy and Leadership	x	x				x
Vogus et al.	2007	IEEE International Conference on Systems, Man and Cybernetics, 2007	x					x
Yamauchi et al.	2007	Journal of Advances in Management Research	x	x			x	
Zhang et al.	2012	International Conference on Enomics Marketing and Management	x					x

Figure 2: Overview literature review part 2

References

Aleksic, A., Stefanovic, M., Arsovski, S. and Tadic, D. (2013). An assessment of organizational resilience potential in SMEs of the process industry, a fuzzy approach. *Journal of Loss Prevention in the Process Industries*, 26 (6), pp. 1238-1245.

Alesi, P. (2008). Building enterprise-wide resilience by integrating business continuity capability into day-to-day business culture and technology. *Journal of Business Continuity & Emergency Planning*, 2 (3), pp. 214-220.

Bhamra, R., Dani, S. & Burnard, K. (2011). Resilience: the concept, a literature review and future directions. *International Journal of Production Research*, 49 (18), pp. 5375-5393.

Blohowiak, D. (1996). After the downsizing: building a resilient organization in a radical change environment. *National Productivity Review*, 16 (1), pp. 3-6.

Boote, D. N. & Beile, P. (2005). Scholars before researchers: On the centrality of the dissertation literature review in research preparation. *Educational researcher*, 34 (6), pp. 3-15.

Burnard, K. & Bhamra, R. (2011). Organisational resilience: development of a conceptual framework for organizational responses. *International Journal of Production Research*, 49 (18), pp. 5581-5599.

Comfort, L. K., Sungu, Y., Johnson, D. & Dunn, M. (2001). Complex systems in crisis: anticipation and resilience in dynamic environments. *Journal of Contingencies and Crisis Management*, 9 (3), pp. 144-158.

Cooper, C.L., Flint-Taylor, J. & Michael Pearn. (July 2013). Building Resilience for Success. *Retrieved from http://www.palgraveconnect.com/pc/doifinder/10.1057/9781137367839*

Crichton, M. T., Ramsay, C. G. &Kelly, T. (2009). Enhancing Organizational Resilience Through Emergency Planning: Learnings from Cross-Sectoral Lessons. *Journal of Contingencies and Crisis Management*, 17 (1), pp. 24-37.

Dalziell, E. & McManus, S. (2004). Resilience, vulnerability, and adaptive capacity: implications for system performance. *University of Canterbury*. Civil and Natural Resources Engineering.

De Carvalho, P. V. R., De Souza, A. P. & Gomes, J. O. (2012). A computerized system to monitor resilience indicators in organizations. *Work: A Journal of Prevention, Assessment and Rehabilitation*, 41 pp. 2803-2809.

Elwood, A. (2009). Using the disaster crunch/release model in building organizational resilience. *Journal of Business Continuity & Emergency Planning*, 3 (3), pp. 241-247.

Everly, G. S. (2011). Building a Resilient Organizational Culture. [online] *Available at: http://blogs.hbr.org/2011/06/building-a-resilient-organizat/* [Accessed: 23 Mar 2014].

Faustenhammer, A. & Gössler, M. (2011). Preparing for the next crisis: what can organizations do to prepare managers for an uncertain future? *Business Strategy Series*, 12 (2), pp. 51-55.

Fiksel, J. (2003). Designing resilient, sustainable systems. *Environmental science & technology*, 37 (23), pp. 5330--5339.

Fleming, R. S. (2012). Ensuring Organizational Resilience in Times of Crisis. *Journal of Global Business Issues*, 6 (1), pp. 31-34.

Frese, E., Graumann, M. & Theuvsen, L. (2012). Organisation, Organisationstheorien und Organisationsgestaltung. In: *Frese, E., Graumann, M. and Theuvsen, L. eds. 2012. Grundlagen der Organisation.* Wiesbaden: Gabler Verlag, pp. 20-28.

Gibson, C. A. & Tarrant, M. (2010). A 'conceptual models' approach to organizational resilience. *Australian Journal of Emergency Management*, 25 (2), p. 6.

Gilbert, C., Eyring, M. & Foster, R. (2012). Two routes to resilience. *Harvard Business Review*, 90 (12), pp. 67-73.

Gilly, J., Kechidi, M. & Talbot, D. (2013). Resilience of organizations and territories: The role of pivot firms. *European Management Journal*.

Goodman, P. S., Ramanujam, R., Carroll, J. S., Edmondson, A. C., Hofmann, D. A. & Sutcliffe, K. M. (2011). Organizational errors: Directions for future research. *Research in Organizational Behavior*, 31 pp. 151-176.

Hart, C. (1998). Doing a literature review. London: *Sage Publications*.

Horne, J. F. & Orr, J. E. (1997). Assessing behaviors that create resilient organizations. *Employment Relations Today*, 24 (4), pp. 29-39.

Janellis. (2014). [online] Available at: *http://www.janellis.com.au/files/nrteUploadFiles/42F092F2012103A063A23AM.pdf* [Accessed: 20 Mar 2014].

Kay, Robert (2012). Patterns of prediction The basis of resilient organizations. *Keeping Good Companies*, 64 (10), pp. 588-592.

Lee, A. V., Vargo, J. & Seville, E. (2013). Developing a Tool to Measure and Compare Organizations' Resilience. *Natural Hazards Review*, 14 (1), pp. 29-41.

Lengnick-Hall, C. A., Beck, T. E. & Lengnick-Hall, M. L. (2011). Developing a capacity for organizational resilience through strategic human resource management. *Human Resource Management Review*, 21 (3), pp. 243-255.

Mallak, L. A. (1998). Measuring resilience in health care provider organizations. *Health Manpower Management*, 24 (4), pp. 148-152.

Mallak, L. A. (1998). Putting Organizational Resilience to Work. *Industrial Management*, 40 (6), pp. 8-13.

Mannen, D., Hinton, S., Kuijper, T. & Porter, T. (2012). Sustainable Organizing A Multiparadigm Perspective of Organizational Development and Permaculture Gardening. *Journal of Leadership \& Organizational Studies*, 19 (3), pp. 355-368.

Manring, S. L. (2007). Creating and managing interorganizational learning networks to achieve sustainable ecosystem management. *Organization & Environment*, 20 (3), pp. 325--346.

Mccoy, J. & Elwood, A. (2009). Human factors in organizational resilience: Implications of breaking the psychological contract. *Journal of Business Continuity & Emergency Planning*, 3 (4), pp. 368-375.

Mccutcheon, D. M. & Meredith, J. R. (1993). Conducting case study research in operations management. *Journal of Operations Management*, 11 (3), pp. 239-256.

Mcmanus, S., Seville, E., Brunsdon, D. & Vargo, J. (2007). Resilience management: a framework for assessing and improving the resilience of organizations. *University of Canterbury*, New Zealand.

Neilson, G. L. & Pasternack, B. A. (2005). Results. New York: *Crown Business*.

Paton, D., Smith, L. & Violanti, J. (2000). Disaster response: risk, vulnerability and resilience. *Disaster prevention and Management*, 9 (3), pp. 173-180.

Pellissier, R. (2011). The Implementation of Resilience Engineering to Enhance Organizational Innovation in a Complex Environment. *International Journal of Business & Management*, 6 (1), pp. 145-164.

Pulley, M. L. (1997). Leading resilient organizations. *Leadership in action*, 17 (4), pp. 1-5.

Reilly, E. T. (2006). [online] Available at: http://www.amanet.org/hri-agility06.pdf [Accessed: 31 Mar 2014].

Robb, D. (2000). Building Resilient Organizations. *OD PRACTITIONER*, 32 (3), pp. 27-32.

Roberts, K. H. (1989). New challenges in organizational research: high reliability organizations. *Organization & Environment*, 3 (2), pp. 111-125.

Rüegg-Stürm, J. (2005). The new St. Gallen management model. Houndmills (Basingstoke, Hampshire): *Palgrave Macmillan*.

Sanchis, R. & Poler, R. (2013). Enterprise Resilience Assessment: A Categorisation Framework of Disruptions. In: Iglesias, C. and Perez Rios, J. eds. 2013. *Book of Proceedings of the 7th International Conference on Industrial Engineering and Industrial Management - XVII Congreso de Ingeniería de Organización*, pp. 603-610.

Scimagojr.com. (2014). *Scimago Journal & Country Rank*. [online] Available at: http://www.scimagojr.com/index.php [Accessed: 06 Mar 2014]

Seville, E., Brunsdon, D., Dantas, A., Le Masurier, J., Wilkinson, S. & Vargo, J. (2008). Organisational resilience: Researching the reality of New Zealand organizations. *Journal of business continuity & emergency planning*, 2 (3), pp. 258-266.

Smith, D. & Fischbacher, M. (2009). The changing nature of risk and risk management: The challenge of borders, uncertainty and resilience. *Risk Management*, pp. 1-12.

Starr, R., Newfrock, J. & Delurey, M. (2003). Enterprise resilience: managing risk in the networked economy. *Strategy and Business*, pp. 70-79.

Stephenson, A., Seville, E., Vargo, J. & Roger, D., (2012). Benchmark resilience: A study of the resilience of organizations in the Auckland Region. *Resilient Organisations Research Report 2010/03b*, pp. 1-49. Online at: http://www.resorgs.org.nz

Sudmeier-Rieux, K. I. (2014). Resilience - an emerging paradigm of danger or of hope?. *Disaster Prevention and Management*, 23 (1), pp. 67-80.

Sullivan-Taylor, B. & Branicki, L. (2011). Creating resilient SMEs: why one size might not fit all. *International journal of production research*, 49 (18), pp. 5565-5579.

Sutcliffe, K.M. & Vogus, T.J. (2003). Organizing for Resilience. In Cameron, K., Dutton, J.E., & Quinn, R.E. (Eds.), Positive Organizational Scholarship. San Francisco: *Berrett-Koehler*. Chapter 7 pp: 94-110.

Trim, P. R., Jones, N. A. & Brear, K. (2009). Building organizational resilience through a designed-in security management approach. *Journal of Business Continuity & Emergency Planning*, 3 (4), pp. 345-355.

Ungericht, B. & Wiesner, M. (2011). Resilienz: Zur Widerstandskraft von Individuen und Organisationen. *ZfO*, 80(3), pp. 188-194.

Tweedy, F. (2009). Resilience in turbulent times - does your organization have what it takes?. human resources. *Hrinz conference paper 2009*, pp. 10-11.

Välinkangas, L. & Romme, A. G. L. (2012). Building resilience capabilities at "Big Brown Box, Inc.". *Strategy & Leadership*, 40 (4), pp. 43-45.

Vogus, T. J. & Sutcliffe, K. M. (2007). Organizational resilience: towards a theory and research agenda. *Systems, Man and Cybernetics, 2007. ISIC. IEEE International Conference*, pp. 3418-3422.

Yamauchi, S., Morisaki, S., Watanabe, C. & Tou, Y. (2007). A resilient structure as a survival strategy for Japan's chemical industry amidst megacompetition. *Journal of Advances in Management Research*, 4 (1), pp. 29-48.

Zhang, R. & Liu, W. 2012. Organizational Resilience Perspective: Facilitating Organizational Adaptation Analysis. *International Proceedings of Economics Development & Research*, 28, p. 55-59.

Section III: Group and Team Aspects

Team Dynamics

Annika Franziska in der Beek, Florian Pahl

Abstract. Despite the fact that much is published about team dynamics, still little is known on how these phenomena and dynamics evolve and develop over time. Cronin et al. (2011) defined research gaps concerning team dynamics and provide a literature review of studies published in 2010. The goal of this article is to investigate the status quo of research on team dynamics published after 2010. Out of several reviewed studies, this contribution provides an overview of different research streams within the field of team dynamics and examines the studies in response to the existing research gaps. Despite new research approaches that fill the research gaps, it is still a long way to go until the topic of team dynamics is fully investigated and understood.

Keywords: Teams, groups, group dynamics, roles

1 Introduction

People working together within a team are able to produce higher quality outputs than one individual alone, in other words "the whole is more than the sum of its parts" (Jones & George 2007, p. 389). To promote synergies and to manage teams effectively, a profound knowledge about teams and their underlying dynamics is necessary.

While studying groups at the workplace, McGrath (1986) noted that group research is focused on "group statics" rather than on "group dynamics". Yet, more than 25 years later this has not completely changed (Cronin, Weingart & Todorova 2011). Although we know that teams are dynamic entities, they are rarely studied as such. Research often uses cross-sectional approaches that are not able to account for cross-level dynamics nested within group and individual levels (Kozlowski & Klein 2000; McGrath, Arrow & Berdahl 2000). This paper will review theoretical developments within the research on team dynamics in response to research gaps identified by Cronin, Weingart and Todorova in 2011 and will conclude with a critical appraisal and avenues for future research.

2 Teams and Team Dynamics

Similar to groups, teams exist in every social context. Shifting back in time some hundred years ago, teams were mainly known within the fields of physical labor and sports. Today teams are also well known within the working context. As the complexity of tasks increases, more persons are needed to solve those tasks sufficiently. Teams can show a huge diversity regarding their focus, composition and design.

A team can be defined as "a group whose members work intensely with one another to achieve a specific common goal or objective (Jones et al. 2007, p. 388). Considering the qualities of teams, it becomes obvious that teams are groups. Teams possess all the basic characteristics of a group: interaction, goals, interdependence, structure and unity. Therefore, teams are groups but differ from groups in the level of intensity (Forsyth 2010; Jones et al. 2007). Keeping in mind the context under which teams usually perform, it becomes obvious that they possess these qualities to a more extreme degree and therefore can be described as hyper-groups (Forsyth 2010).

Team dynamics can be defined as "the ways in which groups function and, ultimately, their effectiveness hinge on group characteristics and processes" (Jones et al., 2007, p.398). By reviewing leading books about teams and group dynamics as well as different journal articles (e.g. Forsyth 2010; Jones et al. 2007) it becomes obvious that the field of "team dynamics" is a broad topic that covers various parts and therefore can be subdivided into eight key research streams (*Figure 2*):

- Size, Structure and Roles
- Development and Processes
- Leadership
- Diversity
- Cohesion and Climate
- Performance and Productivity
- Cognition and Learning
- Creativity and Innovation

These research streams may also be combined with each other so that one study might touch different research streams, like team diversity, creativity and team performance.

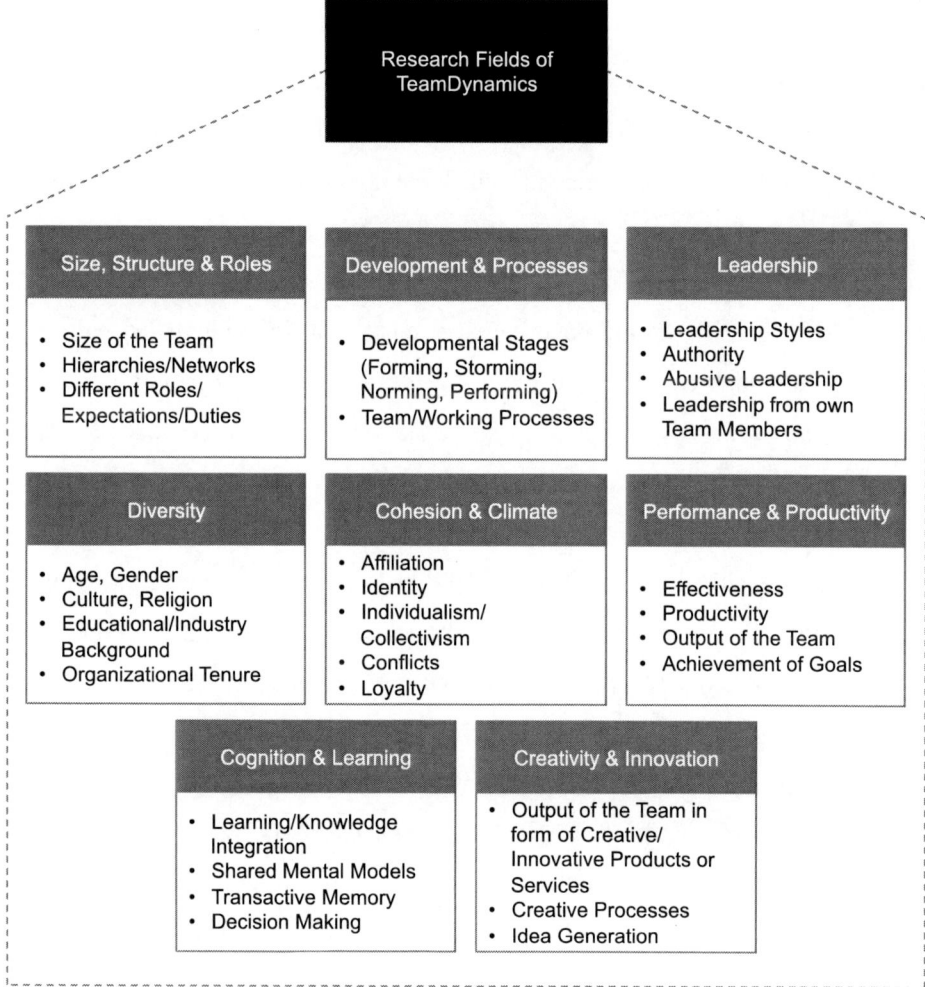

Figure 1: Eight Research Streams in Team Dynamics Research.

3 Effects of Team Dynamics

Whatever the reseach field, in general there can be made a clear distinction in the literature between positive and negative effects of group dynamics. The arguments of the different authors are grouped below.

3.1 Positive Effects of Group Dynamics

Schulze, Mojzisch and Hardt (2009) have a focus on the positive effects of group dynamics. They state that [...] *"groups outperform individuals due to group-to-individual transfer, which denotes group members becoming more accurate individually during group interaction"* (Schultze, Mojzisch, & Schulz-Hardt 2009). This statement has already been made by other researchers (Hackman & Morris 1975); however the underlying mechanisms have not been proved yet. Even though they tried to fill this research gap by their paper it offers an issue for further research as the proof is still not provided.

Haynes (2012) identifies some positive experiences that individuals have through joining a group, such as [...] *"receiving support, encouragement and validation, learning by observing the behaviors and consequences of the actions of others, achieve a sense of belonging and connectedness, share common problems and receive personal feedback"* (Haynes 2012).

One factor also positively influencing group dynamics is social sharedness. Shared knowledge helps in the group decision making process. However, a potential threat here is biased knowledge (Tindale, Smith, Dykema-Engblade, & Katharina 2012).

Another point is perceived positive reaction to group activities by its members. Members of a group are generally more satisfied with their performance where one of the main reasons is that [...] *"groups fulfill their members' social and emotional needs"* (Levine & Moreland 1998). But this only applies if the members feel attached to the group (Abrams & Hogg 2001) and if this is the case the individuals are more committed to goals (Lewin 1958).

Hill (1982) tested through experiments that [...] *"group performance was usually superior to individual performance because of the group's ability to pool their resources, to correct errors, and to use qualitatively different learning strategies"* (Hill 1982). As identified by several authors group members' capacity to learn and cognitive stimulation can also contribute to positive group dynamics. There is evidence for observational learning in studies conducted by Davis and Restle (1963) where 3 word puzzles where analyzed first by individuals and later on by a group.

The results suggest that pace and correctness of the answers increased or at least not decreased. The cognitive stimulation occurring in groups can lead to new ideas or can create a complex solution to a bigger problem (Maier 1970).

As already mentioned above diversity and multiculturalism in groups become more important at the contemporary workplace. There is a high degree of intercultural interaction in multicultural groups and it is therefore interesting to see positive effects of group dynamics in diverse groups. Resolving issues in a group tends to enhance the engagement of the individuals and the multiculturalism promotes creative thinking and brainstorming processes. Also the danger of 'group thinking' which tends to appear in homogenous groups is diminished (Stahl, Maznevski, Voigt, & Jonsen 2010). Mannix and Neale (2005) found out that the […] *"differing cultural perceptions in a multicultural work group produce solutions, ideas and decisions that are highly creative and high in quality"* (Mannix & Neale 2005). Those effects of group dynamics in multicultural teams can be found on the positive side; negative implications derived from the literature are provided in the next paragraph.

3.2 Negative Effects of Group Dynamics

Work in groups can have benefits which are proved by the 80% of large organizations using work groups (Forsyth 1999). But group dynamics can also have negative effects. Hackmann (1998) says that even well designed groups fail if they do not have access to the appropriate resources. Rogers and Senturia (2013) identify four negative consequences of group dynamics: *conformity, group polarization, obedience to authority and bystander effect.*

They refer to an experiment by psychologist Solomon Asch where a group was asked to choose which of three lines was the same length as a prototype line, nearly every subject chose correctly when acting alone. Then he put every participant in a group which has been instructed to choose a wrong line and 75% confessed that they agreed with the group at least once even though they knew that the answer was wrong. Goncalo and Duguid (2007) found out during an experiment that the conformity pressure *[...] "may be a viable mechanism for boosting group creativity, but only among those who lack creative talent"* (Goncalo & Duguid 2007). That implicates that those individuals forced to be part of group waste their creativity due to *conformity.*

Group polarization may lead likeminded people in a group to more extreme decisions. It can have positive effects when it comes to quit smoking or diet programs (El-Shinnawy & Vinze 1998). But the negative implications are weighing more especially when it comes to business decisions. It has been found out by Williams and Taormina (1993) through a study project that there is polarization in businesses and that the more unanimously the group consensus is the higher is the degree of polarization. The polarization dynamic can be moderated by the presence of one dissenting member (Williams & Taormina 1993).

Also when it comes to *obedience to authority* it may affect the result and outcome of work in a negative way. It is important for a company's operation that there is a certain degree of obedience in order not to disturb the work flow (Snell 1999). However, if the decision of a superior is never questioned this may have disastrous consequences. Rogers and Senturia (2013) refer to the case where a KLM flight took off even though another machine was on the runway and it turned out that it never would have happened if the whole crew had not applied the 'captain is always right' principle.

The *bystander effect* is another important point. Individuals are expected to better react when the company is in danger than groups would do. If the group is ignoring harm it is likely that individuals also ignore the problem which can have dangerous implications for organizations (Gerstein 2008).

Coming to the issue of group dynamics in multicultural teams once again, several negative effects can be identified. One point would be the different views on life of the different cultures. This can lead to fundamentally different opinions, focusses and solutions to problems (Hopkins, Hopkins & Gross 2005). Additionally communication problems can be a big issue. Not only in terms of the language barrier. Different cultures tend to express themselves differently and interpret answers and conduct in a different way. Brett, Befahr and Kern (2006) come up with the example of a Korean and an American employee within a work group where they are asked to give feedback. Silence in this context could be interpreted as wisdom by the Korean and as a lack of interest by the American. Perceived cultural power inequality is another point contributing to negative effects of multiculturalism in group dynamics. Employees from areas of the world with a strong cultural background tend to be seen by employees with not such a strong cultural background as potentially more powerful. Thereby the engagement and the participation in core processes of the perceived less powerful group members can be lowered (Foldy, Rivard & Buckley 2009). All above issues contribute to lowering performance and effectiveness due to negative group dynamics.

4 Literature Review on Team Dynamics after 2010

Since 2010 a growing body of empirical research on team dynamics has been published. In order to conduct a comprehensive review covering the literature on team dynamics from 2011 to 2014, this article first identifies research gaps evolving from Cronin et al. (2011) and further refers to approaches for closing these gaps. This article is based on secondary research and reviews 80 studies on team dynamics. *Figure 3* visualizes the four areas lacking of sufficient research.

Research Gaps from Cronin et al. (2011)
1. Observation of groups over time.
2. Investigation of cause-effect relationships is unidirectional.
3. Analysis of evolutionary states is mostly convergent.
4. Context in group development is underutilized.

Figure 2: Research Gaps identified by Cronin et al. (2011).

Only articles published within top management journals were reviewed, focusing on management, human resources, organizational aspects and specialized on team research. Using the search engine EBSCO Host and the search engines associated with the publishers of the respective journals, articles containing the keywords "group" or "team", that address one of the key research streams introduced in chapter one were retrieved. No research approaches were excluded and therefore also theoretical articles without empirical data collection methods were collected. After reviewing the literature, each article was coded on (i) which key elements it deals with, (ii) which research gaps it addresses, and (iii) which methodological approach it uses.

4.1 Research Gap 1: Observation of Groups over Time

Although there is a huge body of research investigating dynamics within teams, much of this research follows a cross-sectional approach that is not able to capture cause-and-effect relationships. Furthermore, it only shows one snapshot of a group and is not able to capture dynamics, since cross-sectional approaches do not focus on changes over time (Cronin et al. 2011). Out of 80 studies reviewed, 38 use longitudinal approaches and 32 cross-sectional approaches. The remaining 10 focus on theory building.

Authors	Research Streams	Approach Referring to Research Gap
Bresman, & Zellmer-Bruhn (2013)	Size, Structure & Roles Cognition & Learning	Longitudinal design Structured interviews, quantitative questionnaires from multiple source
Colquitt, LePine, Zapata, & Wild (2011)	Cohesion & Climate Performance & Productivity	Longitudinal design Critical incident interviews, quantitative questionnaires, archive data
Kane, & Rink (2011)	Development & Processes Diversity Cohesion & Climate	Longitudinal design Team simulation, observation
Majchrzak, More, & Faraj (2012)	Diversity Cognition & Learning	Longitudinal design Case studies, observations of different teams, interviews
Miron-Spector, Erez, & Naveh (2011)	Diversity Cognition & Learning Creativity & Innovation	Longitudinal Design Structured interviews, quantitative questionnaires, rankings on team innovation

Figure 3: Featured studies referring to Research Gap 1.

Since there is actually little known about the phenomenon of team development, it might make sense to approach research questions using qualitative, explorative data collection methods (Edmondson et al. 2007). Within the literature reviewed, 21% used a qualitative research approach and 7% mixed qualitative and quantitative methods. An overview of featured studies is given in *Figure 4*.

Considering longitudinal studies that use qualitative or mixed data collection methods, there are different ways on how data are collected. Interviews at different points are a common method on how to assess longitudinal qualitative data. To make data collection more valid, it can be mixed with other methods: Colquitt et al. (2011) investigated the evolution and the consequences of trust among firefighter teams and used interviews to assess critical incidents and paired those with multiple questionnaires and the evaluation of archive data. Miron-Spector, Erez and Naveh (2011) also combined structured interviews, quantitative questionnaires and rankings to investigate team innovation.

Another approach is the use of case studies. Until 2011 few scholars have used case study approaches to study teams (Cronin et al. 2011). By now an increasing number of research contributions integrates them. While case studies arguably have limited generalization potential due to the small sample size, they are nonetheless a valid approach for capturing team dynamics. Bresman and Zellmer-Bruhn (2013) investigated effects of psychological safety on team learning by closely observing different teams (cases) and using questionnaires with multiple source raters. Other research builds on close observations of different cases by attending project meetings over a certain period of time in addition to conducting interviews with participants of the meetings at several points in time (Majchrzak, More & Faraj 2012). Instead of working with cases in their normal settings, it is also possible to arrange simulations of team settings and manipulate certain aspects to observe how team members react to these changing circumstances (Kane & Rink 2011). However, although research in simulation settings makes it possible to better observe certain behaviors, it also causes a lower generalization because of the experimental conditions.

4.2 Research Gap 2: Investigation of cause-effect relationships is unidirectional

The literature review of Cronin et al. (2011) reveals a clear lack of investigation into cause-effect relationships. Indeed, typical longitudinal research approaches are not able to draw conclusions of recursive influences without the examination of feedback loops and networks. Feedback loops and other recursive effects are still rare within the literature. Only 7% of the studies in this literature review deal with these recursive effects. For detailed analysis we could only take into account 5% of the studies, as the rest investigated recursive effects with cross-sectional research approaches. An overview of featured studies is provided in *Figure 5*.

Authors	Research Streams	Approach Referring to Research Gap
Bresman (2013)	Development & Processes Cohesion & Climate Cognition & Learning	Process model of how team members change their routines Process of identification influences the process of continuation and continuation influences new identifications
Schulte, Cohen & Klein (2012)	Size, Structure & Roles Development & Processes Cohesion & Climate	Coevolution of network ties and perceptions of team psychological safety High perception of psychological safety leads to more network ties and more network ties lead to psychological safety
Varella, Javidan, & Waldman (2012)	Size, Structure & Roles Development & Processes Leadership Performance & Productivity	Networks within teams and their interactions with charismatic leadership and group behavior Instrumental networks lead to higher group performance and cooperation and both evolve through instrumental networks
Williams Wooley (2011)	Development & Processes Cohesion & Climate Cognition & Learning	Influence of strategic direction on teams Overall strategic orientation influences the strategy the teams chooses and the effort a team invests, the effort a team wants to invest influences the work strategy a team chooses

Figure 4: Featured studies referring to Research Gap 2.

Schulte, Cohen and Klein (2012) best address this research gap by examining the coevolution of network ties and perceptions of team psychological safety. The investigation covered 10-month longitudinal research design on how psychological safety within teams predicts network ties and could show that a high perception of psychological safety within a team leads to more active network ties. This can be found in asking teammates for advice or see them as friends. Simultaneously, the existence of network ties predicts psychological safety. Therefore, team members adopt the perceptions about a psychological safe team environment from their friends and advisors. Without investigating those network ties, it would be not possible to see these multidirectional relationships.

Also Varella, Javidan and Waldman (2012) investigated the role of networks within teams and their interactions with charismatic leadership and group behavior. They could show that charismatic leadership has a positive influence on group cooperation and that group cooperation is associated with higher tie density of instrumental networks and a higher group performance. Furthermore, the relationship between cooperation and performance evolves through instrumental networks.

Williams Wooley (2011) investigated team dynamics with a process model and integrated a recursive effect into her research on how the strategic orientation of a team influences different parts of the team process. The overall strategic orientation therefore influences the strategy the team chooses, the extent to which a team relies on internal or external knowledge and skills and the effort and motivation a team invests. The effort a team wants to invest and the motivation of the team in turn affect the work strategy the team adopts. Bresman (2013) also investigates a process model on how teams change their routines by drawing on the experience of others. He identified that changing routines follows four distinct sub-processes and that the process of continuation, that determines if a group continues to rely on a certain routine, entails a feedback loop that influences the identification process again.

4.3 Research Gap 3: Analysis on evolutionary states is still mostly convergent

Research about convergence within teams far outnumbered research on differentiation (Cronin et al. 2011). While reviewing actual research, it becomes obvious that a huge variety of divergent aspects is considered (e.g. age, ethic, religious, gender, temporal, educational etc.).Around 30% of the studies reviewed address the issue of diversity. One main point of interest is how team diversity is related to team performance (42%), creativity and innovation (20%) and to cohesion and climate (42%). Some studies also covered two aspects cohesion and climate and performance. Still, most research on team dynamics and diversity focuses on convergence and not on differentiation of team members. As we are interested in the dynamics of diverse teams, we will only consider longitudinal approaches more closely. An overview of featured studies is presented in *Figure 6*.

One example referring to the convergence of diverse groups over time is the research of Mäs, Flache, Takács and Jehn (2013). Mäs et al. (2013) investigated effects of demographic diversity on team dynamics and found out that teams with a high demographic diversity tend to experience more subgroup polarization in the beginning but are likely to overcome it in the long run. Furthermore, Zhu (2014) could demonstrate similar findings, namely that demographic homogeneity weakens the group polarization effect. A possible explanation for those findings is that team members adapt to each other and therefore become more convergent.

Authors	Research Streams	Approach Referring to Research Gap
Boerner, Linkohr, & Kiefer (2011)	Diversity Performance & Productivity	Age diversity, diversity in educational background and industry experience have a positive impact on management teams in the short run but not in the long run
Mäs, Flache, Takács, & Jehn (2013)	Development & Processes Diversity	High demographic diversity leads to more subgroup polarization in the beginning but is likely to fade away in the long run
Nederveen-Pieterse, van Knippenberg, & van Dierendonck (2013)	Leadership Diversity Cohesion & Climate Performance & Productivity Cognition & Learning	Performance within diverse teams is higher when teams have the same goal Orientation, especially high learning approach and low performance avoidance
Zhu (2014)	Development & Processes Diversity Cohesion & Climate Performance & Productivity	Low demographic diversity weakens the group polarization effect

Figure 5: Featured studies referring to Research Gap 3.

Boerner, Linkohr and Kiefer (2011) could show that age diversity, diversity in educational background and industry experience only have a positive impact on management teams in the short run but not in the long run. These findings, however, are contextual factors that cannot be changed. Therefore we can see a development regarding the influence of diversity factors on team performance over time, but we also deal with fixed factors that do not develop to more differentiation over time.

4.4 Research Gap 4: Context in group development is underutilized

Contexts have a huge impact on team dynamics. In 2002 Hackman identified conditions under which groups "automatically flourish". Other scholars followed and also found out that contextual are highly important for groups (e.g. Sterman 1989). By now, the context of teams has been mainly considered in the case of control variables. Nevertheless, "to fully appreciate the context, researchers must look beyond the often mundane contextual control variables" (Cronin et al. 2011, p. 591). Within this literature review, around 43% of the studies explicitly considered the context of teams beyond control variables. For validity reasons we only considered longitudinal studies. An overview of featured studies is presented in *Figure 7*.

Context variables can be seen from internal and external perspectives, where internal contextual variables might be variables like leadership or the number of collaboration of team members. External factors can be organizational structure or economic environment like high volatility.

Starting with internal factors, especially team leadership gained a lot of attention. For example, Liu, Lioa and Loi (2012) could show that abusive leadership behavior and abusive team supervision has a negative impact on team creativity and innovation. Plunkett Tost, Gino and Larrick (2013) could demonstrate that the subjective experience of power increases the leaders' tendency to verbally dominate social interactions, which in turn leads to a lower team performance. Highly extraverted leaders in turn can help teams to achieve a higher overall performance (Grant, Gino, & Hofman 2011).

Shifting to external variables influencing teams, Gibson and Dibble (2013) investigated how fluidity within teams is related to overall team performance and could show that teams are more effective under conditions of low fluidity. Changing environmental factors are also important for action teams (e.g. firefighter, surgery) and their learning behavior or trust. (e.g. Vashdi, Bamberger, & Erez 2013).

Another emerging topic is the investigation of geographically dispersed teams, and if teams that do not work together physically can be as productive as teams that are working together very close and physically present. Pazos and Beruvides (2011) could compared face-to-face and computer-supported teams and could show that there are no differences in overall performance in both teams and that there are even no differences in performance changes over time between the two media.

Authors	Research Streams	Approach Referring to Research Gap
Gibson, & Dibble (2013)	Size, Structure, & Roles Performance & Productivity	External factors Teams are more effective under conditions of low fluidity/fluctuation
Grant, Gino, & Hofman (2011)	Leadership Cohesion & Climate Performance & Productivity	Internal factors Highly extraverted leaders help teams to achieve a higher performance
Liu, Lioa, & Loi (2012)	Leadership Cognition & Learning	Internal factors Abusive team leadership has a negative impact on creativity and innovation
Pazos, & Beruvides (2011)	Cohesion & Climate Performance & Productivity Cognition & Learning	External factors No differences in overall performance between face-to-face or computer-supported teams
Plunkett Tost, Gino, & Larrick (2013)	Leadership Performance & Productivity Cognition & Learning	Internal factors Subjective experience of power increases leaders' tendency to verbally dominate interactions which leads to lower team performance
Vashdi, Bamberger, & Erez (2013)	Leadership Cohesion & Climate Performance & Productivity	External factors Learning of action teams (e.g. hospital teams, firefighter) under changing environmental circumstances

Figure 6: Featured studies referring to Research Gap 4.

5 Critical Review and Conclusion

Research gap 1 is only partly closed. Although many studies use longitudinal approaches to study team dynamics, the same amount builds its research still on cross-sectional approaches and therefore does not capture real dynamics and developments. Even fewer studies build their assumptions on studies that use cross-sectional approaches and do not explore basic assumptions via qualitative research methods. In the future more studies should follow qualitative and longitudinal approaches to achieve more valid results. This is, however, extremely difficult as close observations over moths or years are costly and time consuming.

Research gap 2 is not closed yet. Still, only few authors investigate team variables as unidirectional, which may lead to misinterpretations regarding cause and effect relationships. However, research on multidirectional states is highly sophisticated. Methodological approaches need to account for the separation of measured effects and for measures nested within different levels. One solution for future research might be to proceed like Schulte et al. (2012), by using longitudinal research approaches and SIENA (Simulation Investigation for Empirical Network Analysis). The software is able to differentiate between changes over time within team members and of the complete team network and therefore accounts for reciprocity and transitivity (Snijders 2005).

Research Gap 3 is not closed yet. Most research considering divergent states investigates this in relationship with team performance or focuses on evolving similarity of divergent team members over time. The problem of the research on convergence over time is that there are no methods available yet to validate that the group caused members to become more different. Research that tries to address that gap mainly using longitudinal approaches and controls for possible variables that also might have an influence on the tested effects. Nevertheless, these are still not valid approaches and more attention needs to be focused on this issue.

Research Gap 4 has been considerably addressed. A huge body of research addresses the context under which teams perform, considering micro and macro variables. However, as the environment is constantly changing, also the context under which team dynamics evolve is changing. Therefore, research on context variables will still be of a high importance for future research.

References

Abrams, D., & Hogg, M. A. (2001). Collective identity: Group membership and social conception. *Blackwell Handbook of Social Psychology*, pp. 425-460.

Argawal, V. (2012). Managing the diversified team: challenges and strategies for improving performance. *Team Performance Management, 18,* 384-400. doi: 10.1108/13527591211281129

Bartel, C.A., & Wiesenfeld, B.M. (2013). The Social Negotiation of Group Prototype Ambiguity in Dynamic Organizational Contexts. *Academy of Management Review, 38,* 503-524. doi: 10.5465/amr.2011.0300

Bechky, B.A., & Okhuysen, G.A. (2011). Expecting the Unexpected? How SWAT Officers and Film Crews Handle Surprises. *Academy of Management Journal, 54,* 239-261. doi: 10.5465/AMJ.2011.60263060

Berg, R.W. (2012). The Anonymity Factor in Making Multicultural Teams Work: Virtual and Real Teams. *Business Communication Quarterly, 75,* 404-424. doi: 10.1177/1080569912453480

Boerner, S., Linkohr, M., & Kiefer, S. (2011). Top management team diversity: positive in the short run, but negative in the long run? *Team Performance Management, 17,* 328-353. doi: 10.1108/13527591111182616

Borek, L. (2011). Team structural constellations and intra-team conflict. *Team Performance Management, 17,* 405-417. doi: 10.1108/13527591111182652

Boyer O'Leary, M., Mortensen, M., & Williams Wooley, A. (2011). Multiple Team Membership: A theoretical Model of its Effects on Productivity and Learning for Individuals and Teams. *Academy of Management Review, 36,* 461-478.

Braun, F.C., Avital, M., & Mart, B. (2012). Action-centred team leadership influences more than performance. *Team Performance Management, 18,* 176-195. doi: 10.1108/13527591211241015

Bresman, H. (2013). Changing Routines: A Process Model of Vicarious Group Learning in Pharmaceutical R&D. *Academy of Management Review, 56,* 35-61. doi: 10.5465/amj.2010.0725

Bresman, H., & Zellmer-Bruhn, M. (2013). The Structural Context of Team Learning: Effects of Organizational and Team Structure on Internal and External Learning. *Organization Science, 24,* 1120-1139. doi: 10.1287/orsc.1120.0783

Brett, J., Behfar, K., & Kern, M. C. (2006). Managing Multicultural Teams. *Harvard Business Review*, pp. 84-91.

Breugst, N., Patzelt, H., Shepherd, D.A., & Aguinis, H. (2012). Relationship Conflict Improves Team Performance Assessment Accuracy: Evidence From a Multilevel Study, *Academy of Management Learning & Education, 11,* 187-206. doi: 10.5465/amle.2011.0032

Bruns, H.C. (2013). Working Alone Together: Coordination in Collaboration across Domains of Expertise. *Academy of Management Journal, 56,* 62-83. doi: 10.5465/amj.2010.0756

Bunderson, J.S., Van der Vegt, G.S., & Sparrowe, R.T. (2014). Status Inertia and Member Replacement in Role-Differentiated Teams. *Organization Science, 25,* 57-72. doi: 10.1287/orsc.2013.0835

Carton, A.M., & Cummings, J.N. (2012). A Theory of Subgroups in Work Teams. *Academy of Management Review, 37,* 441-470. doi: 10.5465/amr.2009.0322

Clopton, A.W. (2011). Social Capital and Team Performance. *Team Performance Management, 17,* 369-381. doi: 10.1108/13527591111182634

Colquitt, J.A., LePine, J.A., Zapata, C.P., & Wild, R.E. (2011). Trust in Typical and High-Reliability Contexts: Building and Reacting to Trust among Firefighters. *Academy of Management Journal, 54,* 999-1015. doi: 10.5465/amj.2006.0241

Cronen, M.A., Weingart, L.R., & Todorova, G. (2011). Dynamics in Groups: Are We There Yet? *The Academy of Management Annals, 5,* 571-612. doi: 10.1080/19416520.2011.590297

Cummings, J.N., & Haas, M.R. (2011). So many teams, so little time: Time allocation matters in geographically dispersed teams. *Journal of Organizational Behaviour, 33,* 316-341. doi: 10.1002/job.777

Daspit, J., Tillman, C.J., Boyd, N.G., & Mckee, V. (2013). Cross-functional team effectiveness. An examination of internal team environment, shared leadership, and cohesion influences. *Team Performance Management, 19,* 34-56. doi: 10.1108/13527591311312088

Davis, J. H., & Restle, F. (1963, February). The analysis of problems and prediction of group problem solving. *The Journal of Abnormal and Social Psychology*, pp. 103-116.

Dierendorff, E.C., & Ellington, J.K. (2012). Members Matter in Team Training: Multilevel and Longitudinal Relationships Between Goal Orientation, Self-Regulation, and Team Outcomes. *Personnel Psychology, 65,* 661-703. doi: 10.1111/j.1744-6570.2012.01255.x

Edmondson, A.C., & McManus, S.E. (2007). Methodological fit in management field research. *Academy of Management Review, 32,* 1155-1179. doi: 10.5465/AMR.2007.26586086

El-Shinnawy, M., & Vinze, A. S. (1998, June 1). Polarization and Persuasive Argumentation: A Study od Decision Making in Group Settings. *MIS Quarterly*, pp. 165-198.

Erez, M., Lisak, A., Harush, R., Glikson, E., Nouri, R., & Shokef, E. (2013). Going Global: Developing Management Students' Cultural Intelligence and Global Identity in Culturally Diverse Groups. *Academy of Management Learning & Education, 12,* 330-355. doi: 10.5465/amle.2012.0200

Erkutlu, H. (2012). The impact of organizational culture on the relationship between shared leadership and team proactivity. *Team Performance Management, 18,* 102-119. doi: 10.1108/13527591211207734

Foldy, G. E., Rivard, P., & Buckley, T. R. (2009). Power, Safety, and Learning in Racially Diverse Groups. *Academy of Management Learning & Education*, pp. 25-41.

Forsyth, D. R. (1999). *Group Dynamics (3rd ed.).* Pacific Grove: Brooks/Cole.

Forsyth, D.R. (2010). *Group Dynamics.* Wadsworth: Cengage Learning.

Gardner, H.K., Gino, F., & Staats, B.R. (2012). Dynamically Integrating Knowledge in Teams: Transforming Resources into Performance. *Academy of Management Journal, 55,* 998-1022. doi: 10.5465/amj.2010.0604

Gerstein, M. S. (2008, January 1). Organizational Bystanders. *People & Strategy*, pp. 16-18.

Gibson, C.B., & Dibble, R. (2013). Excess May Do Harm: Investigating the Effect of Team External Environment on External Activities in Teams. *Organization Science, 24,* 697-715. doi: 10.1287/orsc.1120.0766

Gong, Y., Kim, T.Y., Lee, D.R., & Zhu, J. (2013). A Multilevel Model of Team Goal Orientation, Information Exchange, and Creativity. *Academy of Management Journal, 56,* 827-851. doi: 10.5465/amj.2011.0177

Goncalo, J. A., & Duguid, M. M. (2007, October 2). Follow the crowd in a new direction: When conformity pressure facilitates group creativity (and when it does not). *Organizational Behavior and Human Decision Processes*, pp. 14-23.

Grant, A.M., Gino, F., & Hofman., D.A. (2011). Reversing the Extraverted Leadership Advantage: The Role of Employee Proactivity. *Academy of Management Journal, 54,* 528-550. doi: 10.5465/AMJ.2011.61968043

Haas, H., & Nüesch, S. (2012). Are multinational teams more successful? *The International Journal of Human Resource Management, 23,* 3105-3113. doi: 10.1080/09585192.2011.610948

Hackman, R. J. (1998, February 1). Why Teams Don't Work. *Theory and Research on Small Groups*, pp. 245-268.

Hackman, J. (2002). *Leading teams: Setting the stage for great performance.* Boston: Harvard Business School Press.

Hackman, R. J., & Morris, C. G. (1975). Group Tasks, Group Interaction Process, and Group Performance: A Review and Proposed Integration. *Advances in experimental social psychology*, pp. 47-99.

Hannah, S.T., Walumbwa, F.O., & Fry, L.W. (2011). Leadership in Action Teams: Team Leader and Members' Authenticity, Authenticity Strength, and Team Outcomes. *Personnel Psychology, 64,* 771-802. doi: 10.1111/j.1744-6570.2011.01225.x

Haynes, N. M. (2012). *Group Dynamics - Basics and Pragmatics for Practitioners.* Maryland: University Press of America.

Higgins, M.S., Weiner, J., & Young, L. (2012). Implementation teams: A lever for organizational change. *Journal of Organizational Behaviour, 33,* 366-388. doi: 10.1002/job.1773

Hill, G. W. (1982). Group Versus Individual Performance: Are N+1 Heads Better Than One? *Psychological Bulletin*, pp. 517-539.

Hirst, G., van Knippenberg, D., Chen, C.H., & Sacramento, C.A. (2011). How Does Bureaucracy Impact Individual Creativity? A Cross-Level Investigation of Team Contextual Influences on Goal Orientation – Creativity Relationships. *Academy of Management Journal, 54,* 624-641. doi: 10.5465/AMJ.2011.61968124

Hoffman, B.J., Bynum, B.H., Piccolo, R.F., & Sutton, A.W. (2011). Person-Organization Value Congruence: How Transformational Leaders Influence Work Group Effectiveness. *Academy of Management Journal, 54,* 779-796. doi: 10.5465/AMJ.2011.64870139

Hollenbeck, J.R., Beersma, B., & Schouten, M.E. (2012). Beyond Team Types and Taxonomies: A Dimensional Scaling Conceptualization for Team Description. *Academy of Management Review, 37,* 82-106. doi: 10.5465/amr.2010.0181

Honts, C., Prewett, M., Rahael, J., & Grossenbacher, M. (2012). The importance of team processes for different team types. *Team Performance Management, 18,* 312-327. doi: 10.1108/13527591211251104

Hopkins, W. E., Hopkins, S. A., & Gross, M. A. (2005). Cultural Diversity Recomposition and Effectiveness in Monoculture Work Groups. *Journal of Organizational Behaviour*, pp. 949-964.

Huang, J.C. (2012). The relationship between conflict and team performance in Taiwan: the moderating effect of goal orientation. *The International Journal of Human Resource Management, 23,* 2126-2143. doi: 10.1080/09585192.2012.664961

Jones, G.R., & George, J.M. (2007). *Essentials of Contemporary Management.* New York: McGraw-Hill.

Kane, A.A., & Rink, F. (2011). Newcomers as Active Agents: Team Receptivity to Integrating vs. Differentiating Strategies. *Academy of Management Annals,* 1-6. doi: 10.5464.AMBPP.2011.235.a

Kozlowski, S.W.J., & Klein, K.J. (2000). A multilevel approach to theory and research in organizations: Contextual, temporal, and emergent processes. In K.J. Klein & S.W.J. Kozlowski (Eds.) *Multilevel theory, research, and methods in organizations: Foundations, extensions, and new directions* (pp.3-90). San Francisco: Jossey-Bass.

Lanaj, K., Hollenbeck, J.R., Ilgen, D.R., Barnes, C.M., & Harmon, S.J. (2013). The Double-Edged Sword Of Decentralized Planning in Multiteam Systems. *Academy of Management Journal, 56,* 735-757. doi: 10.5465/amj.2011.0350

Levesque, L.L., Wilson, J.M., & Wholey, D.R. (2001). Cognitive divergence and shared mental models in software development project teams. *Journal of Organizational Behavior, 22,* 135-144. doi: 10.1002/job.87

Levine, J. M., & Moreland, R. L. (1998, January 1). Small Groups. *Handbook of Social Psychology,* pp. 415-469.

Lewin, K. (1958). Group decision and social change. *Readings in Psychology,* pp. 197-211.

Liu, D., Liao, H., & Loi, R. (2012). The Dark Side Of Leadership: A Three-Level Investigation of the Cascading Effect of Abusive Supervision on Employee Creativity. *Academy of Management Journal, 55,* 1187-1212. doi: 10.5465/amj.2010.0400

Lorinkova, N.M., Pearsall, M.J., & Sims, H.P. (2013). Examining The Differential Longitudinal Performance Of Directive Versus Empowering Leadership Teams. *Academy of Management Journal, 56,* 573-596. doi: 10.5465/amj.2011.0132

Maier, N. R. (1970). *Problem Solving and Creativity in Individuals and Groups.* Belmont: Brooks/Cole.

Majchrzak, A., More, P.H.B., & Faraj, S. (2012). Transcending Knowledge Differences in Cross-Functional Teams. *Organization Science, 23,* 951-970. doi:10.1287/orsc.1110.0677

Mannix, E., & Neale, M. A. (2005). What Differences Make a Difference? The Promise and Reality of Diverse Teams in Organizations. *Psychological Science in the Public Interest,* pp. 31-55.

Marques Santos, C., & Passos, A.M. (2013). Team mental models, relationship conflict and effectiveness over time. *Team Performance Management, 19,* 363-385. doi: 10.1108/TPM-01-2013-0003

Martin, J.A. (2011). Dynamic Managerial Capabilities and the Multibusiness Team: The Role of Episodic Teams in Executive Leadership Groups. *Organization Science, 22,* 118-140. doi: 10.1287/orsc.1090.0515

Mäs, M., Flache, A., Takács, K., & Jehn, K.A. (2013). In the Short Term We Divide, in the Long Term We Unite: Demographic Crisscrossing and the Effects of Faultlines on Subgroup Polarization. *Organization Science, 24,* 716-736. doi: 10.1287/orsc.1120.0767

McGrath, J.E. (1986). Studying groups at work: Ten critical needs for theory and practice. In Goodman P.S. and Associates (Eds), *Designing effective work groups* (pp. 362-392). San Francisco: Jossey-Bass

McGrath, J.E., Arrow, H., & Berdahl, J.L. (2000). The study of groups: Past, present, and future. *Personality and Social Psychology Review, 4,* 95-105. doi: 10.1207/S15327957PSPR0401_8

Metiu, A., & Rothbard, N.P. (2013). Task Bubbles, Artifacts, Shared Emotion, and Mutual Focus of Attention: A Comparative Study of the Microprocesses of Group Engagement. *Organization Science, 24,* 455-475. doi: 10.1287/orsc.1120.0738

Miron-Spector, E., Erez, M., & Naveh, E. (2011). The Effect of Conformist and Attentive-To-Detail Members on Team Innovation: Reconciling the Innovation Paradox. *Academy of Management Journal, 54,* 740-760. doi: 10.5465/AMJ.2011.64870100

Mohammed, S., & Nadkarni, S. (2011). Temporal Diversity and Team Performance: The Moderating Role of Team Temporal Leadership. *Academy of Management Journal, 54,* 489-508. doi: 10.5465/AMJ.2011.61967991

Muethel, M., Gehrlein, S., & Hoegl, M. (2012). Socio-Demographic Factors and Shared Leadership Behaviors in Dispersed Teams: Implications for Human Resource Management. *Human Resource Management, 51,* 525-548. doi: 10.1002/hrm.21488

Naidoo, L.J., Scherbaum, C.A., Goldstein, H.W., & Graen, G.B. (2011). A Longitudinal Examination of the Effects of LMX, Ability, and Differentiation on Team Performance. *Journal of Business Psychology, 26,* 347-357. doi: 10.1007/s10869-010-9193-2

Nederveen-Pieterse, A., van Knippenberg, D., & van Dierendonck, D. (2013). Cultural Diversity and Team Performance: The Role of Team Member Goal Orientation. *Academy of Management Review, 56,* 782-804. doi: 10.5465/amj.2010.0992

Nishii, L.H. (2013). The Benefits of Climate for Inclusion for Gender Diverse Groups. *Academy of Management Journal, 56,* 1754-1774. doi: 10.5465/amj.2009.0823

O'Neill, R., Murphy, V., Mogle, J., MacGregor, K.L., MacKenzie, M.J., Parekh, M., & Pearson, M. (2013). Are Systems-Centred ® teams more collaborative, productive and creative? *Team Performance Management, 19,* 201-221. doi: 10.1108/TPM-04-2012-0015

Owens, B.P., Johnson, M.D., & Mitchell, T.R. (2013). Expressed Humility in Organizations: Implications for Performance, Teams and Leadership. *Organization Science, 24,* 1517-1538. doi: 10.1287/orsc.1120.0795

Pazos, P., & Beruvides, M.G. (2011). Performance patterns in face-to-face and computer-supported teams. *Team Performance Management, 17,* 83-101. doi: 10.1108/13527591111114729

Plunkett Tost, L., Gino, F., & Larrick, R.P. (2013). When Power makes Others Speechless: The Negative Impact of Leader Power on Team Performance. *Academy of Management Journal, 56,* 1465-1486. doi: 10.5465/amj.2011.0180

Quian, C., Cao, Q., & Takeuchi, R. (2013). Top Management Team Functional Diversity and Organizational Innovation in China: The Moderating Effects of Environment. *Strategic Management Journal, 34,* 110-120. doi: 10.1002/smj.1993

Quigley, N.R. (2013). A Longitudinal, Multilevel Study of Leadership Efficacy Development in MBA Teams. *Academy of Management Learning & Education, 12,* 579-602. doi: 10.5465/amle.2011.0524

Raes, A.M.L., Heijltjes, M.G., Glunk, U., & Roe, R.A. (2011). The Interface of the Top Management Team and the Middle Managers: A Process Model. *Academy of Management Review, 36,* 102-126. doi: 10.5465/AMBPP.2008.33718412

Roberson, Q.M., & Williamson, I.O. (2012). Justice in Self-Managing Teams: The Role of Social Networks in the Emergence of Procedural Justice Climates. *Academy of Management Journal, 55,* 685-701. doi: 10.5465/amj.2009.0491

Rogers, P., & Senturia, T. (2013, December 03). *Decision Insights.* Retrieved February 19, 2014, from How Group Dynamics Affect Decisions: http://www.bain.com/publications/articles/how-group-dynamics-affect-decisions.aspx

Schippers, M.C., Homan, A.C., & van Knippenberg, D. (2013). To reflect or not to reflect: Prior Team Performance as a boundary condition of the effects of reflexivity on learning and final team performance. *Journal of Organizational Behavior, 34,* 6-23. doi: 10.1002/job.1784

Schulte, M., Cohen, N.A., & Klein, K.J. (2012). The Coevolution of Network Ties and Perceptions of Team Psychological Safety. *Organization Science, 23,* 564-581. doi: 10.1287/orsc.1100.0582

Schultze, T., Mojzisch, A., & Schulz-Hardt, S. (2009, November 5). Why groups perform better than individuals at quantitative judgment tasks. *Organizational Behavior and Human Decision Processes*, pp. 24-36.

Sessa, V.I., London, M., Pingor, C., Gullu, B., & Patel, J. (2011). Adaptive, generative, and transformative learning in project teams. *Team Performance Management, 17,* 146-167. doi: 10.1108/13527591111143691

Shamsie, J., & Mannor, M.J. (2013). Looking Inside the Dream Team: Probing Into the Contributions of Tactic Knowledge as an Organizational Resource. *Organization Science, 24,* 513-529. doi: 10.1287/orsc.1120.0741

Shea, A. (2011). Lighting the route to success. Efficient team implementation processes with the team managerial coping flowchart. *Team Performance Management, 17,* 7-22. doi: 10.1108/13527591111114684

Shin, S.J., Kim, T.Y., Lee, J.Y., & Bian, L. (2012). Cognitive Team Diversity and Individual Team Member Creativity: A Cross-Level Interaction. *Academy of Management Review, 55,* 197-212. doi: 10.5465/amj.2010.0270

Snell, R. S. (1999, July 1). Obedience to Authority and Ethical Dilemmas in Hong Kong Companies. *Business Ethics Quarterly*, pp. 507-526.

Snijders, T.A.B. (2005). Model for longitudinal network data. In P.J. Carrington, J. Scott, S. Wasserman (Eds.) *Models in Social Network Analysis,* pp. 215-247. Cambridge University Press, Cambridge, Uk.

Stahl, G. K., Maznevski, M. L., Voigt, A., & Jonsen, K. (2010). Unravelling the Effects of Cultural Diversity in Teams: A Meta-Analysis of Research on Multicultural Work Groups. *Journal of International Business Studies*, pp. 690-709.

Sterman, J.D. (1989). Misperceptions of feedback in dynamic decision making. *Organizational Behavior and Human Decision Process, 43,* 301-335. doi: 10.1007/978-3-642-74946-9_3

Stigliani, I., & Ravasi, D. (2012). Organizing Thoughts and Connecting Brains: Material Practices and the Transition from Individual to Group-Level Prospective Sensemaking. *Academy of Management Journal, 55,* 1232-1259. doi: 10.5465/amj.2010.0890

de Stobbeleir, K.E.M., Ashford, S.J., & Buyens, D. (2011). Self-Regulation of Creativity at Work: The Role of Feedback-Seeking Behaviour in Creative Performance. *Academy of Management Journal, 54,* 811-831. doi: 10.5465/AMJ.2011.64870144

Sudhakar, G.P., Farooq, A., & Patnaik, S. (2011). Soft factors affecting the performance of software development teams. *Team Performance Management, 17,* 187-205. doi: 10.1108/13527591111143718

Summers, J.K., Humphrey, S.E., & Ferris, G.R. (2012). Team Member Change, Flux in Coordination, and Performance: Effects of Strategic Core Roles, Information Transfer, and Cognitive Ability. *Academy of Management Journal, 55,* 314-338. doi: 10.5465/amj.2010.0175

Tindale, S. R., Smith, C. M., Dykema-Engblade, A., & Katharina, K. (2012, January 1). Good and Bad Group Performance: Same Process - Different Outcomes. *Group Processes and Intergroup Relations*, pp. 603-618.

Tsai, W.C., Chi, N.W., Grandey, A.A., & Fung, S.C. (2011). Positive group affective tone and team creativity: Negative group affective tone and team trust as boundary conditions. *Journal of Organizational Behavior, 33,* 638-656. doi: 10.1002/job.775

Tuuli, M.M., Rowlinson, S., Fellows, R., & Liu, A.M.M. (2012). Empowering the project team: the impact of leadership style and team context. *Team Performance Management, 18,* 149-175. doi: 10.1108/13527591211241006

Varella, P., Javidan, M., & Waldman, D.A. (2012). A Model of Instrumental Networks: The Role of Socialized Charismatic Leadership and Group Behavior. *Organization Science, 23,* 582-595. doi: 10.1287/orsc.1100.0604

Vashdi, D.R., Bamberger, P.A., & Erez, M. (2013). Can Surgical Team Ever Learn? The Role of Coordination, Complexity, and Transitivity in Action Team Learning. *Academy of Management Journal, 56,* 945-971. doi: 10.5465/amj.2010.0501

Vough, H. (2012). Not All Identifications Are Created Equal: Exploring Employee Accounts For Workgroup, Organizational, and Professional Identification. *Organization Science, 23,* 778-800. doi: 10.1287/orsc.1110.0654

Voxted, S. (2011). Traditional and non-traditional employees in production teams. *Team Performance Management, 17,* 299-310. doi: 10.1108/13527591111159027

Wagner, J.A., Humphrey, S.E., Meyer, C.J., & Hollenbeck, J.R. (2012). Individualism-collectivism and team member performance: Another look. *Journal of Organizational Behavior, 33,* 946-963. doi: 10.1002/job.783

Wells, J.E., & Peachey, J.W. (2011). Turnover intentions. Do leadership behaviors and satisfaction with the leader matter? *Team Performance Management, 17,* 23-40. doi: 10.1108/13527591111114693

Williams Wooley, A. (2011). Playing Offense vs. Defense: The Effects of Team Strategic Orientation on Team Process in Competitive Environments. *Organization Science, 22,* 1384-1398. doi: 10.1287/orsc.1100.0617

Williams, S., & Taormina, R. (1993, April 1). Unanimous Versus Majority Influenceson Group Polarization in Business Decision Making. *Journal of Social Psychology*, pp. 199-205.

Wilson, J., Crisp, C.B., & Mortensen, M. (2013). Extending Construal-Level Theory to Distributed Groups: Understanding the Effects of Virtuality. *Organization Science, 24,* 629-644. doi: 10.1287/orsc.1120.0750

Wong, E.M., Ormiston, M.E., & Tetlock, P.E. (2011). The Effects of Top Management Team Integrative Complexity and Decentralized Decision Making on Corporate Social Performance. *Academy of Management Review, 54,* 1207-1228. doi: 10.5465/amj.2008.0762

Wood, S., Michaelides, G., & Thomson, C. (2011). Team approach, idea generation, conflict and performance. *Team Performance Management, 17,* 382-404. doi: 10.1108/13527591111182643

Yang, S.B., & Guy, M.E. (2011). The Effectiveness of Self-Managed Teams in Government. *Journal of Business Psychology, 26,* 531-541. doi:10.1007/s10869-010-9205-2

Yu, K.Y.T., & Cable, D.M. (2011). Unpacking cooperation in teams. Incorporating long-term orientation and civic virtue in the study of informational diversity. *Team Performance Management, 17,* 63-82. doi: 10.1108/13527591111114710

Zhang, Z., Waldman, D.A., & Wang, Z. (2012). A Multilevel Investigation of Leader-Member Exchange, Informal Leader Emergence, and Individual and Team Performance. *Personnel Psychology, 65,* 49-78. doi: 10.1111/j.1744-6570.2011.01238.x

Zhu, D.H. (2014). Group Polarization in Board Decisions About CEO Compensation. *Organization Science, 25,* 552-571. doi: 10.1287/orsc.2013.0848.

Virtual Teams

Stefan Wieland, Jens Wolf

Abstract. Virtual teams have become an integral part in the everyday work of organizations. They disregard time and location dependent borders and enable organizations to make use of the most qualified employees for specific projects. This is facilitated by the advancement of electronic means of communication. The aim of this article is to give a brief overview of the current status of literature on virtual teams. First, the term "virtual teams" is defined and the areas where they occur are summarized. Then, virtual teams' most important benefits are compiled. The article then reports on the findings of different authors in terms of critical success factors. Thereafter, several areas that have not been addressed in the existing literature are exposed and research questions are developed. These questions provide a basis for future research. Finally, the article ends with a conclusion of what the current state of the literature says about virtual teams.

Keywords: Virtual teams, trust, communication, team leadership, global leadership

1 Introduction

As a result of growing competition in marketplaces, companies had to find new ways of staying flexible in order to persist. One new organizational form that deals with this challenge is the virtual team. It offers companies the opportunity to stay flexible in bringing together the best employees worldwide to work on certain projects irrespective of their physical location (Townsend et al., 1998). Virtual teams are the solution to the challenge of connecting knowledge workers from different locations, different time zones, and diverse cultural backgrounds (Nemiro et al., 2008).

Within the past decade there has been a notable increase in the employment of virtual teams, and this trend is expected to continue (Schumacher & Poehler, 2009; Benetytė & Jatuliavičienė, 2013). The popularity of virtual teams with organizations is ever-increasing (Cascio, 2000; Walvoord et al., 2008). As main reasons for this, Hertel et al. (2005) provide the ever-growing decentralization and globalization of work processes. Several authors opine that nowadays it is almost impossible to find working teams that are not virtual to a certain degree (Martins et al., 2004; Kirkman & Mathieu, 2005). Plump & Ketchen Jr. (2013) believe that virtual teams' presence will even accelerate due to the improvement of information technology in terms of cost, speed, and effectiveness. It is expected that over the next few years, well over a billion employees will work in virtual teams (Johns & Gratton, 2013).

The aim of this article is to provide an overview of the literature on virtual teams, to identify gaps in research, and to conclude by summarizing what the current literature says. As a result of the literature analysis, three major topics emerged as major factors influencing the success of virtual teams. These are trust, communication, and leadership. Figure 1 illustrates the structure of this article.

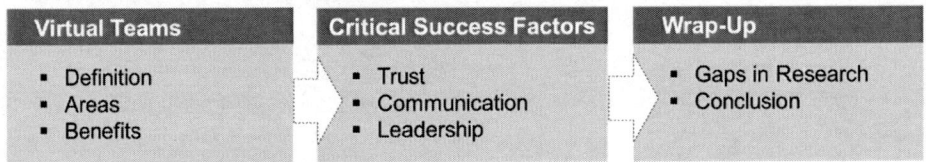

Figure 1: Structure of the Article

2 Definition of Virtual Teams

Before clarifying what virtual teams are, it is important to define the term "team" in general. A widely accepted definition is given by Katzenbach and Smith (1993, p.45):

> "A team is a small number of people with complementary skills who are committed to a common purpose, performance goals, and approach for which they are mutually accountable."

Thanks to the existence of information and communication technology, it is not necessary anymore for teams to be in the same place and to meet face-to-face (Chudoba et al., 2005). Instead, virtual teams use interaction media such as chat, email, audio conference, and video conferencing to communicate with each other. The more a team uses these media to communicate, the higher is its grade of virtuality (Hertel et al., 2005; Berry, 2011). According to Gignac (2005, p.21):

"The virtual team is defined as a group of knowledge workers who are geographically dispersed but not necessarily distributed across expansive geographic locations. They are working toward a common purpose and goal and using electronic communication as their primary medium."

Other authors add the aspect of possible time differences within which virtual teams are working (Alavi & Yoo, 1997; DeSanctis & Poole, 1997; Lipnack & Stamps, 1997; Jarvenpaa & Leidner, 1999; Gassmann & von Zedtwitz, 2003; Hosseini et al., 2013; Jang, 2013; Zander et al., 2013). Often virtual teams only exist for a short time because they are formed in order to fulfill specific needs (Townsend, 1998; Chase, 1999). The majority of authors agree with the definitions mentioned above. However, a small group of researchers use a different approach to defining virtual teams. In fact, these researchers exclude the geographical dispersion and electronic communication from their definitions. Instead, they set their focus on processes in which virtual teams keep on redeveloping themselves over and over again (Hale & Whitlam, 1997; Mowshowitz, 1997; Katzy, 1998; Venkatraman & Henderson, 1998).

3 Areas of Virtual Teams

Townsend et al. (1998) summarize several areas in which virtual teams are best suitable. Project engineering, sales, marketing, and consulting seem to fit since individuals in these domains already work a lot via telephone. Moreover, these jobs are especially service and knowledge oriented, as well as customer-oriented and dynamic. Cascio and Shurygailo (2003) share similar insights since they see the predominant use of virtual teams for employees who spend a small percentage of their time in the office. Examples are consultants and sales people. Nemiro (2002) explicitly clarifies that virtual teams are not appropriate in certain other businesses. New Product Development (NPD) has maybe been most researched among the areas of virtual teams. In this specific context, Martínez-Sánchez et al. (2006) and McDonough et al. (2001) argue that the virtual collaboration integrates NPD workers from inside and outside the company along the supply chain. Zhang et al. (2008) emphasize the effectiveness and efficiency of cross-functional projects in the engineering process.As a general characteristic of virtual teams, Dafoulas and Macaulay (2002) hereby support the fact that team members may belong to different companies. Badrinarayanan and Arnett (2008) also see a greater degree of individuals' involvement in this development process due to virtual networks.Anderson et al. (2007) emphasize the complexity of products nowadays, which automatically affords much more collaboration with the suppliers involved. For instance, the production of a new car requires the involvement of different companies along the supply chain as manufacturing partners. In their case study, May and Carter (2001) illustrate the concrete benefits in the European automotive industry – which are speedy time-to-market, low-cost, and better quality.

Virtual teams in Research and Development (R&D) also play an outstanding role in small and medium enterprises (SMEs), since they rely more on external resources. However, IT in SMEs is still lacking behind compared to corporations and needs to be continuously improved in order to stay competitive (Sharma & Bhagwat, 2006). The literature review of Ale Ebrahim et al. (2009) – which includes a review of leading researchers in this field – provides extensive research on virtual teams in SMEs. Nevertheless, Boehe (2007) states that multinational corporations are more likely to have global, integrated R&D network structures than smaller companies.

Managing sales teams, as another distinct area of virtual teaming, has been little researched yet, although Rapp et al. (2010) point out that there is huge relevance. To date, Badrinarayanan et al. (2011) provide the only conceptual framework for global virtual sales teams' effectiveness. Another recent research area is online education of virtual team members (Erez et al., 2013). Here authors acknowledge reduced training expenses for companies due to e-learning (Badrinarayanan & Arnett, 2008) or better culturally diverse preparation for future managers in business schools (Taras et al., 2012; Pless et al., 2011).

4   Benefits of Virtual Teams

Working in virtual teams offers numerous advantages for organizations. One crucial advantage is virtual teams' independence of space and time (Lurey &

Raisinghani, 2001; Berry, 2011). Especially the fact that virtual teams do not know any location-dependent borders offers organizations the opportunity to use the most qualified employees for certain projects (Bell & Kozlowski, 2002; Hunsaker & Hunsaker, 2008). Rosen et al. (2007) see the importance of this particularly when it comes to very complex and highly specialized tasks. By utilizing virtual teams, organizations are able to deploy more qualified workers, and consequently achieve better results (Martins et al., 2004; Rice et al., 2007; Chen et al., 2008). In a case study, Lee-Kelley & Sankey (2008) demonstrated that virtual teams constitute an important benefit for projects where cross-functional or cross-boundary skilled inputs are needed. Further advantages of virtual teams revealed in the case study are cost savings – especially travel costs – and the opportunity to hold large meetings by means of technologies transmitted via internet. Many other authors agree on the advantage of cost savings and add time savings as another benefit (Cascio, 2000; Lipnack & Stamps, 2000; McDonough et al., 2001; Fuller et al., 2006; Kankanhalli et al., 2006; Olson-Buchanan et al., 2007; Bergiel et al., 2008). A reduction of the time-to-market is an additional benefit that is frequently stated (May and Carter, 2001; Kušar et al., 2004; Zhang et al., 2004; Mulebeke & Zheng, 2006; Sorli et al., 2006; Guniš et al., 2007; Chen, 2008; Ge & Hu, 2008; Shachaf, 2008). As time is often equated with costs, a shorter time-to-market again leads to cost savings (Rabelo & Speller Jr., 2005).

5 Critical Success Factors for Virtual Teams

When looking at the current literature about virtual teams, three challenges keep emerging that are often addressed. These can be considered as critical success factors for virtual teams: trust, communication, and leadership (see Figure 2).

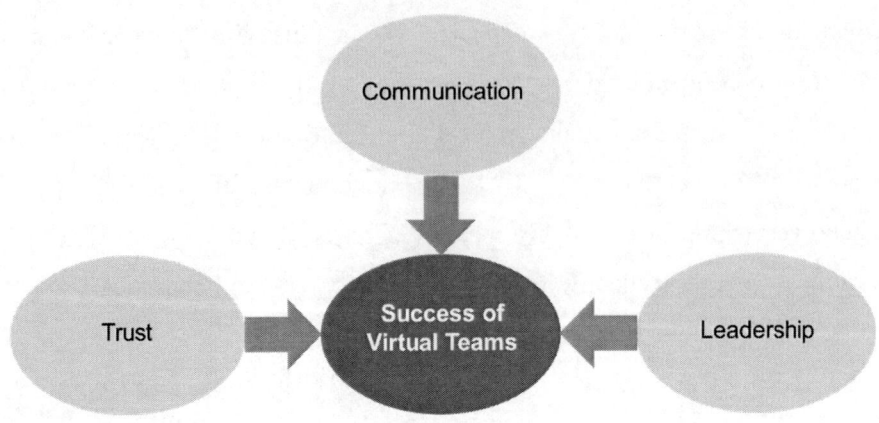

Figure 2: Critical Success Factors for Virtual Teams

Hereinafter is a summary of the literature about these three critical success factors.

5.1 Trust

Researching trust in virtual teams is quite new and some years ago hardly any literature was available that dealt with this topic (Benetytė & Jatuliavičienė, 2013). In 2013, an online simulation game with 98 participating Master's students from four different continents analyzed what affects the performance of virtual teams. The study found out that trust among team members was the most important driver (Phadnis & Caplice, 2013). Other authors agree that trust influences the performance of virtual teams and ascertain a strong link between a high level of trust and a high performance of virtual teams (Khan, 2012; Hosseini et al., 2013; Pinjani & Palvia, 2013). A common source of difficulties when trying to develop trust in virtual teams is the involvement of different cultures (Bell and Kozlowski, 2002; Boutellier et al., 2002; Griffith et al., 2003; Jacobs et al., 2005; Paul et al., 2005; Munkvold & Zigurs, 2007; Badrinarayanan & Arnett, 2008; Dubé & Robey, 2009; Schumacher & Poehler, 2009; Jang, 2013). In this case, the degree of trust in virtual teams is typically low. This can be changed by improving the communication among the team members (Lepsinger & DeRosa, 2011; Benetytė & Jatuliavičienė, 2013). However, Zander et al. (2013) found out that it is generally a difficult task for virtual teams to achieve a high degree of trust due to the lack of personal meetings and common experiences. Pinjani and Palvia (2013) agree that the lack of personal meetings complicates the building of trust. In order to improve trust, Nyström and Asproth (2013) recommend that there should be one or more personal meetings of the team members before the virtual team starts to work. Jansson (2005), by contrast, argues that personal meetings are not necessarily needed to build trust.

5.2 Communication

Schumacher et al. (2008) describe the communication quality in virtual teams as one of the most important success factors. An often addressed issue for virtual teams is that the communication in virtual teams is worse than in traditional teams. This can even develop to the extent that the communication entirely stops (Cascio, 2000; Kirkman et al., 2002; Baskerville & Nandhakumar, 2007; Rosen et al., 2007; Taifi, 2007). In contrast, Lee-Kelley & Sankey (2008) observed something totally different in their case study already mentioned earlier in this article. They even noticed an over-communication among virtual team members. Brandt et al. (2011) conclude that there is no consensus on whether electronic communication methods improve or distract the work of virtual teams. Depending on the chosen method, specific problems can emerge. For instance, Chhay and Kleiner (2013) discovered that email as main communication method can alienate the members of a virtual team because this is a very anonymous method. However, Berry (2011) states that computer-based communication in virtual teams is referred to as being more task-focused than the communication in traditional teams. According to the author, this is because the communication via computer contains less social interaction. For Johns and Gratton (2013), despite all the advantages of virtual teams, this missing social interaction is the flip side of the coin. Furthermore, Maynard et al. (2012) figured out that communication in virtual teams can lead to time loss because it is necessary to interpret and understand what has been communicated. O'Kelly (2013) detected that virtual teams need more communication than traditional teams due to the lack of a shared workplace. Therefore, Martins and Schilpzand (2011) as well as Goman (2012) advise that virtual teams have to agree on standards and expectations for the communication. Nyström and Asproth (2013) offer a new approach by emphasizing that the use of modern communication technologies is not necessary as they do not feature any value themselves. Instead, if simple communication tools can serve the purpose, they are absolutely sufficient.

5.3 Leadership

Like trust and communication, leadership can be considered as an essential success factor for virtual teams (Bell & Kozlowski, 2002; Yoo & Alavi, 2004). A pioneering role in research on leadership in virtual teams can be attributed to Kayworth and Leidner (2002). The authors carried out a study with thirteen virtual teams from several locations in Europe and North America. The study revealed that virtual team leaders have to act like mentors and demonstrate much understanding toward team members in order to be effective. Furthermore, they have to possess strong communication skills. Since this study, not much has happened in the field of research on virtual team leadership for several years. In their review about empirical research on the management of virtual teams, Hertel et al. (2005) illustrated the lack of research that deals with leadership in virtual teams. Malhotra et al. (2007) as well as Badrinarayanan and Arnett (2008) ascertained the same research gap. Eventually, since 2011 many authors have dealt with this lack of research. Zander et al. (2013) identified three challenges that can be attributed particularly to virtual team leaders. These are goal alignment, knowledge transfer, and motivation. Other than Zander et al. (2013), Berry (2011) discovered four skills a virtual team leader should possess: communication, creating expectations, assigning available resources, and forming desired behaviors. The author named the ability to point out the meaningfulness and significance of virtual teamwork as the main challenge. Lepsinger and DeRosa (2011) highlight that research has shown that leadership and a higher team performance are highly linked in virtual teams. In accordance with Zander et al. (2013), the authors attach great importance to goal alignment. The main challenges for virtual team leaders according to Pinjani and Palvia (2013) are knowledge sharing, trust building, navigation of personality issues, and, once more, goal alignment. A study conducted by the Oracle Corporation found out that the main challenges of virtual team leadership are on the one hand giving a clear direction, and on the other hand communicating effectively with team members from different time zones (Hunsaker & Hunsaker, 2008). What really sticks out from all contributions is the importance they attach to goal alignment. In addition, all mentioned leadership characteristics are somehow related to communication and the leaders' ability to convince.

6 Gaps in Research

Particularly over the past decade, a lot of research has been done on the field of virtual teams. However, there are still areas that have not been fully covered by previous research. The areas where further research is needed, are visualized in Figure 3.

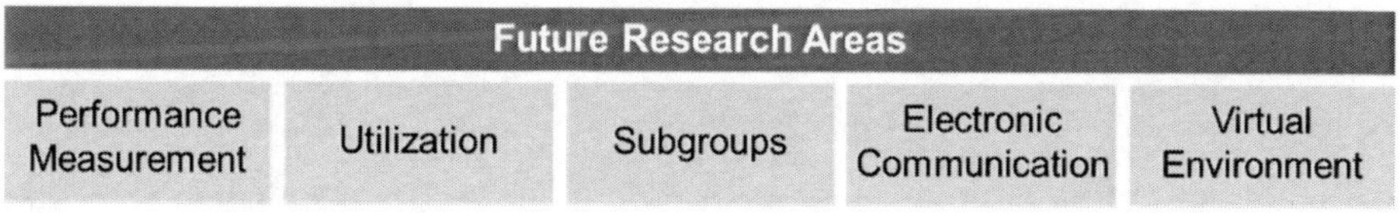

Future Research Areas				
Performance Measurement	Utilization	Subgroups	Electronic Communication	Virtual Environment

Figure 3: Areas for Future Research on Virtual Teams

The probably most important gap that has not yet been closed is the question of how to measure the performance of virtual teams. Future research should define key performance indicators and identify tools that are best to measure these (Hosseini et al., 2013). Furthermore, future research should investigate in what situations the use of virtual teams is appropriate (Badrinarayanan et al., 2011). Besides, the importance of subgroups within virtual teams should be further examined as these might have a considerable impact (Mortensen et al., 2010). It would be interesting to know if there are stronger and weaker subgroups (Webster and Wong, 2008). Earlier in this article, it was already mentioned that there is no consensus in current literature on whether electronic communication methods improve or distract the work of virtual teams (Brandt et al., 2011). Therefore, future research should take on this topic to explore whether the reliance on electronic means of communication impairs the cooperation among team members (Mortensen et al., 2010). What is more, future research should focus on how the virtual environment should be designed (Nyström & Asproth, 2013). For this, a study that analyzes which team members communicate with each other, how often, and by means of which tools could be helpful (Khan, 2012).

7 Conclusion

Virtual teams are more important than ever these days, and regarding their increased significance to the real business world, there is no end in sight. The aim of this article was to give an overview of what recent literature says about virtual teams. In the main part of this article, the authors categorized the literature into three critical success factors – trust, communication, and leadership – which offer both opportunities and challenges. Special attention should be devoted to these three key drivers. A strong connection between trust and success of virtual teams can be observed according to several authors. Many authors agree that trust in virtual teams is usually low and they are aware of the complexity that is affiliated with trust building. Different approaches exist on how to tackle this challenge. Furthermore, the current literature agrees that communication is very important for the success of virtual teams. However, there is no agreement on how to use the variety of electronic communication methods in the right way. Leadership is a quite new area in terms of research on virtual teams. Various researchers have been dealing with this issue over the past few years. The main focus in literature regarding leadership in virtual teams is on the one hand the alignment of goals, and on the other hand communication and the leaders' convincibility.

Clearly, this article has been limited to a brief overview of what the literature displays about virtual teams based on selected areas. There are other interesting topics that could not be addressed in this article, such as different types of virtual teams, a detailed comparison with traditional face-to-face teams, or practical application areas of virtual teams. Despite the already large amount of literature on virtual teams, there are still unresearched – or at least underresearched – areas. In the previous section, the authors have compiled the main questions that still remain unanswered. These questions may provide useful indications for future research.

References

Alavia, Maryam, and Yoo, Youngjin (1997), *Is Learning in Virtual Teams Real?*, Boston: Harvard Business School Press.

Ale Ebrahim, Nader, Ahmed, Shamsuddin, and Taha, Zahari (2009), Virtual R&D Teams in Small and Medium Enterprises: A Literature Review, *Scientific Research and Essays*, 4, 13, 1575-1590.

Anderson, Anne H., McEwan, Rachel, Bal, Jay, and Carletta, Jean (2007), Virtual Team Meetings: An Analysis of Communication and Context, *Computers in Human Behavior*, 23, 5, 2558-2580.

Badrinarayanan, Vishag, and Arnett, Dennis B. (2008), "Effective Virtual New Product Development Teams: An Integrated Framework", *Journal of Business & Industrial Marketing*, 23, 4, 242-248.

Badrinarayanan, Vishag, Madhavaram, Sreedhar, and Granot, Elad (2011), "Global Virtual Sales Teams (GVSTs): A Conceptual Framework of the Influence of Intellectual and Social Capital on Effectiveness", *Journal of Personal Selling & Sales Management*, 31, 3, 311-324.

Baskerville, Richard, and Nandhakumar, Joe (2007), "Activating and Perpetuating Virtual Teams: Now That We're Mobile, Where Do We Go?", *IEEE Transactions on Professional Communication*, 50, 1, 17-34.

Bell, Bradford S., and Kozlowski, Steve W.J. (2002), "A Typology of Virtual Teams: Implications for Effective Leadership", *Group & Organization Management*, 27, 1, 14-49.

Benetytė, Donata, and Jatuliavičienė, Gražina (2013), "Building and Sustaining Trust in Virtual Teams within Organizational Context", *Regional Formation & Development Studies*, 2, 10, 18-30.

Bergiel, Blaise J., Bergiel, Erich B., and Balsmeier, Phillip W. (2008), "Nature of Virtual Teams: A Summary of their Advantages and Disadvantages", *Management Research News*, 31, 2, 99-110.

Berry, Gregory R. (2011), "Enhancing Effectiveness on Virtual Teams", *Journal of Business Communication*, 48, 2, 186-206.

Boehe, Dirk M. (2007), Product Development in MNC Subsidiaries: Local Linkages and Global Interdependencies, *Journal of International Management*, 13, 4, 488-512.

Boutellier, Roman, Gassmann, Olivier, Macho, Holger, and Roux, Manfred (2002), "Management of Dispersed Product Development Teams: The Role of Information Technologies", *R&D Management*, 28, 1, 13-25.

Brandt, Virginia, England, William, and Ward, Susan (2011), "Virtual Teams", *Research Technology Management*, 54, 6, 62-63.

Cascio, Wayne F. (2000), "Managing a Virtual Workplace", *The Academy of Management Executive*, 14, 3, 81-90.

Cascio, Wayne F., and Shurygailo, Stan (2003), E-Leadership and Virtual Teams, *Organizational Dynamics*, 24, 1, 217-238.

Chase, Nancy (1999), "Learning to Lead a Virtual Team", *Quality*, 38, 9, 76.

Chen, Tsung-Yi (2008), "Knowledge Sharing in Virtual Enterprises via an Ontology-Based Access Control Approach", *Computers in Industry*, 59, 5, 502-519.

Chen, Tsung-Yi, Chen, Yuh-Min, and Chu, Hui-Chuan (2008), "Developing a Trust Evaluation Method between Co-Workers in Virtual Project Team for Enabling Resource Sharing and Collaboration", *Computers in Industry*, 59, 6, 565-579.

Chhay, Rathtana V., and Kleiner, Brian H. (2013), "Effective Communication in Virtual Teams", *Industrial Management*, 55, 4, 28-30.

Chudoba, Katherine M., Wynn, Eleanor, Lu, Mei, and Watson-Manheim, Mary B. (2005), "How Virtual are We? Measuring Virtuality and Understanding its Impact in a Global Organization", *Information Systems Journal*, 15, 4, 279-306.

Dafoulas, Georgios, and Macaulay, Linda (2002), Investigation Cultural Differences in Virtual Software Teams, *The Electronic Journal of Information Systems in Developing Countries (EJISDC)*, 7, 4, 1-14.

DeSanctis, Gerardine, and Poole, Marshall S. (1997), "Transitions in Teamwork in New Organizational Forms", *Advances in Group Processes*, 14, 157-176.

Dubé, Line, and Robey, Daniel (2009), "Surviving the Paradoxes of Virtual Teamwork", *Information Systems Journal*, 19, 1, 3-30.

Erez, Miriam, Lisak, Alon, Harush, Raveh, Glikson, Ella, Nouri, Rikki, and Shokef, Efrat (2013), Going Global: Developing Management Students' Cultural Intelligence and Global Identity in Culturally Diverse Virtual Teams, *Academy of Management Learning & Education*, 12, 3, 330-355.

Fuller, Mark A., Hardin, Andrew M., and Davison, Robert M. (2006), "Efficacy in Technology-Mediated Distributed Teams", *Journal of Management Information Systems*, 23, 3, 209-235.

Gassmann, Oliver, and Zedtwitz, Maximilian von (2003), "Trends and Determinants of Managing Virtual R&D Teams", *R&D Management*, 33, 3, 243-262.

Ge, Zehui, and Hu, Qiying (2008), "Collaboration in R&D Activities: Firm-Specific Decisions", *European Journal of Operational Research*, 185, 2, 864-883.

Gignac, Francine (2005), *Building Successful Virtual Teams*, Boston: Artech House.

Goman, Carol K. (2012), "Virtual Teams", *Sales & Service Excellence*, 12, 8, 6.

Griffith, Terri L., Sawyer, John E., and Neale, Margaret A. (2003), "Virtualness and Knowledge in Teams: Managing the Love Triangle of Organizations, Individuals, and Information Technology", *MIS Quarterly*, 27, 2, 265-287.

Guniš, Adrian, Šišlák, Ján, and Valčuha, Štefan (2007), "Implementation of Collaboration Model within SMEs" in *Digital Enterprise Technology: Perspectives and Future Challenges*, ed. Pedro Filipe Cunha and Paul G. Maropoulos, New York: Springer, 377-384.

Hale, Richard, and Whitlam, Peter (1997), *Towards the virtual organization*, London: McGraw-Hill Publishers.

Hertel, Guido, Geister, Susanne, and Konradt, Udo (2005), "Managing Virtual Teams: A Review of Current Empirical Research", *Human Resource Management Review*, 15, 1, 69-95.

Hosseini, Reza M., Chileshe, Nicholas, Ghoddousi, Parviz, Jahanshahloo, Gholam R., Katebi, Ali, and Saeedi, Mohsen (2013), "Performance Evaluation for Global Virtual Teams (GVTs): Application of Data Envelopment Analysis (DEA)", *International Journal of Business and Management*, 8, 19, 122-136.

Hunsaker, Phillip L., and Hunsaker, Johanna S. (2008), "Virtual Teams: A Leader's Guide", *Team Performance Management*, 14, 1/2, 86-101.

Jacobs, Jef. C., Moll, Jan. H. van, Krause, Paul, Kusters, Rob J., Trienekens, Jos J.-M., and Brombacher, Aarnout C. (2005), "Exploring Defect Causes in Products Developed by Virtual Teams", *Information and Software Technology*, 47, 6, 399-410.

Jang, Chyng-Yang (2013), "Facilitating Trust in Virtual Teams: The Role of Awareness", *Advances in Competitiveness Research*, 21, 1/2, 61-77.

Jansson, Eva (2005), *Working together when Being apart: An Analysis of Distributed Collaborative Work through ICT from an Organizational and Psychosocial Perspective*, Stockholm: Tekniska Högskolan.

Jarvenpaa, Sirkka L., and Leidner, Dorothy E. (1999), "Communication and Trust in Global Virtual Teams", *Organization Science*, 10, 6, 791-815.

Johns, Tammy, and Gratton, Lynda (2013), "The Third Wave of Virtual Work", *Harvard Business Review*, 91, 1, 66-73.

Kankanhalli, Atreyi, Tan, Bernard C.Y., and Wei, Kwok-Kee (2006), "Conflict and Performance in Global Virtual Teams", *Journal of Management Information Systems*, 23, 3, 237-274.

Katzenbach, Jon R., and Smith, Douglas K. (1993), *The Wisdom of Teams: Creating the High-Performance Organization*, Boston: Harvard Business School Press.

Katzy, Bernhard R. (1998), "Design and Implementation of virtual organizations" in *Proceedings of the Thirty-First Hawaii International Conference on System Sciences*, Vol. 4, ed. Dolk, Daniel R., Los Alamitos, California: IEEE Computer Society, 142-151.

Kayworth, Timothy R., and Leidner, Dorothy E. (2002), "Leadership Effectiveness in Global Virtual Teams", *Journal of Management Information Systems*, 18, 3, 7-40.

Khan, Mohammad S. (2012), "Role of Trust and Relationships in Geographically Distributed Teams: Exploratory Study on Development Sector", *International Journal of Networking and Virtual Organisations*, 10, 1, 40-58.

Kirkman, Bradley L., Rosen, Benson, Gibson, Cristina B., Tesluk, Paul E., and McPherson, Simon O. (2002), "Five Challenges to Virtual Team Success: Lessons from Sabre, Inc.", *The Academy of Management Executive*, 16, 3, 67-79.

Kirkman, Bradley L., and Mathieu, John E. (2005), "The Dimensions and Antecedents of Team Virtuality", *Journal of Management*, 31, 5, 700-718.

Kušar, Janez, Duhovnik, Jože, and Grum, Janez (2004), "How to Reduce New Product Development Time", *Robotics and Computer-Integrated Manufacturing*, 20, 1, 1-15.

Lee-Kelley, Liz, and Sankey, Tim (2008), "Global Virtual Teams for Value Creation and Project Success: A Case Study", *International Journal of Project Management*, 26, 1, 51-62.

Leenders, Roger T., Van Engelen, Jo M.L., and Kratzer, Jan (2003), Virtuality, Communication, and New Product Team Creativity: A Social Network Perspective, *Journal of Engineering and Technology Management*, 20, 1, 69-92.

Lepsinger, Rick, and DeRosa, Darlene (2011), "Five Ways to Create Successful Virtual Teams", *Baseline*, July/August, 111, 12.

Lipnack, Jessica, and Stamps, Jeffrey (1997), *Virtual Teams: Reaching across Space, Time, and Organizations with Technology*, New York: John Wiley & Sons.

Lipnack, Jessica, and Stamps, Jeffrey (ed.) (2000), *Virtual Teams: People Working across Boundaries with Technology* (2nd ed.), New York: John Wiley & Sons.

Lurey, Jeremy S., and Raisinghani, Mahesh S. (2001), "An Empirical Study of Best Practices in Virtual Teams", *Information & Management*, 38, 8, 523-544.

Malhotra, Arvind, Majchrzak, Ann, and Rosen, Benson (2007), "Leading Virtual Teams", *Academy of Management Perspectives*, 21, 1, 60-70.

Martínez-Sánchez, Angel, Pérez-Pérez, Manuela, De-Luis-Carnicer, Pilar, Vela-Jiménez, Ma José (2006), Teleworking and New Product Development, *European Journal of Innovation Management*, 9, 2, 202-214.

Martins, Luis L., Gilson, Lucy L., and Maynard, Travis M. (2004), "Virtual Teams: What Do We Know and Where Do We Go from Here?", *Journal of Management*, 30, 6, 805-835.

Martins, Luis L., and Schilpzand, Marieke C. (2011), "Global Virtual Teams: Key Developments, ResearchND Gaps, and Future Directions" in *Research in Personnel and Human Resources Management*, ed. Aparna Joshi, Hui Liao, and Joseph J. Martocchio, Bingley (UK): Emerald Group Publishing Limited, 1-72.

May, Andrew, and Carter, Chris (2001), "A Case Study of Virtual Team Working in the European Automotive Industry", *International Journal of Industrial Ergonomics*, 27, 3, 171-186.

Maynard, Travis M., Mathieu, John E., Rapp, Tammy L., and Gilson, Lucy L. (2012), "Something(s) Old and Something(s) New: Modeling Drivers of Global Virtual Team Effectiveness", *Journal of Organizational Behavior*, 33, 3, 342-365.

McDonough, Edward F. III, Kahn, Kenneth B., and Barczak, Gloria (2001), "An Investigation of the Use of Global, Virtual, and Collocated New Product Development Teams", *Journal of Product Innovation Management*, 18, 2, 110–120.

Mortensen, Mark, Caya, Olivier, and Pinsonneault, Alain (2010), "Virtual Teams *Computer Supported Cooperative Work: The Journal of Collaborative Computing* Research" in *MIT Sloan School Working Paper 4738-09*, ed. S.P. Kothari, Cambridge: MIT Sloan School of Management, 1-37.

Mowshowitz, Abbe (1997), "virtual organization", *Communications of the ACM*, 40, 9, 30-37.

Mulebeke, James A.W., and Zheng, Li (2006), "Incorporating Integrated Product Development with Technology Road Mapping for Dynamism and Innovation", *International Journal of Product Development*, 3, 1, 56-76.

Munkvold, Bjørn E., and Zigurs, Ilze (2007), "Process and Technology Challenges in Swift-Starting Virtual Teams", *Information and Management*, 44, 3, 287-299.

Nemiro, Jill E. (2002), The Creative Process in Virtual Teams, Creativity Research Journal, 14, 1, 69-83.

Nemiro, Jill. E., Beyerlein, Michael M., Bradley, Lori, and Beyerlein, Susan (ed.) (2008), *The Handbook of High-Performance Virtual Teams: A Toolkit for Collaborating across Boundaries* (1st ed.), San Francisco: Jossey-Bass.

Nyström, Christina A., and Asproth, Viveca (2013), "Virtual Teams – Support for Technical Communication?", *Journal of Organisational Transformation & Social Change*, 10, 1, 64-80.

O'Kelly, Allison (2013), "Planning and Managing a Virtual Work Team", *MWorld*, 12, 2, 12-13.

Olson-Buchanan, Julie B., Rechner, Paula L., Sanchez, Rudolph J., and Schmidtke, James M. (2007), "Utilizing Virtual Teams in a Management Principles Course", *Education + Training*, 49, 5, 408-423.

Paul, Souren, Seetharaman, Priya, Samarah, Imad, and Mykytyn Jr., Peter (2005), "Understanding Conflict in Virtual Teams: An Experimental Investigation Using Content Analysis" in *Proceedings of the 38th Hawaii International Conference on System Sciences*, ed. Ralph H. Sprague, Los Alamitos, California: IEEE Computer Society, 1-10.

Phadnis, Shardul, and Caplice, Chris (2013), "Global Virtual Teams: How Are They Performing?", *Supply Chain Management Review*, 17, 4, 8-9.

Pinjani, Praveen, and Palvia, Prashant (2013), "Trust and Knowledge Sharing in Diverse Global Virtual Teams", *Information & Management*, 50, 4, 144-153.

Pless, Nicola M., Maak, Thomas, and Stahl, Günter K. (2011), Developing Responsible Global Leaders through International Service-Learning Programs: The Ulysses Experience, Academy of Management Learning & Education, 10, 2, 237-260.

Plump, Carolyn M., and Ketchen Jr., David J. (2013), "Navigating the Possible Legal Pitfalls of Virtual Teams", *Journal of Organization Design*, 2, 3, 51-55.

Rabelo, Luis, and Speller Jr., Thomas H. (2005), "Sustaining Growth in the Modern Enterprise: A Case Study", *Journal of Engineering and Technology Management*, 22, 4, 274-290.

Rapp, Adam, Ahearne, Michael, Mathieu, John, and Rapp, Tammy (2010), Managing Sales Teams in a Virtual Environment, International Journal of Research in Marketing, 27, 2, 108-118.

Rice, Daniel J., Davidson, Barry D., Dannenhoffer, John F., and Gay, Geri K. (2007), "Improving the Effectiveness of Virtual Teams by Adapting Team Processes", *Computer Supported Cooperative Work: The Journal of Collaborative Computing*, 16, 6, 567-594.

Rosen, Benson, Furst, Stacie, and Blackburn, Richard (2007), "Overcoming Barriers to Knowledge Sharing in Virtual Teams", *Organizational Dynamics*, 36, 3, 259-273.

Schumacher, Marinita, Le Cardinal, Julie, and Mekhilef, Mounib (2008), "A Competence Management Methodology for Virtual Teams – A Systematic Approach to Support Innovation Processes in SMEs" in *Proceedings DESIGN 2008 – the 10th International Design Conference*, Vol. 1, ed. D. Marjanovic, M. Storga, N. Pavkovic, and N. Bojcetic, Dubrovnik: The Design Society, 993-1000.

Schumacher, Terry, and Poehler, Lance (2009), "The Virtual Team Challenge: Is It Time for Training?", *International Journal of Innovation & Technology Management*, 6, 2, 169-181.

Shachaf, Pnina (2008), "Cultural Diversity and Information and Communication Technology Impacts on Global Virtual Teams: An Exploratory Study", *Information and Management*, 45, 2, 131-142.

Sharma, Milind K., and Bhagwat, Rajat (2006), Practice of Information Systems: Evidence from Select Indian SMEs, *Journal of Manufacturing Technology Management*, 17, 2, 199-223.

Sorli, Mikel, Stokic, Dragan, Gorostiza, Alvaro, and Campos, Ana (2006), "Managing Product/Process Knowledge in the Concurrent/Simultaneous Enterprise Environment", *Robotics and Computer-Integrated Manufacturing*, 22, 5/6, 399-408.

Taifi, Nouha (2007), "Organizational Collaborative Model of Small and Medium Enterprises in the Extended Enterprise Era Lessons to Learn from a Large Automotive Company and its Dealers' Network" in *EC-TEL 2007 PROLEARN Doctoral Consortium – 2nd European Conference on Technology Enhanced Learning*, Vol. 288, ed. Katherine Maillet, Tomaz Klobucar, Denis Gillet, and Ralf Klamma, Crete, Greece: CEUR Workshop Proceedings, 22-31.

Taras, Vas, Caprar, Dan V., Rottig, Daniel, Sarala, Riikka M., Zakaria, Norhayati, Zhao, Fang, Jiménez, Alfredo, Wankel, Charles, Lei, Weng Si, Minor, Michael S., Bryła, Paweł, Ordeñana, Xavier, Bode, Alexander, Schuster, Anja, Vaiginiene, Erika, Froese, Fabian J., Bathula, Hanoku, Yajnik, Nilay, Baldegger Rico, and Huang, Victor Z. (2012), A Global Classroom? Evaluating the Effectiveness of Global Virtual Collaboration as a Teaching Tool in Management Education. *Academy of Management Learning & Education*, 12, 3, 4-14.

Townsend, Anthony M., DeMarie, Samuel M., and Hendrickson, Anthony R. (1998), "Virtual Teams: Technology and the Workplace of the Future", *The Academy of Management Executive*, 12, 3, 17-29.

Venkatraman, Narayanan, and Henderson, John C. (1998), Real Strategies for Virtual Organizing, *Sloan Management Review*, 40, 1, 33-48.

Walvoord, Ashley A.G., Redden, Elizabeth R., Elliott, Linda R., and Coovert, Michael D. (2008), "Empowering Followers in Virtual Teams: Guiding Principles from Theory and Practice", *Computers in Human Behavior*, 24, 5, 1884-1906.

Webster, Jane E., and Wong, W.K.P. (2008), "Comparing Traditional and Virtual Group Forms: Identity, Communication and Trust in Naturally Occurring Project Teams", *The International Journal of Human Resource Management*, 19, 1, 41-62.

Yoo, Youngjin, and Alavi, Maryam (2004), "Emergent Leadership in Virtual Teams: What Do Emergent Leaders Do?", *Information & Organization*, 14, 1, 27-58.

Zander, Lena, Zettinig, Peter, and Mäkelä, Kristiina (2013), "Leading Global Virtual Teams to Success", *Organizational Dynamics*, Special Issue: Global Leadership, 42, 3, 228-237.

Zhang, Shusheng, Shen, Weiming, and Ghenniwa, Hamada (2004), "A Review of Internet-Based Product Information Sharing and Visualization", *Computers in Industry*, 54, 1, 1-15.

Zang, Yufeng, Gregory, Mike, and Shi, Yongjiang (2008), Global Engineering Networks (GEN): Drivers, Evolution, Configuration, Performance and Key Patterns, Journal of Manufacturing Technology Management, 19, 3, 299-314.

Leading International Teams

Christina Ungerer, Jan Plachta

Abstract. Teamwork across cultural, spatial and time-related boundaries became a common practice in the face of worldwide economic and technological advancements. For many companies this form of work organization is a necessity nowadays, allowing them to build competitive advantages. Leading global teams entails unique challenges, particularly in the most relevant cases of virtual and multicultural teams. These two settings represent overlapping areas of research and are in the focus of this contribution on leading international teams. Many authors studied the cause-and-effect relationship between leadership behavior and group performance. Various recommendations and practical guidelines for leaders have been derived from the primary research conducted. A range of authors analyzed characteristics of effective global leaders. In general, however, literature about leading international teams is found to be scarce. Hence, potential areas of further research are highlighted at the end of this article.

Keywords: Teamwork, cultural differences, internationalisation, team, group, cross-cultural leadership

1 Introduction

The emergence of global markets and the decreasing importance of national boundaries add to new realities companies have to face (Keegan & Green 2013; Aritz & Walker 2014). Cost pressures, the increasing global integration, as well as potential benefits from sharing information worldwide, have led to new forms of organizing work. The way multinational companies manage their activities differs substantially from common practices just a decade ago (Zander, Zettinig & Mäkelä 2013). A major trend in recent years is the increased use of global teamwork in order to cope with the high pressure for innovation, to bundle resources and to enable quick reactions to changing demands and market diversity (Chevrier 2003; Brennan & Braswell 2005; Bachman and Wolf 2007; Smith 2008; Zander, Mockaitis & Butler 2012).

The diversity typically prevailing in international teams can lead to greater performance, but may result in conflicts instead (Chevrier 2003; Humes & Reilly 2008).

Different perspectives of the team members bring about an increased conflict potential but at the same time potentially higher creativity (Stahl et al. 2007). Earley and Masakowski (2000) conducted an extensive study about the effects of heterogeneity in transnational teams and found that highly heterogeneous teams can outperform modestly heterogeneous and homogenous ones. These opposing dynamics are a main characteristic of global teams and have to be managed wisely.

However, teams may not only be considered as being international due to the diverse nature of the team members. Another important area of research and discussion arises from geographically dispersed teams. Literature suggests that firms increasingly make use of so-called "virtual teams" or "global virtual teams" (Bell and Kozlowski 2002; Brake 2006; Mukherjee et al. 2012).

Leadership is one of the main factors influencing team performance and determining success (Hackman & Wageman 2005a; Yukl 2012; Sohmen 2013). With the emergence of global teams, the leadership task became much more complex, since the dimensions of diversity and distance need to be handled. In these times of constant change, effective leadership is even more critical (Stephenson 2011; Gundersen, Hellesoy & Raeder 2012).

This article aims at shedding light on the current state of research on leading international teams. According to Zander, Mockaitis and Butler (2012), despite the considerably augmented use of multinational teams, knowledge concerning leadership is still limited. Though hardly any authors deal with the topic as a whole, available literature on the associated research areas on the contrary seems massive. Thousands of articles on leadership, team dynamics, multicultural research and diversity management are available. Theoretically, all of them add to the topic.

2 Structure and Scope

The structure and focus of this contribution are illustrated in the following figure. It visualizes the contextual framework of the topic as well as the relationship between the areas of interest with respect to leading international teams (Figure 1).

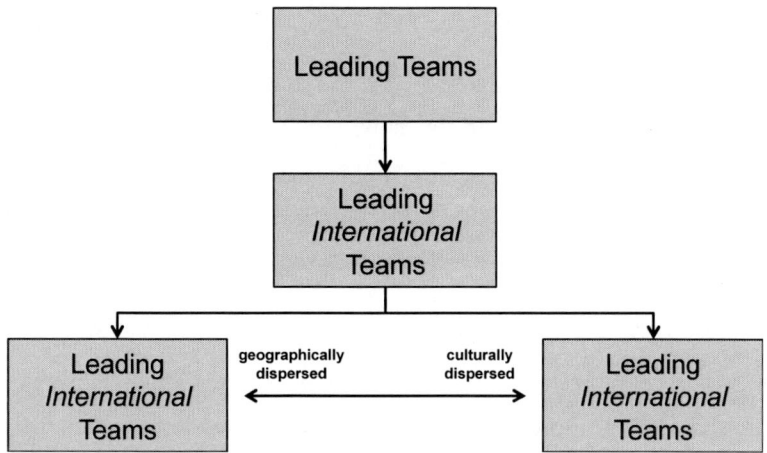

Figure 1: Structure and scope of this paper

Two major dimensions of the 'international' component of leading teams are geographical distance and cultural diversity. The leadership challenges involved in the latter become even more complex when the team in addition is of virtual nature and vice versa. Diversity characteristics other than culture have been excluded from this article as they are less exclusive to global teams: gender, age, profession, experience etc. also are of relevance within local national teams. Some further explanations concerning the article's scope can be found in appendix 1 if required.

For readers with less background knowledge, an extra section on leading teams can be found in appendix 2. This article starts with investigating the two chosen areas of leading international teams, followed by a brief section on resulting implications for global leaders. Suggestions for further research complete the contribution.

3 Global Virtual Teams: Leading over distance

3.1 Definition and Relevance

In virtual teams, members work together to reach a common goal by using electronic information and communication technology[1] rather than having face-to-face interactions, often being situated in more than one location either within one coun-

---

[1] Frequently used technological means of communication and collaboration include email, telephone, portals, team workspaces, shared calendaring, instant messaging applications, web-conferencing, and content management systems (Brennan and Braswell 2005, p.48).

try or across nations (Hetel, Geister & Konradt (2005); Joshi, Lazarova & Liao 2006; Lane et al. 2009; GPM 2012). Global virtual teams are situated in several countries and basically faced with the same challenges as virtual teams in a single nation, which justifies the relevance of the literature. In addition, however, they are often described as nationally, linguistically, and culturally diverse (Zander, Zettinig & Mäkelä 2013).

According to a study by Forrester Consulting, 40% of employees work in virtual teams (Vilet 2012). In Mandzuk's survey (2014) 99% of managers indicated that at least some employees in are involved in virtual teamwork. Additionally, this type of work organization is believed to further increase in the next years (Vilet 2012; Zander, Zettinig & Mäkelä 2013). Nearly all sources, whether directly or indirectly by their findings, acknowledge unique leadership challenges for virtual team leaders and also the need for specific leadership skills (e.g. Colfax, Santos, and Diego 2009). A rich body of literature on team leadership has been elaborated, but usually face-to-face meetings are an underlying assumption (Joshi, Lazarova, & Liao 2009). Hence, literature on leading global virtual teams is rather limited (Kayworth and Leidner 2001; Malhotra, Majchrzak, and Rosen 2007; Nader, Shamsuddin, and Zahari 2009).

3.2 Leadership Challenges and Recommendations

Authors list a lot of different barriers associated with leading virtual teams before they explore ways of positively influencing team performance by recommending effective leader traits, skills, or behavior patterns to overcome those challenges. Attempts to sort and classify the challenges failed, as I realized every additional source names new ones and authors use diverse dimensions. Some refer to complicating task areas such as communication, technology, culture and logistics (Kayworth and Leidner 2001), whereas others focus on processes critical to success including "goal alignment" and "knowledge sharing" (Zander, Zettinig, and Mäkelä 2013), and others even specify challenges arising for the whole team, for example "getting started" or "building engagement" and then give potential leader responses

(Cordery et al. 2009). To put it in a nutshell and being consonant with Brake (2006), leaders of virtual teams have to cope with isolation and confusion. Frequently named challenges refer to building trust, handling technology, and ensuring effective communication (Uber Grosse 2002; Nader, Shamsuddin, and Zahari 2009; Mockaitis and Butler 2012).

The range of recommendations is also far too broad to include a holistic overview in this contribution. However it appears that many authors conduct surveys, interviews or experiments and derive best practices or give advice in the form of practical guidelines (Uber Grosse 2002; Zigurs 2002; Malhotra, Majchrzak, and Rosen 2007; Cordery et al. 2009; DeRosa 2009a; Quisenberry and Burrell 2012; Akin & Rumpf 2013). Ideas include for example giving concrete recommended leader actions such as "Do what you say you will do; be consistent and predictable" as one contribution to build swift trust and finally reach at "building community", one of two major strategies named by Brake (2006).

3.3 Three Research Approach Categories

In order to shed light on the causes and effects of leading global virtual teams, most authors concentrate on *leadership theories* in combination with primary research. Cogliser et al. (2012) used the trait approach, one of the oldest perspectives on leadership, to find out which of the big five personality factors are most important for leaders. She recommends deploying persons who are both conscientious and agreeable. However the focus is clearly on using leadership style theories, which for instance resulted in emphasizing the importance of inspirational leadership[2] as a significant predictor of trust (Joshi, Lazarova, and Liao 2006 and 2009), detecting the strong positive effect of transformational leadership on performance in virtual teams compared to face-to-face (Purvanova and Bono 2009), or in suggesting behavior-based leadership theory as being superior to trait- or contingency-based approaches (Kayworth and Leidner 2001). A quite contrary perspective is provided

---

[2] Inspirational Leadership behaviors represent the motivational component of transformational leadership (Joshi, Lazarova, and Liao 2006).

by Lurey and Raisinghani (2001), whose survey resulted in a merely moderate leadership influence on team performance. Team processes and team member relationships were of greater relevance.

Adding the dimension of time, some authors distinguish several *team phases*. These elaborations seem to be of rather theoretical nature and usually lack primary research. Zander, Zettinig, and Mäkelä (2013) consider three phases ("welcoming", "working" and "wrapping up") and give leadership recommendations for each. Mukherjee et al. (2012) discusses the relevance and implications of five lifecycle stages.

The third literature category may be described as *'other approaches'*. DeRosa (2009b) focuses on the group performance level and distinguishes performance enhancers for less effective teams and such for already effective ones to perform even better. Characterizing different forms of virtual teams, another approach offers leadership implications and recommendations for various team types (Bell and Kozlowski 2002).

4 Culturally Diverse Teams: Leading diversity

4.1 Relevance of Leadership in Culturally Diverse Groups

Hofielen and Broome (2000) ask whether "Leading International Teams" is a new discipline of management and argue yes, due to the unique challenges arising from the considerable influence of cultural differences such as language, mentalities, mind-sets and habits. Multicultural teams have been a focus in literature for years (Stahl et al. 2010). Since diverse teams can perform better than heterogeneous ones but also exhibit greater conflict potential (Stahl et al. 2007), many authors researched on the critical success factors. What is the link between team diversity and performance? Suggested criteria include the team's task focus (Hambrick et al. 1998), the underlying perspective on diversity taken by individuals (Ely and Thomas 2001), whether groups successfully apply the MBI model of high performance and consequently become "creators" (Distefano and Maznevski 2000) or reach at creating a "hybrid culture" over time (Earley and Mosakowski 2000; Hajro and Pudelko 2012), and the team members' goal orientation (Pieterse, Knippenberg, and Dierendonck 2013).

All those factors are important for leaders to know, since they are in the position to influence on them and have the chance to leverage performance if they recognize and manage cultural diversity in their team as an asset (Iles and Hayers 1997; Sujansky 2004a; Humes and Reilly 2008; Stahl et al. 2010). For example Ochieng and Price (2010) conducted 20 expert interviews in Kenya and the UK to determine the influence of communication on the success of multicultural construction project teams. They found communication can be effective if leaders demonstrate awareness of cultural variation.

4.2 Practical Approaches to Leadership

"Developing excellent communication skills is absolutely essential to effective leadership. The leader must be able to share knowledge and ideas to transmit a sense of urgency and enthusiasm to others. If a leader can't get a message across clearly and motivate others to act on it, then having a message doesn't even matter."

— Gilbert Amelio, President and CEO of National Semiconductor Corp.

Source: http://www.leadershipnow.com/communicationquotes.html

Similar to this advising citation, the majority of literature seems to be practitioners-oriented. Communication issues are the most frequently named issues in multicultural teams, since different perspectives, habits, and languages provoke misunderstandings. An often read recommendation for leaders of culturally diverse groups, as a first step towards successful leadership, is to build awareness and understanding that cultural differences do exist. Consequently, it is important to include these by allowing every member to contribute (Gwynne 2009; Jackson 2009; Agrawal 2012).

Quite a few authors did primary research and derived practical advice, concrete strategies or a best practice guide for leaders. Aiming at detecting the strategies used by project leaders to overcome cultural issues, Chevrier (2003) conducted a comparative study among project groups with several engineers of different European countries. Her analysis resulted in three (not exclusive) cross-cultural practices that are commonly used: not paying attention to differences, entering into a trial-and-error process and develop relationships, or resorting to professional or corporate culture. Chevrier suggests a fourth one since leaders commented they were lacking better solutions: using a cultural mediator.

Other authors deducting practical advice from their research include Banks and Waisfisz (1993) who used Hofstede's cultural dimensions to develop a training program, Brett, Behfar, and Kern (2006) who used interviews to elaborate a practical guide for managers, Humes and Reillys' (2008) project team simulations resulted in accumulated best practices, and Luhar who (2012) concluded from semi-structured interviews that cultural awareness, team orientation and clear communication are three factors that can make successful leaders. Sujansky (2004b) has chosen a different approach by giving leaders warning of five leadership traps that need to be avoided in order to generate high team performance.

4.3 Leadership Theories

When testing task- and relationship-oriented leadership on different team processes in their field study, Bachman and Wolf (2007) could provide evidence for the significant influence of leadership styles on multicultural team processes. Hellesoy, Gundersen, and Raeder (2012) state a positive relationship between transformational leadership and performance, work adjustment and job satisfaction. The positive effects of considerate leadership on team functioning in diverse teams have been substantiated by Homan and Greer (2013). They attribute the success of considerate leadership to the team leader's ability to see group members as unique individuals.

However there are limitations to these findings, as Aritz and Walker (2014) point to. Showing how team member participation, contribution and at times feelings of inclusion and satisfaction are influenced by different leadership styles, their research makes also clear that not all approaches are successful with all cultural groups. This viewpoint is further supported by the work of Barmeyer and Davoine (2006) who demonstrate how expectations and preferences with respect to leadership differ between French and German team members. Certain leadership behavior is perceived differently by group individuals. Ochieng and Price (2009) present "leadership style" as one of eight key influencing factors on the effectiveness of multicultural project teams. Interestingly, the interviewed Kenyan and UK groups did not prefer the same styles.

Another perspective on the topic is given by the extensive research project GLOBE (Global Leadership and Organizational Behavior), which conceptualized worldwide leadership differences. More than 60 cultures and 17,000 managers were studied to gain understanding on leadership, cultural values, and industry performance. The results show some universal and some culture-specific leader behaviors (Maznevski and DiStefano 2000); Javidan et al. 2006; Dorfman et al. 2012).

If national culture to a certain degree determines team leader behavior and in addition the team members are culturally diverse – one can imagine how complex the leadership task becomes. To think further, if clear communication is the mean to overcome these challenges, but the team may be globally dispersed and relying on technology, 'leading international teams' for sure requires special skills.

5 Implications for Global Leadership

Global leadership requires much more than purely technical skills (e.g. Kuesten 2013). Soft-skills, for instance the ability to style-switch and adapt to diverse situations intuitively are becoming essential for leaders (e.g. Lane et al. 2009). Integrity, vision and commitment are important, but global leaders today need three additional skills: leading through influence, making decision quickly, and staying on top of the big picture (Stephenson 2001). Terms such as "global mindset" and "cultural intelligence" are frequently mentioned in recent literature (Earley and Mosakowski 2004; Cohen 2010, Zander, Mockaitis and Butler 2012).

Managers of international teams must be able to combine task and relationship oriented leadership when the time is right (Gratton and Erickson 2007), or even more general be able to deal with paradox and contradiction by taking multiple leadership roles at the same time (Holt and Seki 2012). Mentoring and empathy towards other team members is considered crucial as well (Kayworth and Leidner 2002). Leaders need to show authority but avoid running into verbal dominance which reduces team communication and performance (Plunkett Tost, Gino, and Larrick 2013). According to Butler et al. (2012), global managers need to be "boundary spanners", "bridge makers", and "blenders". Much more could be said about essential traits of a global leader, however, the general trend appears to foster constant learning about the own underlying behavioral triggers and those of others, building relationships and trust, and hence ensure clear communication, avoid conflicts and create a shared sense of purpose.

6 Research Gaps and Resulting Suggestions for Further Research

Comprehensive literature on leading international teams, including the two chosen focus areas, still has to emerge. Hardly any sources researched on leadership with language differences or on technological communication means, though both were often mentioned as leader challenges. Most of the existing work is either of very generalist nature, or too specific. Zander, Mockaitis, and Butler (2012) suggest three just emerging research areas: "global team leaders as boundary spanners, bridge makers, and blenders", "people-oriented leadership" and "leveraging global team diversity". In addition, they question whether bicultural leaders are the better ones.

Potential for future research is also given by the question whether teams are still the same, or whether new forms of contemporary collaboration need further analysis (Ancona, Bresman, and Caldwell 2009; Wageman, Gardner, and Mortensen 2012). Investigating the effectiveness of shared leadership is an interesting research gap (Pearce, Manz, and Sims 2009), but also the creation of leadership roles in self-managed teams. Literature on leading different team types and leadership types generally lacks. Examining the determinants of leaders' behavior change is also a topic of interest, as well as how useful different leadership styles are at different team phases (Purvanova and Bono 2009).

Regarding multicultural teams, analyzing in depth which cultural factors require specific leadership styles would support existing research. More guidelines on effective communication are useful for practitioners (Ochieng and Price 2010). Comparing what constitutes a good leader as perceived by multicultural team leaders and members seems to be a valuable research opportunity. Due to the complexity and volatility of the issues involved in 'leading international teams', a general need for more literature on various associated topics is stated.

Appendix

Appendix 1 – Explanation for the Chosen Scope of the Article

Some further limitations and explanations regarding the scope of this article shall be mentioned here in case there are questions left from the reader's point of view. First, the focus is placed on teams that are already composed, since the preliminary step of finding the right people for the team is not mainly linked to team leadership. Second, I decided not to go too deep into leadership theories, since this is a far too broad topic to cover and the specific leadership challenges arising in the setting of international teams are not bringing about new leadership theories, but rather particular adjustment needs to concrete situations. However, I added a section on leading teams to the appendix, where some background on leadership theories is provided. Third, the terms 'global' and 'international' are used interchangeable in this work. Whether 'leading' and 'managing' are synonyms is seen controversially in literature. Depending on the definition of the two terms, there is evidence for both views (Kelly 2009; Lane et al. 2009). In this paper, leadership is seen as one aspect of management on the team level and management as part of leadership on the task level. Therefore some sources referring to managing international teams are used where the content is considered appropriate.Furthermore, I have used 'team' and 'group' as synonyms in some sections, since literature does so as well.

Teamwork seems to have become so common, that some sources do not even consider it as a separate topic: books on 'leading' in a global context automatically assume leading a *team*, so some of the implications of rather general literature have been included where appropriate. Many sources overlapped: I used literature on leading diverse teams where the implication was equally true for multicultural teams. Literature about leading virtual teams automatically often assumes they are global, or at least state that one of the main challenges arises if the team is of diverse nature – which is why also in the 'global virtual team' section I included literature on virtual teams that are not explicitly 'global'.

Appendix 2 – A Literature Guide to Leadership and the Context of Teams

Team Types and Their Relevance for Leadership

Every team is unique regarding team members, specific tasks, environment in which it operates, and processes (Lane et al. 2009). Many studies on leading teams refer to a very specific type of team, for example new product teams (Jassawalla and Sashittal 2000), senior management teams (Wageman et al. 2008) or external audit teams (Notgrass, Conner, and Bell 2013), which are then studied in a particular setting or industry. Such studies, though based on research in very specific contexts, often result in general recommendations for team leaders, for instance foster clear communication, guide and share the team's burdens, and many more. This supports what Lane et al. (2012) states: some characteristics of effective, high-performing teams are universal, regardless of the team composition.

Yet in some distinctive types of teams that are discussed in literature, the leader's influence on team effectiveness may be limited. Self-managed teams with an external leader came up (e.g. Manz and Sims 1987), which belong to the category of shared leadership teams in which the role of the leader is not to be seen in a single person but in all team members (Park and Kwon 2013).

How Leadership Theories Evolved and Apply to Teams

In the past seventy years, different approaches to leadership evolved in literature. One of the main questions in research asked which aspects of behavior explain a leader's influence on the performance of a team, work unit, or organization. Theories first concentrated on leaders' inborn *traits* such as stress tolerance, self-confidence and integrity. Then *techniques* used by leaders were put forward, management by objectives or by delegation are two popular ones. In the next phase, leadership *styles* (behavior patterns) became the primary research focus, for instance participative or authoritarian. Task-oriented versus relationship-oriented leadership gained attention afterwards, which is sometimes classified to leadership styles as well and the change-oriented dimension was added. Finally leadership *roles* such as being a "moderator" emerged. Moreover, situational leadership as a consequence from the contingency theory[3] of leadership deals with style adjustments depending on the context requirements (Kelly 2009; GPM 2012; Yukl 2012). Thousands of studies have been conducted on leadership in the context of teams, but researcher used a variety of approaches and constructs, making a comparison of literature difficult (Lane et al. 2009; Piccolo et al. 2012; Yukl 2012). Limitations of studies and various definitions of what for instance constitutes team "performance" or "efficiency" add to this challenge. Yukl (2012) was found as an author who tried to structure existing literature on a broader base. He used a hierarchical taxonomy encompassing 15 specific leader behaviors and their influence on team effectiveness as deducted from prior research to provide a framework for future research.

Nearly all sources agree on the fact that leadership does have an influence on team performance (Kingston 2007; Prabhakar 2008; Thamhain 2009). However, Hackman and Wageman (2005) for example challenge this by arguing that team leaders are not as influential on team performance as literature suggests. They focused on the options that remain to leaders under constraint circumstances and derive recommended actions.

What Team Leadership Literature Focuses on

Most authors give recommendations based on research and leadership theories, but there is a second group of authors who give concrete advice they gained from own experience. For instance Wilkins (2013) says leading teams is all about having a vi-

---

[3] Perspective suggesting that leaders must adjust their style in a manner consistent with aspects of the context, which leads to the conclusion that there is no ideal leadership style (Kelly 2012, p.176).

sion, sharing it and inspiring team members through example, whereas Eikenberry (2013) states that the best team leaders need to master the art of silence, meaning to know when they should let the team find the solution.

Interestingly, whenever transformational leadership has been part of a study where the effects of different leader styles and behaviors on team performance were compared, there was evidence that transformational leadership[4] causes the most significant impact (e.g. Kuo 2004; Piccolo et al. 2012; Notgrass, Conner, and Bell 2013). Judge and Piccolo (2004) analyzed the relative validity of transformational, transactional and laissez-faire leadership and came to the same conclusion. However they also substantiate that since transactional and transformational leadership are so highly related, the effects can hardly be separated.

For a range of authors, team leadership also goes along with the right timing. Wageman, Fisher, and Hackman (2009) for example argue that timing is vital for team leaders. They distinguish between highly predictable and unpredictable moments of team openness to actions and deem best leaders exhibit good timing in both. Ethical or responsible leadership is a relatively new field of research (Yukl 2012), which for instance Politis (2013) advanced by examining the relation between the two constructs "authentic" and "servant" leadership.

Recent literature seems to emphasize the increasing importance of soft-skills relative to technical leader skills. According to Thamhain (2009), effective leaders are "social architects" and Sohmen (2013) developed a framework of eight soft-skills, stating that "leadership is more than science".

---

[4] Transformational leadership involves identifying the need for change and consequently causing shifts in the beliefs, needs and values of followers (group members). Transformational leaders attempt to raise awareness for the importance and value of the work and convince team members to put the goals before self-interest. This requires leaders to have a vision, self-confidence, and inner strength to guide through inspiration. The change is accomplished with the commitment of the followers.
Transactional leadership involves giving team members something in return for their compliance: give something group members want for something the team leader wants (Kelly 2009, p. 180).

References

Agrawal, Vidhi (2012), 'Managing the Diversified Team: Challenges and Strategies for Improving Performance', *Team Performance Management*, 18, 7/8, 384-400.

Akin, Niyazi, and Jörg Rumpf (2013), 'Führung Virtueller Teams', *Gruppendynamik und Organisationsberatung*, 44, 373-387.

Ancona, Deborah, Henrik Bresman, and David Caldwell (2009), ‚Six Steps to Leading High-Performing X-Teams', *Organizational Dynamics*, 38, 3, 217-224.

Aritz, Jolanta, and Robyn C. Walker (2014), 'Leadership Styles in Multicultural Groups: Americans and East Asians Working Together', *International Journal of Business Communication*, 51, 1, 72-92.

Bachmann, Anne, and Joachim Wolf (2007), 'Führung multikultureller Teams: Eine Konzeptualisierung und empirische Analyse der Notwendigkeit unterschiedlicher Führungsstile', *Zeitschrift für Betriebswirtschaft*, 77,10, 1035-1064.

Banks, Paul, and Bob Waisfisz (1993), 'Managing International Teams: A Practical Approach to Cultural Problems', *Journal of Strategy Change*, 2, 309-318.

Barmeyer, Christoph I., and Eric Davoine (2006), 'Interkulturelle Zusammenarbeit und Führung in internationalen Teams: Das Beispiel Deutschland – Frankreich', *Zeitschrift für Führung und Organisation*, 1, 35-39.

Bell, Bradford S., and Steve W. J. Kozlowski (2002), 'A Typology of Virtual Teams: Implications for Effective Leadership', *Group & Organization Management*, 27, 2, 14-49.

Brake, Terence (2006), 'Leading Global Virtual Teams', *Industrial and Commercial Training*, 38, 3, 116-121.

Brennan, Michael, and Paul Braswell (2005), 'Developing and Leading Effective Global Teams', *Human Capital*, 3, 44-48.

Brett, Jeanne, Kristin Behfar, and Mary C. Kern (2006), ‚Managing Multicultural Teams', *harvard Business Review*, November, 84-91.

Butler et al. (2012), 'The Global Leader as Boundary Spanner, Bridge Maker, and Blender', *Industrial and Organizational Psychology*, 5, 2, 240-243.

Chevrier, Sylvie (2003), 'Cross-Cultural Management in Multinational Project Groups', *Journal of World Business*, 38, 141-149.

Cogliser, Claudia C. et al. (2012), 'Big Five Personality Factors and Leader Emergence in Virtual Teams: Relationships With Team Trustworthiness, Member Performance Contributions, and Team Performance', *Group and Organization Management*, 37, 6, 752-784.

Cohen, Stephen L. (2010), 'Effective Global Leadership Requires a Global Mindset', *Industrial and Commercial Training*, 42, 1, 3-10.

Cordery, John et al. (2009), 'Leading Parallel Global Virtual Teams: Lessons from Alcoa', *Organizational Dynamics*, 38, 3, 204-216.

Colfax, Richard S., Annette T. Santos, and Joann Diego (2009), ‚Virtual Leadership: A Green Possibility in Critical Times But Can it Really Work?', *Journal of International Business Research*, 8, 2, 133-139.

DeRosa, Darleen (2009a), 'Improving Performance by Emulating the Best', *Leadership in Action*, 29, 2, 17-19.

DeRosa, Darleen (2009b), 'Virtual Success The Keys to Effectiveness in Leading from a Distance', *Leadership in Action*, 28, 6, 9-11.

Distefano, Joseph J., and Martha L. Maznevski (2000), 'Creating Value with Diverse Teams in Global Management', *Organizational Dynamics*, 29, 1, 45-63.

Dorfman, Peter et al. (2012), 'GLOBE: A Twenty Year Journey Into the Intriguing World of Culture and Leadership', *Journal of World Business*, 47, 504-518.

Earley, Christopher P., and Elaine Mosakowski (2000), 'Creating Hybrid Team Cultures: An Empirical Test of Transnational Team Functioning', *Academy of Management Journal*, 43, 1, 26-49.

Earley, Christopher P., and Elaine Mosakowski (2004), 'Cultural Intelligence', *Harvard Business Review,* October, 139-146.

Eikenberry, Kevin (2013), 'Leading Teams? Use Smart Silence', *Executive Leadership*, February, 4.

Ely, Robin J., and David A. Thomas (2001), 'Cultural Diversity at Work: The Effects of Diversity Perspectives on Work Group Processes and Outcomes', *Administrative Science Quarterly,* 46, 229-273.

GPM Deutsche Gesellschaft für Projektmanagement e.V. (2012), *Kompetenzbasiertes Projektmanagement*, 5th ed., Nürnberg: GPM.

Gratton, Lynda, and Tamara J. Erickson (2007), 'Eight Ways to Build Collaborative Teams', *Harvard Business Review,* November, 102-109.

Gundersen, Goran, Bjorn Tore Hellesoy, and Sabine Raeder, 'Leading International Project Teams: The Effectiveness of Transformational Leadership in Dynamic Work Environments', *Journal of Leadership & Organizational Studies*, 19, 1, 46-57.

Gwynne, Peter (2009), 'Managing Culturally Diverse Teams', *Research Technology Management,* January-February, 68f.

Hackman, Richard J., and Ruth Wageman (2005a), 'A Theory of Team Coaching', *Academy of Management Review*, 30, 2, 269-287.

Hackman, Richard J., and Ruth Wageman (2005b), 'When and How Team Leaders Matter', *Research in Organizational Behavior,* 26, 37-74.

Hajro, Aida, and Markus Pudelko (2012), 'Multinational Teams: How Team Interactions Mediate Between Cultural Differences and Team Performance', *Academy of Management Annual Meeting Proceedings.*

Hambrick, Donald C. et al. (1998), 'When Groups Consist of Multiple Nationalities: Towards a New Understanding of the Implications', *Organization Studies*, 19, 2, 181-205.

Hanson, Darren, Cecily Ward, and Paul Chin (2012), 'Leading Virtual Teams Across National and Cultural Boundaries', *International Leadership Journal,* 4, 3, 1-17.

Hertel, Guido, Susanne Geister, and Udo Konradt (2005), 'Managing virtual teams: A review of current empirical research', *Human Resource Management Review*, 15, 69-95.

Hofielen, Gerd, and Jim Broome (2000), 'Leading International Teams: A New Discipline?', *Zeitschrift für Organisationsentwicklung*, 4, 1-8.

Holt, Katherine, and Kyoko Seki (2012), ‚Global Leadership: A Developmental Shift for Everyone', *Industrial and Organizational Psychology,* 5, 196-215.

Homan, Astrid C., and Lindred L. Greer (2013), 'Considering Diversity: The Positive Effects of Considerate Leadership in Diverse Teams, *Group Processes & Intergroup Relations,* 16, 1, 105-125.

Humes, Michelle, and Anne H. Reilly (2008), 'Managing Intercultural Teams: The eOrganization Exercise', *Journal of Management Education,* 32, 1, 118-137.

Iles, Paul, and Paromjit Kaur Hayers (1997), 'Managing Diversity in Transnational Project Teams: A Tentative Model and Case Study', *Journal of Managerial Psychology,* 12, 2, 95-117.

Jackson, Terence (2009), 'Managing Cultural Differences: Understanding of Different Mentalities is Key to Managing a Multicultural Team', *ThirdSector,* March, 21.

Jassawalla, Avan R., and Hemant C. Sashittal (2000), 'Strategies of Effective New Product Team Leaders', *California Management Review,* 42, 2, 34-51.

Javidan, Mansour et al. (2006), 'In the Eye of the Beholder: Cross Cultural Lessons in Leadership from Project GLOBE', *Academy of Management Perspectives,* February, 67-90.

Joshi, Aparna, Mila B. Lazarova, and Hui Liao (2006), 'A Cross-Level Study of Identification in Geographically Dispersed Teams: The Role of Leadership, Academy of Management Best Conference Paper.

Joshi, Aparna, Mila B. Lazarova, and Hui Liao (2009), 'Getting Everyone on Board: The Role of Inspirational Leadership in Geographically Dispersed Teams', *Organization Science,* 20, 1, 240-252.

Judge, Timothy A., and Ronald F. Piccolo (2004), 'Transformational and Transactional Leadership: A Meta-Analytic Test of Their Relative Validity', *Journal of Applied Psychology*, 98, 5, 755-768.

Kayworth, Timothy R., and Dorothy E. Leidner (2001), 'Leadership Effectiveness in Global Virtual Teams', *Journal of Management Information Systems,* 18, 3, 7-40.

Keegan, Warren J. and Mark C. Green (2013), *Global Marketing,* 7th ed., Boston: Pearson Education, Inc.

Kelly, Phil (2009), *International Business and Management,* Singapore: South-Western Cengage Larning EMEA.

Kingston, George (2007), Literature Review on 'Leading Project Teams: An Introduction to the Basics of Project Management and Project Team Leadership' by Anthony T. Cobb, in *Journal of Production Innovation Management,* 24, 280-281.

Kuesten, Carla (2013), book review on 'Leading Global Project Teams: The New Leadership Challenge' by Martinelli, Russ, Tim Rahschulte, and Jim Waddel (2010), *Journal of Production and Innovation Management,* 30, 2, 400-402.

Kuo, Chia-Chen (2004), 'Research on Impacts of Team Leadership on Team Effectiveness', *The Journal of American Academy of Business,* September, 266-277.

Lane, Henry W. et al. (2009), *International Management Behavior – Leading with a Global Mindset,* 6th ed., Croydon: Wiley.

Luhar, Ketan (2012), 'Leading International Project Teams', Master of Science Thesis (Project Management) Chalmers University of Technology, Sweden, and Northumbria University, UK.

Lurey, Jeremy S., and Mahesh S. Raisinghani (2001), 'An empirical study of best practices in virtual teams', *Information & Management*, 38, 523-544.

Malhotra, Arvind, Ann Majchrzak, and Benson Rosen (2007), 'Leading Virtual Teams', *Academy of Management Perspectives*, February, 60-70.

Mandzuk, Christina (2014), 'Challenges of Leading a Virtual Team: More Than Meets the Eye', *T+D*, January, p.20.

Manz, Charles C., and Henry P. Sims (1987), 'Leading Workers to Lead Themselves: The External Leadership of Self- Managing Work Teams', *Administrative Science Quarterly*, 32, 106-128.

Maznevski, Martha L., and Joseph J. DiStefano (2000), 'Global Leaders are Team Players: Developing Global Leaders Through Membership on Global Teams', *Human Resource Management,* 39, 2&3, 195-208.

Mukherjee, Debmalya et al. (2012), 'Leading virtual teams: how do social, cognitive, and behavioral capabilities matter?', *Management Decision*, 50, 2, 273-290.

Nader, Ale Ebrahim, Ahmed Shamsuddin, and Taha Zahari (2009), 'Virtual Teams: a Literature Review', *Australian Journal of Basic and Applied Sciences*, 3, 3, 2653-2669.

Notgrass, David, Charlene Conner, and Thomas J. Bell III (2013), 'Leading External Auditing Teams: The Correlation Between Leaders' Behaviors and Team Dynamics of Cohesion and Conflict', *International Journal of Business and Public Administration*, 10, 2, 1-14.

Ochieng, Edward Godfrey, and Andrew David Price (2009), 'Framework for managing multicultural project teams', *Engineering, Construction and Architectural Management*, 16, 6, 527-543.

Ochieng, Edward Godfrey, and Andrew David Price (2010), 'Managing cross-cultural communication in multicultural construction project teams: The case of Kenya and UK', *International Journal of Project Management*, 28, 449-460.

Park, Jong Gyu, and Bora Kwon (2013), 'Literature Review on Shared Leadership in Teams', *Journal of Leadership, Accountability and Ethics*, 10, 3, 28-36.

Pearce, Craig L., Charles C. Manz, and Henry P. Sims (2009), 'Where Do We Go From Here' Is Shared Leadership the Key to Success?', *Organizational Dynamics,* 38, 3, 234-238.

Piccolo Ronald F. et al. (2012), 'The relative impact of complementary leader behaviors: Which matter most?', *The Leadership Quarterly,* 23, 567-581.

Pieterse, Anne Nederveen, Daan van Knippenberg, and Dirk van Dierendonck (2013), ,Cultural Diversity and Team Performance: The Role of Team Member Goal Orientation', *Academy of Management Journal,* 56, 3, 782-804.

Plunkett Tost, Leigh, Francesca Gino, and Richard P. Larrick (2013), 'When Power Makes Others Speechless: The Negative Impact of Leader Power on Team Performance', *Academy of Management Journal,* 56, 5, 1465-1486.

Politis, John (2013), 'The Relationship Between Team Performance, Authentic and Servant Leadership', *Proceedings of the European Conference on Management, Leadership & Governance,* 237-244.

Prabhakar, Guru Prakash (2008), 'Teams and Projects: A Literature Review', *International Journal of Business and Management*, 3, 10, 3-7.

Purvanova, Radostina K., and Joyce E. Bono (2009), 'Transformational leadership in context: Face-to-face and virtual teams', *The Leadership Quarterly*, 20, 343-357.

Quisenberry, William, and Darrell Norman Burrell (2012), 'Establishing a Cycle of Success by Utilizing Transactional Leadership, Technology, Trust, and Relationship Building on High Performing Self-Managed Virtual Teams', *Review of Management Innovation and Creativity*, 5, 16, 97-116.

Smith, David (2008), 'How to Build an International Team', *MultiLingual*, 19, 12-13.

Sohmen, Victor S. (2013), 'Leadership and Teamwork: Two Sides of the Same Coin', *Journal of IT and Economic Development*, 4, 2, 1-18.

Stahl, Günter K. et al. (2007), 'Unraveling the Diversity-Performance Link in Multicultural Teams: Meta-analysis of Studies on the Impact of Cultural Diversity in Teams', *INSEAD Working Papers Collection*, 36, 1-49.

Stahl, Günter K. et al. (2010), , A look at the bright side of multicultural team diversity', *Scandinavian Journal of Management,* 26, 439-447.

Stephenson, Carol (2011), 'How Leadership Has Changed', *IVEY Business Journal*, July/August.

Sujansky, Joanne G. (2004a), 'Leading a Diverse Team', Credit Union Executive Newsletter, June 14, 6.

Sujansky, Joanne G. (2004b), 'The Five Biggest Traps To Avoid When Leading a Diverse Team', *Occupational Hazards,* August, 23.

Thamhain, Hans J. (2009), 'Leadership Lessons from Managing Technology-Intensive Teams', *International Journal of Innovation and Technology Management*, 6, 2, 117-133.

Uber Grosse, Christine (2002), 'Managing Communication within Virtual Intercultural Teams', *Business Communication Quarterly,* 65, 4, 22-38.

Vilet, Jacque (2012), 'The Challenge and Promise of Global Virtual Teams', http://www.tlnt.com/2012/10/19/the-challenge-and-promise-of-global-virtual-teams/. Accessed 29/03/2014.

Wageman, Ruth, Colin M. Fisher, and Richard J. Hackman (2009), 'Leading Teams When the Time is Right: Finding the Best Moments to Act', *Organizational Dynamics*, 38, 3, 192-203.

Wageman, Ruth, Heidi Gardner, and Mark Mortensen (2012), 'The Changing Ecology of Teams: New Directions for Team Research', *Journal of Organizational Behavior*, 33, 301-315.

Wageman, Ruth et al. (2008), 'Behind the Seniors', *Harvard Business Review'*, January, 38-41.

Wilkins, James (2013), 'Leading Your Team is About Vision', *C&IT*, May, 16.

Yukl, Gary (2012), 'Effective Leadership Behavior: What We Know and What Questions Need More Attention', *Academy of Management: Perspectives*, 26, 4, 66-85.

Zander, Lena, Audra I. Mockaitis, and Christina L. Butler (2012), 'Leading global teams', *Journal of World Business*, 47, 4, 592-603.

Zander, Lena, Peter Zettinig, and Kristiina Mäkelä (2013), 'Leading global virtual teams to success', *Organizational Dynamics*, 42, 3, 228-237.

Zigurs, Ilze (2002), 'Leadership in Virtual Teams: Oxymoron or Opportunity?' *Organizational Dynamics,* 31, 4, 339-351.

ibidem-Verlag

Melchiorstr. 15

D-70439 Stuttgart

info@ibidem-verlag.de

www.ibidem-verlag.de
www.ibidem.eu
www.edition-noema.de
www.autorenbetreuung.de